PLAYWAY to English

Second edition

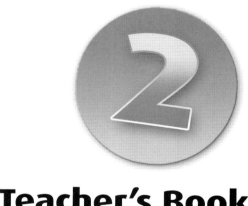

2

Teacher's Book

Günter Gerngross • Herbert Puchta

Introduction

Contents

I. Introduction

Teacher's Book • Playway to English 2 Second edition   © Cambridge University Press and Helbling Languages 2009

I.
Introduction

Playway to English 2 Second edition represents an integrated body of material for teaching English starting in Year 1; its essential characteristic is learning through play. With the aid of the SMILE approach *Playway to English 2* introduces basic listening and speaking skills and engages the children in learning English.

The tried and tested **SMILE approach** is based on the following principles:

S	kill oriented foreign language learning
M	ulti-sensory learner motivation
I	ntelligence-building activities
L	ong-term memory storage through music, movement, rhythm and rhyme
E	xciting stories and games

What is new about *Playway to English 2 Second edition*?

Compared with the previous edition, *Playway to English 2 Second edition* is even more efficient because of the following innovations:

1. A stronger emphasis on outcome in the development of speaking skills:

With the aid of numerous exercises the pupils are systematically encouraged to speak English. An extended range of exercises and a clearer focus on communicative speaking results in the children learning to express themselves on a wide variety of topics and developing an ever expanding repertoire of communicative expressions.

2. Better opportunities for assessment and self-assessment:

Under the heading *Show what you can do*, *Playway* now offers material for self-assessment at regular intervals that the children can use to assess their progress. This is initially done under supervision but then gradually the students are encouraged to assess their progress independently.

3. New content:

- In *Playway 1* the learners are not confronted with the written word. In *Playway 2* the written word is carefully introduced on a word, a sentence and a text level. When the children have heard words, sentences and dialogues and when they have spoken them they are presented with the written form of what they have learned orally so far. Thus the written words serve as an additional memory anchor which speeds up learning.
- Alongside well-established content from the original edition of *Playway* there are also new songs, rhymes and stories.

- Four humorous DVD stories about Mr Matt and his two children, Danny and Daisy, have been added. Each episode is intended to develop listening and visual comprehension in a way that is motivating and fun for the children. They bring the target language to life in an extremely entertaining way, conveying cultural information and providing the children with valuable everyday English phrases and expressions used by children of the same age. In this way the sketches offer a motivating way of developing listening and speaking skills.

4. CLIL
(Content and Language Integrated Learning):

The CLIL pages introduce content from the general curriculum into the English classroom. In this cross-curricular lesson the intention is not so much 'language learning' but 'learning through language'. This means, therefore, that the children work with interesting content from other areas of the curriculum that is new to them. The main aim of these lessons is to cultivate the receptive processing of language, i.e. that the children learn to understand the foreign language in new, meaningful contexts that are important for them. The cross-curricular links promote holistic 'immersion' in English and give foreign language learning additional meaning.

In *Playway to English 2 Second edition* Pupil's Book you will find CLIL activities with the following objectives:

- p. 15 Making a fruit salad.
- p. 29 Being aware of the senses.
- p. 43 Doing sums.
- p. 57 Learning about the lives of earthworms.
- p. 71 The sea. Finding out about ecological matters.
- In addition, in Unit 8 *(On the farm)* a CLIL activity is suggested in the teacher's notes following Lesson 1 (p. 121 in the Teacher's Book).

CLIL activities are suggested in the Teacher's Book to extend the content of the lesson – these link to science, (food, nutrition, nature and the five senses), maths, geography and art (making a cat). The CLIL activities are optional and are well suited to different interests and abilities. Teachers can decide on a case by case basis which of the CLIL activities to carry out with the children according to their level and interests.

5. Steps to creativity (Word Play):

These new activities have been developed especially to give the children an opportunity to be linguistically creative with the help of set structures or models. For example, the children compose their own chant by means of set rhyming words or, with the aid of pictures, they construct a rhyme. In other sections, they are encouraged to change set expressions within a structured framework to make dialogues or role plays as they wish.

6. More user-friendliness:

A clear cross-referencing system in Teacher's Book facilitates the use of *Playway to English* in the lesson. The new active vocabulary of each activity is shown at beginning of each lesson. Each activity is clearly accompanied by a Pupil's Book or Activity Book icon for quick reference. The CD icons give the relevant audio CD track number whilst DVD section references are also given alongside the teaching notes. Transcriptions of all audio CD and DVD texts are included in the teaching notes.

The components of *Playway to English 2 Second edition*

Playway to English 2 Second edition consists of a comprehensive range of teaching materials:

- Teacher's Book
- 3 Audio CDs
- Pupil's Book
- Activity Book and CD-ROM
- DVD (with the Cartoon Stories and Mr Matt Stories)
- Cards Pack (flashcards, word cards and story cards)
- The Max glove puppet

Teacher's Book

The Teacher's Book provides:

- **Information on the structure, components and ways of using the material and also on the desired outcomes.** In addition there is an introduction to the teaching theory of *Playway to English 2*, the educational bases and the principles behind the use of the materials plus a discussion of important issues of classroom management.
- **Comprehensive notes on the individual units.** These notes give a clear overview of the topic in question, the desired outcomes, the learning content, the learning activities and vocabulary plus tips on possible pronunciation difficulties. The main part consists of detailed and well-tried step-by-step instructions for using the individual lesson plans in class. There are also suggestions on how to practise listening comprehension and speaking skills and sub-skills such as vocabulary and pronunciation.

Audio CDs

The three audio CDs contain all the listening exercises, Action Stories, Word Plays, songs and chants, dialogues and interviews plus the listening versions of the cartoon stories and scenes from the Mr Matt sketches. The songs, Word Plays and chants include karaoke versions that can be used to introduce them in stages.

Listening to a foreign language frequently and intensively is an essential requirement for the development of speaking skills. On the CD, the children hear examples of authentic pronunciation and intonation from both child and adult native speakers. Although the teacher represents the most important model for pronunciation and intonation for the children, by using the CD from the start of their learning process the children are given the opportunity to hear a variety of native speakers. In this way they can develop differentiated listening comprehension skills that are not limited to just one attachment figure (the teacher). The CD is, therefore, an ideal resource in preparing the students for meeting different variations of English.

The different types of aural comprehension activities give the children exposure to a variety of models. In the trial phase of *Playway to English 2* it was noted that, in a role play activity, some children were able to imitate the pronunciation of the characters almost perfectly. This is seldom achieved with isolated pronunciation exercises but the various activities

offered in *Playway to English 2* e.g. humorous role plays that encourage the students to identify with the characters through play, emphasise the valuable connection between motivation and pronunciation.

Pupil's Book

The 80-page Pupil's Book has a wide range of illustrations that support the development of the children's listening comprehension and speaking skills.

Key features and activities:

- The illustrations of the songs and chants help the children to quickly master the meaning of written words.
- Many lessons begin with a song, a rhyme or a chant on the CD and invite children to follow it in the book. With the aid of pictures the children learn to understand the texts and gradually to sing or say them.
- There are several action stories in the Pupil's Book. These encourage children to learn phrases in the imperative. Children match the pictures in the Pupil's Book to what they hear, e.g. on p. 22. and do the actions themselves to show that they understand.
- Exercises on vocabulary revision are for playful and multi-sensory consolidation of new words (e.g. Pupil's Book p. 16).
- The model presentation of dialogues with the aid of classroom photos has a similar function. The children look at the photos and at the same time read and/or listen to the mini-dialogues. They learn to say it themselves and also to change it in a creative way (e.g. Pupil's Book p. 24, 28, 37).
- There are exercises that directly build upon the stories. When the children have seen a cartoon story on the DVD, for example, they then complete missing scenes in the picture story with the aid of the picture stickers (see appendix of the Pupil's Book) whilst listening to the audio version on the CD. This engages the children in an active reconstruction of the story.
- There are a wide range of activities to encourage active listening. For example, the children listen to instructions on the CD and complete a set exercise in the Pupil's Book (they draw a picture following spoken instructions, or put pictures in the correct sequence).
- Regular Word Play activities give the children a valuable opportunity to use the language they have learned creatively. After practising a structured chant or rhyme, the children are then encouraged to produce their own version, therefore allowing them to engage with the language in a wholly personal, imaginative way.
- At the end of every second unit the *Show what you can do* section serves as a summary, revision and reinforcement of the main vocabulary in the topics of the preceding two units. The children may – at first with the help of the teacher and, gradually, independently – evaluate their progress for the purpose of self assessment.
- A picture dictionary with all the main vocabulary also in print offers students the chance to revise or consolidate the learning of the new words or phrases after each unit (see Pupil's Book pp. 76–79).

1) Child A points to a picture, covers up the written word or phrase. Child B names it.
2) Child A looks at the picture dictionary for ten seconds and tries to remember as many items as possible. Then they close their eyes and tell child B as many items as they can remember.

3) Child A names a picture and child B points to it.
4) Both children look at the picture dictionary. Child A says the names of all the items except one. Child B has to identify and name it.

Activity Book

The 64-page Activity Book offers a variety of exercises designed to consolidate the language that children have learnt and to assist them in using it creatively in individual, pair and group work. There are a wide range of activities that involve students in a number of different tasks: they listen and complete with numbers or colour; complete logical sequences by drawing pictures; draw, colour and speak, etc.

As a general guideline, the Activity Book is for use at the end of a lesson rather than at the beginning since it helps to consolidate the language that has been practised through various other means.

Key activities:

These are the main methodological steps that the children take when they work with the Activity Book:

- Listening and numbering pictures.
- Matching words, sentences or short texts to pictures.
- Listening, reading and colouring.
- Listening and drawing.
- Decoding anagrams.
- Drawing and speaking.
- Listening and finding items.
- Solving puzzles.
- Completing short texts.
- Finding words in a puzzle.
- Making sentences.
- Doing logical puzzles.

CD-ROM (included in the Activity Book)

This learning software contains not only vocabulary activities but also exercises for use with the songs, chants, rhymes, cartoon stories and action stories in the book, meaning that *Playway to English 2 Second edition* can be supplemented either at home or at school.

System requirements:

Operating systems: Windows 2000, XP, Vista
CPU: Pentium 1 GHz
Memory: 256 MB RAM, (Vista: 512 MB RAM)
Graphics card: min. 800 x 600, 16 bit colour
CD-ROM drive: min. 16x speed
Sound card: full duplex, speakers or headphones

DVD

The DVD contains four Mr Matt stories and eight cartoon stories that present English in a way that is both humorous and informative. At the centre of the Mr Matt stories are Mr Matt and his two children, Danny and Daisy. These sequences are intended to help the children to understand English in the context of a genuine dialogue. The interaction of picture and sound offers important support for the comprehension process. The use of native speakers provides an ideal preparation for understanding English in real situations. The sketches also offer the children important pronunciation models.

In their first school years, children still have a very strong imitative way of learning pronunciation, and classroom research shows that this process is particularly effective when the pronunciation models are appropriately motivating and invite imitation.

The cartoon stories are fully animated. There are also audio versions of them on the CD. This means that the children can listen to a story several times for revision without needing to use a PC or DVD player. Furthermore, the children listen to the audio version after watching the story on the DVD when they do the text-editing exercises in the Pupil's Book, such as completing a picture story by correctly inserting the picture stickers.

Cards Pack

The pack contains 74 flashcards, 117 word cards and 63 story cards to support work in the lesson.

Flashcards

There are flashcards for all the main vocabulary. They are an essential means of conveying the meaning of new words and they help the children to memorise them more effectively. The flashcards also eliminate the task of drawing on the board or producing home-made pictures, thus saving a lot of preparation time for the teacher. The lesson notes give numerous tips on how the flashcards can be used for the reinforcement and revision of vocabulary and in games.
A list of all the flashcards is given in the appendix of the Teacher's Book, p. 156.

Word cards

In addition to the flashcards there are also word cards available. Once the children have understood the meaning of a word or phrase, have listened to it several times and have spoken it the teacher will introduce the written form of the word or phrase. In this way the children will learn to deal successfully with matching words orally and visually.
A list of all the word cards is given in the appendix of the Teacher's Book, p. 157.

Story cards

There are story cards to accompany each of the cartoon stories in *Playway to English 2 Second edition*. After the children have watched a story on DVD, they reconstruct it with the aid of the pictures and picture stickers in the Pupil's Book, then the teacher repeats the story using story cards, mimes and gestures. Alternatively, these two stages can be reversed. The teacher revises the story with the aid of the story cards and gradually the children can join in the reconstruction of the story. Then they complete the exercise in the Pupil's Book.
A list of all the story cards is given in the appendix of the Teacher's Book, p. 156.

The Max glove puppet

The Max glove puppet is used for the visual presentation and modelling of dialogues in the classroom. Teachers can use the puppet to act out a dialogue between two people, helping the children to understand the dialogues better. The Max puppet can also be used to ask the children questions or to act out simple dialogues with them. Short role plays where one child controls the glove puppet are also an option, after the children have seen a story on DVD, for example.

Aims

The aims of *Playway to English 2 Second edition* are:
- to let the children experience, through all the senses, that learning a foreign language is fun.
- to enable the children to experience language as a means of communication in the lesson itself.
- to enable the children to express their own wishes and needs in English.
- to practise reading skills with activities such as matching pictures and words, sentences and pictures, stories and dialogues with speech bubbles.
- to develop listening comprehension and speaking skills.
- to offer a wide range of activities that promote the learning process.
- to contribute to the development of the intellectual, social, emotional and spatial skills of the children.
- to establish foreign language learning as a positive experience for the children from the start. They gather positive learning experiences of finding their creative side when, for example, they learn to compose short texts, rhymes and chants using the models provided and with linguistic assistance.
- to lay the foundations for an open and positive attitude to other peoples and cultures by familiarising the children with another linguistic community.
- to offer teachers concrete teaching models for an innovative and up-to-date foreign language lesson in the primary school and to support them with ideas for integrating foreign language learning into the curriculum.

Contents

Playway to English 2 Second edition is divided into ten topic areas that have been selected according to motivational and age-appropriate criteria and can also be integrated into the main curriculum as they contain elements from other subject areas.

The songs and chants, for example, can be worked on in the music lesson, the action stories and activity games can be integrated into the PE lesson and logical sequences refer to aspects of mathematics. In addition, the CLIL activities referred to above offer links to other topics.

Topics

Characters

Linda, Benny and Max appear frequently as characters in the cartoon stories and also in listening exercises in *Playway to English 2 Second edition*. Max is a fantasy figure who is friends with Benny and Linda. He also steps out of the material as a glove puppet and is used in various activities in the classroom.

Alongside them the characters of Mr Matt, Danny and Daisy from the DVD Mr Matt stories will become familiar to the children.

Activities

The content of the units is taught through various types of texts:
- *Cartoon Stories*
- *Mr Matt Stories*
- *Action Stories*
- *Songs*
- *Chants*
- *Word Plays*

It has been clearly shown that information in a foreign language remains more firmly fixed in the children's memories when what they are learning appeals to them. Most information that reaches our brains via various senses is quickly forgotten. What is retained in our memories is what is relevant to us. Psychologists talk of the 'depth quality' of an experience. For teaching interesting and humorous content, stories, rhymes, songs and chants are particularly suitable.

The activities in *Playway to English 2 Second edition* are designed to be compatible with the interests of Year 2 children and to facilitate their learning. These involve as many of the children's senses as possible.

The combination of interesting content and holistic presentation ensures that the children retain the material and have fun learning English.

Cartoon stories and Mr Matt stories

It is impossible to imagine primary school lessons without stories. There is good reason for this as educational psychologists repeatedly stress the idea that stories make an essential contribution to the cultural, social and emotional development of the child:

The story form is a cultural universal; everyone everywhere enjoys stories. The story, then, is not just some casual entertainment; it reflects a basic and powerful form in which we make sense of the world and experience.[1]

In the foreign-language lesson the children learn to understand longer sequences of events with the aid of stories and gradually become accustomed to descriptive, narrative language. It has been clearly established through research on foreign language in primary schools that stories rate particularly highly in the children's scale of preferences. Stories are strong motivators and remain very strongly anchored in the memory if they are conveyed appropriately. Moreover, they promote the children's enjoyment of theatrical presentation. The children watch the story first on DVD, then the mini-dialogues are practised and next a role play is performed.

The work with the role plays makes an essential contribution to the development of the children's speaking skills. The children's high degree of identification with the content of a story can be seen in the fact that many children succeed in imitating with surprising accuracy the pronunciation and intonation of the roles of the speakers that they have previously heard on the DVD.

---

[1] Egan, K, (1986) *Teaching as Story Telling*, Chicago, University of Chicago Press, p. 2.

Action stories

Action stories are short stories with sentences that can be represented by actions, gestures and mimes. They are performed using the Total Physical Response (TPR) method developed by James Asher[2] to convey language with a multi-sensory approach by first aiming for intensive training of the receptive skills. As already noted above, it is critically important to develop listening comprehension skills. The closer the link between what children hear and a concrete action, the better they can remember the language that they have learned and the easier it is for them to use it productively. In the action stories the children hear a sentence and act it out immediately by imitating the teacher. The sentence is represented physically after it has been heard; in this way, listening comprehension is directly linked to action.

Action stories are a classic example of learning with all the senses. Studies on the use of Total Physical Response show that, for several reasons, this method is well suited to getting the foreign language across to children at beginners' level. The reasons for this are:

- Doing the actions with others allows the child to experience following instructions as an action game. In this game, language and action are inseparable and the meaning of the language is learned directly through the action.
- Action stories are learned in an anxiety-free environment and through play. The actions of the group provide security, particularly for those children who need a little longer to process the language: they can get their bearings by looking at other children in the group and using them as models.
- Right from the start the children learn through the action stories that they can do something in English. This gives an important sense of achievement and strengthens the children's confidence in their own ability to learn a foreign language.
- The development of the children's listening comprehension skills forms an important foundation for their speaking. When working with the action stories the children should first and foremost be listening. Gradually, they will speak along with the teacher and in this way gain self-confidence in their pronunciation and intonation. The primary goal in working with action stories is developing listening comprehension. This means that the teaching/learning goal is achieved when the children can act out the sentences of an action story independently after practising it. It is not the primary goal of working with action stories to have the children immediately recite the story or even to be able to reconstruct it freely.

Songs

Songs are highly valuable for motivating children of primary school age. Singing in groups is fun and children enjoy learning a repertoire of songs during the course of the year. *Playway to English 2 Second edition* offers songs that have been written especially for the individual topics. The advantage of this is that songs consolidate the language presented and the language input can be easily monitored.

Chants

Chants are texts that are recited to a set rhythm. They offer an excellent opportunity to practise pronunciation, intonation and speech rhythm. All the chants in *Playway to English 2 Second edition* have been written especially for the individual topics. When working on a chant the children listen to it on the CD first. In the Pupil's Book the text is represented by the illustrations, so, when listening to the chant a second time, the children follow the chant in the book. In the pilot phase of *Playway to English 2 Second edition* it was found that the pictures were very helpful for the children in mentally reconstructing the text.

Then the children watch the gestures of the teacher, imitate them and speak at the same time. Next the children listen to the first part of the karaoke section (*And now you!*) with gaps (half playback) and say the missing parts of the text. Finally, the children recite the complete text of the chant with the rhythmic support of the karaoke section.

Word Plays – creative tasks

Playway to English 2 Second edition includes tasks that carefully encourage the children to be creative in English. For example, the children listen and read the poem on Pupil's Book p. 36, ex. 6:

Look at me.
My T-shirt's red.
My jacket's green.
My jeans are blue.
Like a parrot in a zoo.

The teacher might then write a skeleton text of the poem on the board:

L a m
M T 's r
…
…
…

The children jointly reconstruct the text.
On Pupil's Book p. 36, ex. 7 the children find the instruction: Draw, write and say. Below is the following gapped text.

Look at me.
My _____ 's _____.
My _____ 's _____.
My _____ are _____.
Like a parrot in a zoo.

Then the teacher might write items of clothing and colour words on the board or simply tell the children to check the spelling of the words in their books.

Then the children create their own poem. The teacher checks it, asks the individual children to read it out to her and finally asks the children to present their poem in class.

When the children ask for words that have not been introduced, write them on the board, say them and ask the children to repeat them.

By involving as many senses as possible the rhymes are retained in the memory long-term. Research findings in primary school English lessons show that children who have forgotten parts of the text can remember them again by recalling the series of actions or the colours and the rhymes.

[2] Asher, J. (1988), *Learning Another Language Through Actions: The Complete Teacher's Guide Book*, Los Gatos, Ca.: Sky Oaks Publications.

ME-page

Each unit in the Activity Book also contains a ME-page. These activities are designed to give the children the opportunity to personalise the language they have used in the class. They are encouraged to complete the activity in a way that is personal to them and are therefore given guided support in using the language creatively.

How to use *Playway to English 2 Second edition* in the lesson

The selection of teaching topics

There are numerous ways of using the material in *Playway to English 2 Second edition* in combination with the topics in the curriculum. The topics have been organised in such a way that the teacher can always find material and activities that link in with the topics currently being taught in the curriculum. See contents on p. 2 for the list of topics.

Lesson overviews

At the start of the teaching notes for each individual lesson an overview box provides a summary of the language used and lists the materials required in that lesson under the following headings:

- Vocabulary, phrases and structures
- Linguistic skills
- Cognitive, motor and social skills
- Cross-curricular integration
- Materials

Lesson plans for the school year

Lessons should always be pre-planned to take into account the situation in individual classes. The following overview gives a summary of the syllabus with suggestions for integration of the individual units of *Playway to English 2 Second edition* into the curriculum for the whole of the school year. It presents a framework that can be used as a basis for individual lesson plans.

Topics	Types of text and activities	Vocabulary, phrases and structures
1 Hello again	• Revision/introduction of vocabulary. Vocabulary games.	• Word groups: colours; toys; school; pets; party; numbers from one to ten. bird/s
	• *Hello again* (song) Listening exercise.	
	• The mouse in the house (Mr Matt story) Listening exercise. Reading exercise.	• *Melon, grapes, pound, pence, two pounds fifty, one pound sixty, fifty-four pence. Receptive: Just a little. Let's eat the melon; Where are the grapes?; Where's the melon?; Two pounds, please.*
	• *The banana skin* (action story) Listen and imitate. Listen and point. Listen and write the numbers.	• *Walk to school; Open your schoolbag; Take out a banana; Eat it; Throw the skin away; Walk on; Ouch.*
		What number is ...?
	• Listen and draw. Guessing the fruit.	• *Peach/es; nut/s; kiwi/s; strawberry/ies; orange/s. Receptive: Close your eyes; open your mouth; What is it?*
	• Find the pattern.	
	• *One apple for Benny* (rhyme) Create your own poem. Word play. Step to creativity. Draw and describe.	• *One (apple) for (Benny); Some (grapes) for (me). My favourite (fruit) is (plums).*
2 Shopping	• *I like potatoes* (chant) Match the words to the pictures.	• *I like potatoes; onions; carrots; green/red peppers; tomatoes; cucumbers; Yummy!; I don't like ...*
	• Write jumbled letters to make words.	
	• Look, read and write numbers. Stick in pictures. Pair work.	• *How many (cucumbers) are there? What do you like? (Maria) likes/doesn't like. What about you?*
	• Listen and write names.	
	• *At a shop* (cartoon story) Act out shop scenes.	• *How much is it?; Two pounds; Here you are; Three onions, please; Thank you; Goodbye.*
	• Picture puzzle.	
	• Make a fruit salad (CLIL activity).	• *Receptive: Cut the apple; Add yoghurt; Mix everything; In my favourite fruit salad there are ...*
Units 1–2 Show what you can do	• Listening activity • Matching activity	Vocabulary from previous units.

Topics	Types of text and activities	Vocabulary, phrases and structures
3 In my house	• Listen and point. • Pair work.	• *sofa; chair; cupboard; curtains; TV; lamp; table; telephone; mat*
	• *The mice are having fun* (song)	• *What colour is the (sofa)?; What colour are the (curtains)?; mice; floor; door; on; family*
	• Listen and read. Create your own poem. Step to creativity.	• *In my room, there's a pink sofa …*
	• Listen and say. Describing rooms. Look and match: Reading exercise. Word ping-pong.	• *Let's watch TV; Listen! A car; They've got a cat!; Let's run!; The TV's on; That's strange; I can smell mice.*
	• *Time for fun!* (cartoon story) Stick-in pictures.	• *Open the cupboard; Ah. A chocolate bar; Climb onto a chair; Take the chocolate bar; Jump down; Ouch! Your foot! You drop the chocolate bar; Your dog grabs the chocolate bar; Shout: "Give it back!"*
	• *The chocolate bar* (action story) Listen and imitate.	• numbers from 11–20; *start/finish; It's my turn/your turn. Eleven plus five is …*
	• Pair work: Arithmetic game. Listen and match. Draw your own room and describe. Step to creativity.	
4 My body	• Listen and write numbers. Point and say activity – point at the body part and say what it is.	• *hand/s; head; ear/s; hair; shoulder/s; arm/s; finger/s; toe/s; leg/s; foot/feet; eye/s; nose; mouth*
	• *Bend your knees* (chant)	• *Bend your knees; Touch your toes; Clap your hands; Touch your nose; Shake your fingers; Touch your hair; Stamp your feet; Jump up high; Grow and grow; Touch the sky.*
	• Listen to the monster descriptions and number.	• Receptive: *My monster has got …; … Close your eyes; Open your eyes.*
	• *Wilbur* (action story)	• *Wilbur gets out of bed; He shakes his arms; He shakes his legs; He bends his knees; He says hello to his dog; Oh no! Wilbur runs into the bathroom; He cleans his teeth.*
	• *Mr Matt keeps fit* (Mr Matt story) Listen and write the numbers.	• Receptive: *Ouch, my back!; Where are we going?; Next, please; I've got an idea; Look at my tooth; Watch me, Megan.*
	• Listen and colour.	• *My tummy/knee/head etc. hurts.*
	• Listening exercise. Pair work. Circle the words.	
	Exercises on the five senses (CLIL activity).	
	• Listen and draw a monster from a description. Draw your own monster and describe it.	• *My monster has got …*

Topics	Types of text and activities	Vocabulary, phrases and structures
Units 3–4 **Show what you can do**	• Listening activity • Matching activity	Vocabulary from previous units.
5 Clothes	• Vocabulary games and activities. Pair work. Clothes sums. Word search.	• *shoes; pullover; woolly hat; skirt; socks; jacket; trainers; T-shirt; dress; hat; cap; jeans*
	• Listen and write.	• *Susan is wearing ...*
	• *Oh no!* (action story) Listen and write the numbers.	• *You're in the swimming pool; Get out of the water; Dry yourself; Put on your jeans; Put on your shoes and socks; Put on your T-shirt; Put on your jacket; Walk out; Oh, no! You're wearing your swimming goggles.*
	• *The woolly hat* (cartoon story) Listen and stick.	
	• Listen and colour. Listen and circle.	• *His (hat) is (blue); He/she's wearing.* *Hurry up; I don't know what to wear; put on; take off.*
	• Colour and say.	• *What colour is the jacket?; What colour are the shoes?; It's blue/...; They're brown/...*
	• Vocabulary games. Reading a poem. Create your own poem.	• Revision: colours Introduction of vocabulary: *zoo; parrot.* *Look at me; My T-shirt's red; My jacket's green; My jeans are blue; Like a parrot in a zoo.*
	• *The T-shirt* (Mr Matt story) Listen and colour. Read, match and colour.	• *I don't like it; Can I try the T-shirt on?; Can I help you?; I'll take the blue jacket; That's nice.*
	• Draw, write and say.	• *My favourite clothes.*
6 Let's count	• Introduction of vocabulary. Listen and colour. Listen and write the numbers. Introduction of written words.	• *thirty; forty; fifty; sixty; seventy; eighty; ninety; a hundred; zero*
	• *Pounds in my piggy bank* (song) Draw lines to join numbers. Number word search. Write the words.	• *piggy bank; camera skateboard; football; hammer*
	• *Clever Joe* (cartoon story) Role play of Clever Joe	• *circus; the maths test; I can't do it.*
	• Listen and colour. Play a game (snakes and ladders) as pair work. Match and write – forming categories. Look and do the sums. (CLIL activity) Match the numbers in figures to the written numbers.	• *I'm so sorry; Let's go to the swimming pool; Tim is ill; Ben is thinking; Anne, come here; Can I try?*

© Cambridge University Press and Helbling Languages 2009

Topics	Types of text and activities	Vocabulary, phrases and structures
Units 5–6 **Show what you can do**	• Listening activity • Matching activity	Vocabulary from previous units.
7 Family	• Vocabulary introduction and revision. Listen and read the poem. Write a poem about your family. • *The racoons and the beaver* (cartoon story) Stick in pictures. Tell the story. Role play with masks/mask-making. • Reading exercise. Listen and order the pictures. • *The clever racoons* (song) Find the odd word out. Sentence building. • Listening exercise. Match the sentences to the pictures. Speaking exercises.	• *family; mum; dad; sister; brother; grandpa; grandma; In Susan's family there's a... racoon* • *river; beaver; cut off his tail* • *I've got an idea; Let's help him; Let's go to the river; Swim across the river; He is happy; We are happy.* • *helpful* • *They smell wonderful; garden*
8 On the farm	• Vocabulary exercises. • *Feed the hens* (action story) Listen and write the numbers. Writing exercise. Folding a cat. (CLIL activity) • *Eddie, the earthworm* (cartoon story) Stick in pictures. Tell the story and role play. • Animal wordsearch. Sentence building. • Reading exercise. • *The earthworm song* (song) • Match the sentences to the pictures. (CLIL activity) Match the sentences to make mini-dialogues. • Reading exercise. Draw and write about your own farm. Step to creativity.	• Revision: *numbers; cat; dog; mouse; duck; butterfly; bee; hen. pig; cow; earthworm; sheep; horse; Is it a cow?* • *eggs; corn; chick.* *Put on your shoes; Take some corn; Go outside; Call the hens; Feed the hens; Go to the hen house; Look for eggs; Pick up an egg; Crack. There's a chick. Feed the cat; Look for the cat; Put on your trainers; Call the cat; Pick up a ball; Go outside.* • *vegetables; trees; flowers.* *Who are you?; Eddie is happy; Bees make honey; Eddie is sad; Hens lay eggs; Everybody loves you.*

Topics	Types of text and activities	Vocabulary, phrases and structures
Units 7–8 **Show what you can do**	• Listening activity • Matching activity	• Vocabulary from previous units.
9 Travelling	• Listen and point at the picture. Write sentences. • Pair work. • *Come to my party* (chant) Listen and write the names. • *Timmy* (cartoon story) Stick in pictures. Telling the story; role play. • Listen and write the numbers. • Find the odd one out – formulating categories. • *Juicy apples* (song) • Pair work: Communication game. Writing exercise. • *First by bike* (rhyme) Create your own poem. Step to creativity. Reading and speaking exercise.	• *car; train; plane; boat; bike; walk; left; right.* • *How do you get to school?; By bus/car...; Go by bus/car.* • *go by plane; a rocket* • *rain; wind; apples; go by bike; go by bus; go by train; peaches; juicy; bus stop; station; walk (faster)* • *What a heavy basket; What a strong wind; Linda goes by bus; Can I have an apple?; What's in your basket?; It starts raining.* • Revision: *What colour is your (train)?* *go by bike; go by bus; go by train; go by bus go by car; go by underground.*
10 Holidays	• *A day on the beach* (Mr Matt story) • *The lake* (action story) Listening exercise. Match the sentences to the pictures. • *The jungle safari* (cartoon story) Stick in pictures. • Telling a story. Writing exercise. • *Holiday boogie* (song) • Listen and colour. Read, match and colour. Read and write the numbers. (CLIL activity). Reading exercise. Writing about your favourite holiday.	• *beach; swimming; sailing; fishing; I'm bored.* • *lake; Jump in; Take off your jeans; Go to the swimming pool; Swim; You're hot; Cool off.* • *tiger; jungle; Let's be quiet; It's asleep.* *Let's jump in; Too late; It's asleep; Careful! Let's be quiet; Look at its big ears.* • *Let's build a sandcastle; Let's go fishing; Let's go swimming; Let's watch TV; Let's go sailing.* *Let's go to the show.*
Units 9–10 **Show what you can do**	• Listening activity • Matching activity	• Vocabulary from previous units.

Basic technology

Working with the flashcards

The purpose of the flashcards is to introduce important new words visually. These suggestions for using them in the lesson are based on the following educational principles:

- Conveying the **meaning** of new words in the foreign language lesson should be carried out **as visually as possible.**
- Always apply the principle **listening precedes speaking**. The children should first of all become accustomed to the pronunciation and intonation of a word before they are asked to repeat it.
- When introducing new words use a **combination of all the senses**. Pictures, pronunciation and intonation and also motor-processing techniques complement each other and help to anchor a word in the long-term memory.
- The **anchoring of the new words** will be all the more long-lasting if the words are repeated often enough. No more than one to two minutes are needed for this. The flashcards are highly suited to such repetition stages.

The following methods have proven successful:

Introduction of vocabulary
- Show the flashcards in order and say the English word at the same time.
- Then stick the cards on the board. Repeat the words in order, then jumbled up, at the same time pointing to the corresponding flashcard.
- Say the words and encourage the children to point to the flashcards, e.g.: *Point to the grapes.*
- Have the children repeat the word after you several times.
- Gradually increase the pace.

Exercises for anchoring the vocabulary in the children's recognition memory:
- Call one child up to the board and say the words in order. The child points to the corresponding flashcards on the board. Call another child to the board, say the words jumbled up and ask the child to point along as you speak.
- Call individual children to the front and ask them to take a card from the board and to give it to another child in the class, e.g.: *Mark, take the skirt, please. Pass it to Lena.* Mark: *Here you are.* Lena: *Thank you.*
  When all the flashcards have been distributed around the class, say: *Stick the lamp on the board.* The child with the corresponding flashcard sticks it back on the board. Continue in this way until all the flashcards are stuck back on the board.
- Call individual children out to the board. Give the following instruction: *Touch the (grapes).* The children touch the corresponding flashcard. Then remove all the flashcards from the board. Ask the children to close their eyes. By turning off the visual channel the children can concentrate completely on the sound pattern. Say the words individually. Change your voice as you do so. Say the words loudly, quietly, in a high voice, in a deep voice, happily, sadly, angrily and encouragingly. The children just listen first of all then they repeat the word exactly as you say it.

Exercises for anchoring words in the children's productive memory
- Hold a flashcard in your hand with the reverse side to the children and ask: *What is it?* The children guess what the word is. When a child has guessed correctly, show the flashcard and reply: *Yes, it is.*
- Stick the flashcards on the board. Then say all the words in order together with the children. Clap twice between each word. Repeat the words a few times but change the activities between the individual words. For example, click your fingers, slap your thighs, stamp your feet, stand up and sit down at the next word.
- Take one flashcard after another, say the words and turn the card over so that only the reverse is visible. When all the flashcards have been turned over, ask: *Who can remember the words?* Have individual children come up, say a word and turn over the card they think is the right one.

Working with the word cards

When the children can pronounce the new words and phrases correctly should the teacher introduce the word cards. When the word cards are introduced for the first time it is important that the teacher should say the words or phrases.
- The following techniques have proved very successful when the children are trying to commit the written words to their long-term memory.
- Put the relevant flashcards on the board.
- The teacher hands out words cards and the children match the flashcards with the word cards.
- Memory game. The children sit in a circle. The teacher puts the flashcards face down on the floor. Then the teacher adds the word cards and says the words. They are also put on the floor face down. Now a child turns over two cards. If the picture and the word are a match, the child can keep them. If not the cards are turned over again and the next child tries their luck.

Using the DVD sequences and the story cards

Not all the language in the DVD sequences or CD versions of the stories are presented in the cartoon story in the Pupil's Book. This is mainly because of the length of the stories but also this serves to encourage the children to listen for the necessary information in order to complete the gap fill in the Pupil's Book.

For using the cartoon story sequences on the DVD we recommend the following steps:

1st stage: Preliminary preparation of important words and phrases
Pre-teach important words or phrases beforehand if necessary – usually with the aid of the flashcards or story cards.

2nd stage: Playing the DVD sequence
Play the DVD sequence – several times if necessary.

3rd stage: Picture sticker activity
The children listen to the audio version of the story on the CD while they are completing the picture story with the picture stickers from the appendix of the Pupil's Book.

4th stage: Evaluation

Go around the class and check whether the children have completed the picture story correctly with the stickers. Alternatively, produce a completed picture story and the children check their work independently.

5th stage: Telling the story

In further stages the story cards or Max the glove puppet can be used to practise and reinforce the story texts through play. They can also be used later on as an ideal way for regular revision of learned material.

- Tell the story with the aid of the story cards. While you are telling the story stick the cards one after the other on the board.
- Tell the story again. While you are telling the story keep stopping and asking the children with corresponding mimes and gestures to reconstruct the story with you. For example, when working on the story … *The racoons and the beaver* (Pupil's Book, pp. 48–49) say: *The racoons are going for …* Children: *A picnic.* Etc.

6th stage: Story reconstruction game

- Distribute the story cards to individual children. Tell the story again. The child with the corresponding picture comes out to the front. Finally, all the children who were given the story cards are standing in the order of the sequence of the story in front of the class. Tell the children to hold the pictures up so that they can be seen clearly by all.
- Tell the story with mistakes. Say: *The racoons are going to school.* Children: *No, they are going for a picnic.* Etc.

Using the Mr Matt stories

For using the Mr Matt stories on the DVD we recommend the following steps:

1st stage: Preliminary preparation of important words and phrases

Pre-teach important words or phrases beforehand if necessary – ideally with the aid of the flashcards.

2nd stage: Playing the DVD sequence

Play the DVD sequence – several times if necessary.

3rd stage: Listening exercise

Play the listening exercise for the Mr Matt stories on the CD (ideally) twice. In their books the children number the scenes depicted in the sketches.

4th stage: Evaluation

Go around the class and check whether the children have correctly numbered the pictures. You can also hold up your book, point to scenes and the children say the corresponding number. In high-ability groups the answers can be checked by you saying: *Picture one.* Children: *I like this T-shirt./This is nice.*

How to use the Max glove puppet

The Max glove puppet performs a variety of functions in the lesson.

- Max should always be placed somewhere visible when you want to signal to the children that an English lesson is starting. When the children see Max, it helps them to recall the language they have already learned and this causes their previous knowledge to be activated unconsciously.
- Max can be used again and again as a model for speaking. Tell the children that he likes them to repeat what he says. The following methodology tips make the use of the Max glove puppet in the lesson particularly effective:
  - Use a distinctive voice for Max by changing your voice slightly. You can also copy the voice of Max in the film. This helps to give Max his own identity in the children's perception, i.e. it makes him seem as real as possible.
  - Take care that Max only makes mouth movements when he is speaking. When you are speaking as yourself Max should not move. This is an important aid to comprehension for the children.
  - When children speak to Max in L1 (their mother tongue) he doesn't understand them. Max should never be used in a mother-tongue lesson because he serves as an important psychological anchor for foreign language use.

How to use the action stories

The action stories are based on the Total Physical Response method through which listening comprehension is consolidated holistically through play. Here is an example for the text of an action story from the topic *Clothes* (Unit 5):

> *You're in the swimming pool.*
> *Get out of the water.*
> *Dry yourself.*
> *Put on your jeans.*
> *Put on your shoes and socks.*
> *Put on your T-shirt.*
> *Put on your jacket.*
> *Walk out.*
> *Oh, no! You're wearing your swimming goggles!*

The following steps have proven very useful in working with the action stories.

1st stage: Listening and imitating

- Model the first statement *(You're in the swimming pool.)* and act it out by pretending to swim.
- Model the next statement and mime it. The children imitate your actions and synchronise their as closely as possible with yours. Repeat this procedere for all the lines in the action story.

2nd stage: Carrying out instructions

- The sequence of instructions and actions is repeated several times until you see that the children can carry them out independently and without difficulty.
- Then give the instructions again in the correct order and the children carry them out. This time you do not do the actions with them. Repeat this several times until you see that the children all understand well.

3rd stage: Carrying out the instructions in jumbled order

- Give the instructions in jumbled order and the children carry them out. Do not do the actions yourself.
- A particular favourite is a game where you give instructions to individual children more and more quickly to see if they can keep up. The game is fun, and practises quick responses to English utterances whilst furthermore increasing the concentration of the children.

4th stage: Listening exercise

- Finally the children open the Pupil's Book. They listen to the instructions on the CD and point along in the book where the pictures are illustrated in jumbled order. Then the children put the pictures in the right order by numbering them. This serves to check and confirm whether individual children can understand the sentences in the action story.

5th stage: Evaluation

- Go around the class and check the children's work.
- Option: In high-ability classes, you can put out an answer key for self-checking. The children go and check their own work themselves.
- Alternatively: Draw six boxes on the board (some action stories have four or six pictures/boxes) that represent the page in the Pupil's Book. Have the children tell you the numbers. Write the numbers in the boxes.

Using the songs

The following steps have proven very successful when used with the songs.

1st stage: Preliminary preparation and playing the song on the CD

Option: Introduce the new words with the aid of the flashcards. If necessary, reinforce important phrases with appropriate actions/gestures or drawings on the board. Play the song twice. The children follow in the book.

2nd stage: Reinforcing the text

Facilitate understanding of the text with corresponding actions or gestures and encourage the children to imitate you. Say the lyrics – several times if necessary in the rhythm of the song.

3rd stage: Singing along

Ask the children to stand in a circle. Hum the tune of the song. Gradually the children join in with you and hum along. When they are all humming, start to sing the words. Sing the song together with the children a few times along with the CD.

4th stage: Singing to the karaoke version of the CD

Sing the song together with the children using the karaoke version of the CD. Sing the song and do the actions.

Using the rhymes

The rhymes in *Playway to English 2 Second edition* have been carefully constructed so that they can be worked on using the multi-sensory method; the children listen to the rhyme, speak and carry out certain movements at the same time. The following steps have proven very useful in practice:

1st stage: Play the rhyme on the CD and present its content in gestures

Play the rhyme on the CD and, at the same time, present its content with the aid of appropriate gestures and actions or point to the corresponding pictures in the book.

2nd stage: Reinforcing the text (1)

Play the rhyme for a second time. Do the corresponding actions to it again or point along in the book. At first the children just watch. Say the rhyme line by line with the support of actions and encourage the children to copy you. Practise the chant with the children one line at a time by saying it out loud and doing the appropriate actions. The children repeat after you and imitate your actions.

3rd stage: Reinforcing the text (2)

The children open their books. Say the lines of the text in random order and the children point to the corresponding pictures in the book.

4th stage: Presentation

Invite any children who feel confident about it to recite the rhyme. The children can also do this in pairs. High-ability groups can also say the rhyme to the playback version of the CD.

5th stage: Step to creativity (only relevant for Word Plays)

Some of the rhymes are used as Word Plays. In that case, the original rhyme gives the children the framework to compose their own rhyme using the pictures in the Pupil's Book as a guide.

Using the chants

All the chants in *Playway to English 2 Second edition* have been written especially for the individual topics and have been carefully constructed so that they can be worked on using the multi-sensory approach. The following steps offer a basic structure for working on the chants:

1st stage: Play the chant on the CD and mime the meaning

Play the chant on the CD and carry out appropriate actions to facilitate the comprehension of the text.

2nd stage: Reinforcing the text (1)

Play the chant a second time on the CD and have the children point along in the book. The text is represented by the illustrations in the Pupil's Book. Say the text line by line. The children do the actions.

3rd stage: Reinforcing the text (2)

Practise the chant with the children by giving two 'instructions' and miming them. The children imitate your actions and repeat after you. Practise the chant in this way one verse at a time, then get the children to repeat the verses rhythmically and mime them.

4th stage: Listening exercise

Play the chant on the CD. The children number the pictures accordingly in the book. This serves to check and confirm whether they can understand the lines of the chant.

5th stage: Using the first playback version of the CD
(And now you!)

Play the CD. The children point to the corresponding pictures in the book and join in the verses. Play the half playback version on the CD. The children point along in the book and recite the missing parts of the text.

6th stage: Using the karaoke version of the CD
(One more time!)

The children now say the whole text to the karaoke section on the CD. Finally, divide the children into two groups. Allocate sections of the chant that can be said by each group; the teaching notes for specific chants offer some suggestions as to how this could be done, e.g. one group takes the part of the speaker with the teacher and the other group repeats. The group that is not speaking carries out the instructions. Repeat this several times.

Developing speaking skills

The development of the children's ability to express themselves in English represents an important aim in the educational concept of *Playway to English 2 Second edition* and in its method of use. Foundations for speaking are first and foremost laid by the children getting to know and understand various sorts of texts (action stories, songs, chants, rhymes, stories, listening exercises) important words, chunks of language, phrases and sentences and absorbing and storing many of them by way of writing exercises. A wide range of exercises serves to consistently build up and systematically extend the children's linguistic expressions. A distinction must be made between so-called 'pre-communicative' and 'communicative' exercises in the course. In the pre-communicative exercises the focus is on the language work. The exercises provide preparation for later communicative exercises. Communicative exercises, on the other hand, are distinguished by the fact that they offer opportunities for speaking that the children want or have to use to express themselves.

Examples for pre-communicative exercises in Playway 2 Second edition
- Games on p. 28 of the Pupil's Book. Child A pretends that her tummy hurts by miming. Child B says, "Your tummy hurts".
- On p. 42 of the Pupil's Book there is the board game snakes and ladders. When the children get onto a certain picture they have to say the word.
- Simple pair work activities. On p. 32 of the Pupil's Book the children listen to items of clothing and point at the pictures and words. Afterwards they work in pairs. Child A points at a picture of a jacket while covering the word with a rubber or pencil sharpener. Child B says the word.

- Checking comprehension. On p. 52 of the Pupil's Book there are pictures and words of animals. The children listen and write numbers next to each picture/word. As a comprehension check the teacher asks: *What's number six?* The children respond by saying the word.

Examples for communicative exercises in Playway to English 2 Second edition
- Simple pair work activities. In Unit 1, p. 7 of the Pupil's Book there is a model for a very simple dialogue. Child A puts a piece of fruit in child B's mouth and asks: *What is it?* Child B who has her eyes closed, tries to guess and says: *A peach.*
- Role plays. The children watch a shopping scene with Max, Benny and Linda on the DVD. After they have put in the missing stickers and listened to the story on the CD the teacher asks them to close their eyes. They listen to the story again. Then the teacher acts out short scenes with the children. Whenever they can't remember their part the teacher helps by whispering the words/phrases/sentences to them. Finally groups of children act out the shopping scene.
- Information gap activities. On p. 35 of the Pupil's Book there are two children in black and white. Child A colours the boy and child B colours the girl. Then child A tells child B how to colour the boy and child B tells child A how to colour the girl.

The use of the English in the here-and-now of the lesson

Increasingly, conversation in class should be carried out in English. It will start off with the teacher speaking English and the children understanding and carrying out what the teacher says. With the appropriate skills it will, however, also be possible to motivate the children to try saying something themselves in English which goes beyond the pre-communicative or communicative exercises described above. You can support the children in this by whispering words or groups of words as prompts whenever necessary. It is also important to emphasise that learning foreign languages and making mistakes belong inseparably together.

Working with *Show what you can do*

- This self-assessment section appears after every two units. It serves the purpose of consolidating the most important words and phrases; the ones that are set as compulsory in the syllabus. The children listen to the CD and match the words/phrases to the pictures by numbering them.
- They then match the written words/phares to the corresponding pictures and the words/phrases that they hear.
- Children and parents should be aware that the words/phrases in the self-assessment are to be mastered as productively as possible, i.e. that the children can use the words/phrases from the self-assessment with as few errors as possible.

Observations from the psychology of learning on the early learning of foreign languages

Requirements of foreign language learning for very young learners

When children start learning English at primary school as a rule they not only already know a few English words but also have a range of basic skills that enable them to learn a new language. These skills have been gained in the process of learning their mother tongue. Learning a foreign language at school builds on these foundations and further develops the skills:

The ability to grasp meaning
Before toddlers know the exact meanings of individual words they are able to understand the sense of complete utterances. Intonation, mime, gesture, and the connection between what is said and their environment helps them to decode what they have heard. In the foreign-language lesson this skill needs to be activated. By doing so, already in very early stages of the foreign-language lesson, the children experience a sense of achievement.

The ability to manage with limited linguistic means
Children often play with language and try to extend their often very limited linguistic options by transferring what they have learned to other contexts and through new creations. Often, for example, L1 words are spoken with an English accent if a child cannot find the right word in English. Observing this gives the teacher insight into important processes in the learning of languages.

The ability to learn indirectly
Primary school children are not very interested in grammatical structures, the system of pronunciation or other formal aspects of language. They are fascinated by a story and try to understand it. They gain pleasure from the sound of new words that the teacher introduces and love copying them. They enjoy chants and songs and enthusiastically do the actions to them when they speak or sing. They want to find the answer in a guessing game and eagerly use the structure that the teacher has introduced when they do this. They act out scenes from a story in class imitating the voices of the characters that they are playing so well that their pronunciation comes very close to the models that they have previously heard on the DVD or CD. In all these cases, and in many others, the children are unconsciously learning important linguistic skills. Here language is not an end in itself but a natural means of reaching communicative goals.

The ability to learn through fantasy and imagination
Children know that role play is a game. At the same time they identify so strongly with the story that it is as if it were actually real. The boundary between make-believe and reality is blurred. Children can better make the foreign language their own in such situations. In this way, the foreignness of the new language is gradually diminished.

The ability to interact and to speak
Children have a natural need to communicate with each other and to adults. This may not always be easy, especially when teachers or parents want to encourage them to listen. However communication is also an important basic skill on which the ability to interact in a foreign language can be built.

Learning languages as a holistic process

Language is communication. By using language we can understand others and make ourselves understood. For many adults learning a foreign language, the conscious explanation of its formal aspects is important. They want to understand how the language works and what rules it follows; they want to know, for example, how different verb tenses are formed and how they are used and try to use their cognitive knowledge about language as an aid to learning a foreign language systematically. Children learn a foreign language in a different way. They pick it up as a holistic process. The **development of listening comprehension** forms one of the important bases of this process. Children learn to understand what they hear, speculating at first about what it might mean. In this process, mime and gesture, realia and other visual aids such as pictures and drawings on the board play an important part in assisting comprehension. Thus, from the beginning, the children can understand the teacher's request to *Stand up.* because the teacher stands up the first time the phrase is used and asks the children to imitate through mime and gesture. When subsequently the teacher gives the same instruction time and again, the children will gradually be able to do it without any prompting. What a child assumes a phrase or question might mean is verified through constant repetition. An anxiety-free atmosphere and a pleasant learning environment are created by praising children for having correctly understood and by patiently helping them when they have misunderstood.

The content of what the children are offered in the new language is of crucial importance in motivating them to work out the meaning of what they hear. If this content is meaningful, interesting, exciting or funny they will be more motivated to try to understand. The pleasure in their ability to understand, for example, a story in the foreign language, increases their self-esteem and heightens their **motivation to learn**.

The same is true for **developing speaking skills**. Songs, rhymes and chants give children the opportunity to gain experience with pronunciation and intonation, through play and without anxiety. The children also practise and repeat important words and expressions in ways that are fun and subconsciously store them in their memories. Stories (cartoon stories and Mr Matt stories) are as valuable an aid in the development of speaking skills when learning a foreign language as they are in the acquisition of the mother tongue. The children memorise important expressions. They learn to understand connections and they can try out simple utterances in communicative contexts in the role plays.

The SMILE approach®

In developing the **SMILE approach**® we were guided by the following basic principles which are based on accepted findings in research in the psychology of learning:

➤ Skill-oriented learning
M
I
L
E

Recent findings in the psychology of learning clearly show that the development of foreign-language skills does not take place independently of general cognitive development. For example, when children are engaged in deciphering the meaning of a sentence that they have heard spoken by the teacher they draw on abilities that they also need for handling tasks in other areas of life. These abilities include solving problems, establishing causal relationships, drawing conclusions based on analogy, etc. For this reason it makes sense to integrate early foreign-language learning into the curriculum as far as possible. This is congruent with the learning style of children of this age group which is still very holistic. Integrating the foreign-language lesson and the curriculum in this way develops the child's general intellectual skills and they promote each other reciprocally.

S
➤ Multi-sensory learner motivation
I
L
E

You need only watch children at play to understand the significance of learning through all the senses. *Playway to English 2 Second edition* aims to constantly activate all the senses as far as possible. This is based on the following concepts of the psychology of learning:

- When our pupils take in information, they do so through the senses: they learn what they see, hear and do.
- The auditory reception of information correlates with the so-called left side of the brain activities. Processing information kinaesthetically – by concrete activity is closely connected to the processing part that is often attributed to the right side of the brain. The visual reception of information can be controlled by either the left or the right side of the brain.
- The better the individual senses are integrated into the presentation of information stage the better the children's reception of the information (multi-sensory reception).
- The reception of information activates the neurological systems (visual, auditory, kinaesthetic) in the processing of information when thinking and remembering. During these processes a multi-sensory activation of the brain heightens children's ability to pay attention and concentrate and to store linguistic information in their long-term memories.
- The fact that most children have different learning styles and have a preference for one sensory channel over another (and can therefore also have weaknesses in one or two sensory channels) underlines the importance of a teaching methodology that takes account of the differing sensory needs of different learners and aims to strike a balance between visual, auditory and kinaesthetic presentation, processing and practice of linguistic information.
- Children love stories (narrative texts) and humorous sketches (dialogues). These stories and sketches remain firmly in the memory when presented in an appropriate multi-sensory way. Words, parts of sentences and sentences (chunks of language) can thus be fixed in the long-term memory.

S
M
➤ Intelligence-building activities
L
E

'Intelligence' is a collective term that covers a range of different human abilities which are all independent of each other. Researchers into intelligence speak of a multiplicity of 'intelligences'.

Howard Gardner, for example, claims that there are seven different areas of intelligence, i.e. 'multiple intelligences'.[3] Modern research into intelligence also clearly indicates that intelligence is not a gift with which human beings are born and which then stays with them for the rest of their lives in the form of a higher or lower IQ (intelligent quotient). Even though the inherited element is not inconsiderable, intelligence is quite clearly influenced by the learning process. Simply put, it can be said that intelligence can be learned. Learning a foreign language at an early age helps develop and stimulate a child's intelligence in a number of ways. All the intelligences named by Howard Gardner are stimulated by the **SMILE** approach:

Area of intelligence	Activation in *Playway to English 2 Second edition* by:
Linguistic intelligence	• Systematically developing the ability to decode the meaning of a foreign language through a great variety of different kinds of text. • Developing the child's hearing of phonemes by exercises in phonetic and articulatory differentiation. • Promoting the pleasure in playing with language. • Promoting unconscious discovery of laws of language. • Offering associative aids to noting vocabulary and phrases.

---

[3] Gardner, H, (1983) *Frames of Mind: the Theory of Multiple Intelligences*. Basic Books.

Area of intelligence	Activation in *Playway to English 2 Second edition* by:
Musical intelligence	• Promoting the ability to differentiate rhythm through chants and rhymes. • Promoting the ability to differentiate tunes through songs.
Interpersonal intelligence	• Developing basic social skills as an intrinsic principle: learning to listen to each other, tolerance of language errors, patience, etc. • Promoting empathy through role play. • Promoting the ability to work in pairs by cooperative tasks.
Kinaesthetic intelligence	• Using the whole body when working on the language through action stories, songs and action games. • Developing fine motor skills through various types of activities: picture stickers, drawing, colouring and craft activities.
Visuospatial intelligence	• Developing visuospatial perception through picture searches (discovery pictures). • Promoting the visual memory through picture puzzles.
Mathematical-logical intelligence	• Developing mathematical-logical intelligence through exercises where the children sort and match. • Encouraging logical perception through logical sequences and activities requiring putting things in order.
Intrapersonal intelligence	• Encouraging the ability to reflect as a basis for one's own speaking.

S
M
I
➢ **Long-term memory storage through**
E   **music, movement, rhythm**
     and rhyme

It is well known that adults can remember rhymes and songs they learned in the earliest stages of childhood. The reason these songs are so well retained is because children learn them using actions and movement. The ability to grasp and carry out rhythmic structuring can almost be seen as an expression of the level of language development of a child. The central function of the rhythmic differentiation ability for the unity of the perception and understanding of language is important for the storage of word and writing content and also of sentence patterns.

S
M
I
L
➢ **Exciting stories and games**

When learning, motivation is highly dependent on whether the learners identify with what they are learning. When children can identify closely with what has been learned it leads to them remembering it better. They remember phrases, parts of sentences and often whole sentences (so-called chunks of language) holistically. Good foreign language learners are characterised by the fact that they can repeatedly transfer such chunks of language to other contexts and thus practise and consolidate the foreign language through play. A learner who identifies with a foreign language makes this foreign language more easily 'their own'. This reduces the 'foreignness' of the foreign language. This principle also plays an important role in the acquisition of good pronunciation. Role plays are a natural component of a child's everyday life. In role play children develop their identity. Identifying with the foreign language and with foreign-language roles and characters in role play in the class helps build up a good pronunciation and intonation.

Learning a language through play is more than just fun and games

'That is by no means to say that learning too must be through play in all these cases. It can also remain associated with effort even during a game...'.[4] Early foreign-language learning is anything but laborious swotting of vocabulary, difficult puzzling over structures or anxiety-ridden battling with correctness of language. Foreign-language learning should not have negative connotations at any age – and yet for some adults it has those associations. *Playway to English 2 Second edition* makes it possible for children to enjoy foreign-language learning from the very beginning by involving them in games, songs, chants, role plays, puzzles and craft activities. For children these activities are fun, and yet they are involved in serious learning as they are doing them. Because of the many elements of play, children seem to completely forget that they are learning. They are so fascinated by the stories, role plays, songs and activities that they seem to take in the language effortlessly and remember it well. The children often cannot wait to be allowed to recite a rhyme or a short dialogue in a role play in front of the class.

The importance of constant revision

Revision is vital for learning a foreign language. This is clearly established in the psychology of learning. The acquisition of a foreign language makes it necessary to acquire a whole range of complex skills that can be summed up, in terms of cognitive psychology, under the heading of *procedural knowledge*. This is a multitude of intertwining cognitive process skills acquired as a complex whole and cannot be compared with the simple learning of facts (declarative knowledge). One of the essential prerequisites for establishing procedural knowledge is that its acquisition requires significantly more time and is stimulated by constant regular practice over a long period of time. Like driving a car, procedural knowledge is established by regular revision.[5] Therefore it is beneficial to revise with the children repeatedly in very short bursts during the lesson. This can be very enjoyable for them; it becomes a demonstration of their own capabilities and thus an essential confirmation of their learning success. It shows you and the children how the foreign language grows and gradually moves into the 'possession' of the children. The applause of the class community and praise from the teacher are not only an outward sign of progress made; they also strengthen the children's self-confidence and increase their motivation.

Playway to English 2 Second edition offers you numerous options for revision:
- Revising the songs and chants regularly.
- Revising the rhymes and also having them recited by individual children.
- Carrying out regular vocabulary revision with the aid of the flashcards.
- Using the DVD or story cards to revise the stories.
- Having the children perform role plays of the stories that lend themselves to it.

Classroom management

The teacher's tasks

In the process of teaching English the teacher has a number of different tasks:
- Conveying linguistic input (in part with the aid of media) and checking that this input has been understood.
- Using the mother tongue (L1) in small doses.
- Establishing routines.
- Encouraging the children to express themselves in the foreign language.
- Reacting to the children's errors in a methodologically correct way.
- Encouraging the children to learn independently.
- Adapting the seating arrangement to suit the type of activity.

Checking comprehension

When we learn a foreign language we are constantly exposing ourselves to the risk of not understanding everything that we hear or see. We try to understand messages holistically and work out what is not understood from the context. In class, the teacher tries to help the children understand as much as possible by conveying the information through different sensory channels (auditory, visual and motor). Watching children when they are performing tasks gives the teacher clues as to how much they have understood. Three patterns of behaviour frequently observed among teachers checking comprehension are **counterproductive**.
These are:
- Constantly translating individual words. This makes the children feel that they can only understand the foreign language when they know every single word. For example, when you teach the sentences in the action story in Unit 5 *(Clothes), Get out of the water.; Dry yourself*, etc. you teach the children to understand the sentences as an integral whole. Translating individual words would be absurd and would hinder the learning process. In contrast, translation in the following case is appropriate. The teacher says: *Touch the shoes.*, etc. to establish whether the children have mastered the English terms for clothes. A child hits every object named. At this point the teacher cannot distinguish whether the child is displaying aggressive behaviour, wants attention or has not understood. The teacher goes to the child and says *Touch the T-shirt*. S/he gives the L1 equivalent for *touch* and shows the child the action once again.

[4] Hans Scheuerl, (1990) Das Spiel [*Play*], Volume 1, Beltz, p. 176.

[5] cf. J. R. Anderson, (1983) *The Architecture of Cognition*, Harvard, University Press.

- The question *Do you understand?* is in most cases counterproductive. Children prefer to say yes to a question rather than go into explaining what they have not understood. It is much more useful to maintain eye contact and watch closely how the children behave and this will enable you to determine whether further aids to comprehension are needed.
- The following pattern of behaviour can frequently be observed during lessons. The teacher gives an instruction in English and then translates it into the L1. The reason for this may be that the teacher is unsure whether or not the children really understand the instruction in English. As soon as the children realise that each instruction is also given in L1, they hardly bother to listen to the English instruction any more. It is therefore recommended that you speak in short sentences, give the children time to think, repeat the instructions patiently and help by using mimes and gestures or, in some cases, support the instructions by drawing on the board or using pictures.

The role of the mother tongue (L1)

In the first months of the children's contact with the foreign language, giving explanations, instructions etc. in the child's first language cannot be avoided. The aim, however, over the course of the school year is to increase the use of the foreign language in conducting the classroom activities. By constantly using classroom phrases it is easy to gradually move over to the foreign language for regular routines. So the children very soon react, e.g. to the request *Let's do an action story.*, by standing up and putting their chairs away to make room for the actions, and to the request *Now work in pairs.*, by moving closer together.

Although the aim is to reduce the use of the mother tongue, there are always situations where it is necessary to translate single words or phrases because they cannot be represented by gestures, pictures, realia, etc. It is unavoidable to explain, for example, the phrase *Let's ...* in *Let's make a ...* with a mother tongue equivalent when it first comes up. *Let's ...* cannot be represented with gestures, pictures, realia etc., and the children must be prevented from coming up with their own interpretation. In contrast, when introducing the word *book* it is pointless to add a translation in addition to showing an actual book. The meaning is made clear by the object. To sum up, the following ground rule should determine the use of the mother tongue. Use as much English as possible and only as much of the mother tongue as is absolutely necessary.

An observation on the children's names

In primary schools there is a tradition of giving the children English names in the English lesson. **Two arguments** for this are usually given:
- Children like to slip into another role.
- When the teacher says for example: *Gerd, can you help me, please*, the articulatory basis is the native language – the child's name – and the teacher then switches into English with the next word.

We are inclined to support the following counterarguments in favour of retaining the child's own name:
- Playing a part in a role play means that a child takes on the identity of a character for the duration of the game. However, Klara becomes Sue in the English lesson, she does not take on another identity. Only the name is changed. The child stays the same person despite the fact that she has been given or has assumed another name.
- The children – and sometimes also the teacher – keep forgetting the English names of their classmates. This leads to confusion in group work and when working with a partner.
- If children are to learn to communicate in the foreign language, then this also means that they should state their own feelings, state of health, preferences etc. When, for example, the teacher encourages Sue (who is actually called Klara), to name her favourite food, Klara talks about herself. Sue's identity is not present.
- If Klara meets another child in the holidays and this child can only communicate in English, if she is asked her name she will answer Klara and not Sue.

Routines

English lessons involve constantly changing classroom scenarios. The children watch and listen to a story and show that they have understood it by putting pictures in order. They learn a song. They practise and revise a rhyme that they already know well. They ask each other for words in pair work, etc.

Alongside these changing scenarios, other processes are constantly taking place at the socio-emotional level. One child is being disruptive, another is trying to get the teacher's attention, a third is explaining an exercise to their partner, another is looking for their pencil or borrowing a rubber, etc.

The teacher tries to guide these processes verbally and non-verbally. The important thing is that the teacher begins to develop routines around all these complex processes using English to an ever-increasing degree.

CLASSROOM LANGUAGE

General instructions:
Let's start.
Listen.
Stand up.
Sit down.
Can you come here?
Can you come to the front?
Show me a/the … .
Bring me a/the … .
Give me a/the … .
Put it here/there.
Open/close the door/window … .
Stop now.
Pay attention.
Stop eating.
Put it in the bin.

Working with vocabulary:
Say the word.
All together.
Say it after/with me.
Say it again.
Now in groups.

Working with the Pupil's Book:
Look at the picture/pictures.
Write the numbers.
Work in/get into pairs.
Colour the … .
Open your books (at page) … .

Working with Songs, Rhymes und Chants:
Sing along.

Giving praise:
Great!
Well done.
Yes, that's right.
What a lovely drawing!
Good./Very good.

Language the children use:
Good morning.
Goodbye.
Hello.
Can I have the (scissors)?
I don't know.
I don't understand.
Can I go to the toilet?
Check, please.
It's my turn.
Sorry!
Thank you.
I can't find my … .
I haven't got … .
What's … in English?

Dealing with linguistic errors

What errors do children make when acquiring a foreign language? Basically, we differentiate between errors that occur in understanding and errors in reproduction or production of language. The errors that can be made at the reproduction stage or in the production of language occur at the levels of pronunciation and intonation, vocabulary and grammar. Three examples may illustrate this:

- In a role play one child says to the other *Go away*. During the performance several children do not succeed in pronouncing the [w] in *away* correctly. The teacher does not interrupt the role play. Even after the role play she does not dwell on the fact that three particular children have made this pronunciation mistake but she practises the [w] with the whole class with other words they already know and points out the exact position of the mouth. It would be naïve to assume that this compensatory practice would have the effect of clearing up problems with the [w] once and for all. The correct pronunciation of sounds and sound combinations, and also the intonation are the result of long practice. Adequate opportunities to hear English in motivating situations, the teacher's good example and short activities that are carried out again and again help the learners to improve their pronunciation and intonation.

- While performing a mini-dialogue a child says: *Here.* instead of *Here you are*. The teacher does not interrupt but practises the phrase again before other pairs present the dialogue.

- When working out a puzzle a child says: *Three nut*. The teacher repeats: *Right, three nuts*. Unlike during a role play, a rhyme or chant where it would be disruptive for the teacher to interrupt the course of the lesson, in this example they acknowledge the correct content of the child's utterance positively and adds the linguistic correction.

Making mistakes is unavoidable when trying to make progress in a foreign language. For this reason, when the teacher corrects the child the tone and context must be clearly helpful so that the child perceives it as such. Correcting in a negative way is counterproductive. The result is that the children no longer dare to speak. Mistakes that occur during activities with the objective of producing correct language (drills, etc.) are corrected immediately. The teacher does not make corrections during role plays and other situations where the children are trying to be linguistically creative. The teacher will show interest in what the child is communicating.
Should certain errors occur repeatedly in these stages then the teacher should consider what activities could be effective in improving the linguistic accuracy as a follow-up.

Learning to learn

Learning to learn can, in its initial stages, start to be developed in the first year of primary school. The aim is for children to gradually gain slight awareness of how they understand what is presented to them, what helps them remember words, phrases and texts and whether or not the pace of the lesson is appropriate for them. In order to achieve this aim, it is important to talk with the children about goals and about their own learning. That does not mean that the teacher takes the position of knowing everything, but that the aim is to take on board what the children say and talk about and what is particularly helpful or hinders their learning progress.

The seating arrangement

Although it is unrealistic to expect the tables in the classroom to be moved round for short periods of English teaching, the following points should, if possible, be considered with respect to the seating arrangement:

- Tables and chairs should be arranged in such a way that the children have enough room in their places to be able to move.
- Ideally there should be space in the classroom to allow the performance of role plays.
- All children should have a clear view of the board.
- If a DVD player is used, the children should be able to sit on the floor in front of the 'stage' like a puppet show.

The role of the parents

In general, the parents of primary school children have a very positive attitude towards the early learning of a foreign language and also want to actively support their children's language development.

It is recommended that at a parents' evening the following points are made:

- The children's early experiences of learning the foreign language should be positive ones. Through these experiences they gain self-esteem and motivation and lose their shyness about expressing themselves in a foreign language.
- Parents should not expect their children to be able to speak English right from the start. Children should first learn to understand linguistic utterances and later be able to respond orally in simple language.
- Using *Playway to English 2 Second edition* in foreign-language lessons will develop the children's intellectual, social, emotional and motor skills.
- Learning a foreign language at an early age stimulates an open-minded attitude towards other people and cultures.
- Point out that it is very important to praise children for the slightest progress in learning. If a child comes home and says *'Today we learned 'yes' and 'no'.'*, they should receive recognition for it.
- If children would like to show what they can do at home, parents should listen patiently and show interest. Errors are a sign of progress in learning. It is quite normal for children to make a lot of errors at the beginning.

- Parents should not ask their children to translate an English sentence into their mother tongue. The children learn the foreign language holistically. They may be able to understand the content of many sentences and phrases but not be able to translate them into the mother tongue.
- Parents should not be disappointed if their child cannot yet say something that has been learned. Some children start talking earlier than others. Parents can support their children in learning English with *Playway to English 2 Second edition* in the following way:
  - Rhymes, songs and chants can be revised. The pictures in the Pupil's Book can be used for support.
  - Parents can play at 'school' with their children and take on the role of the pupil. Children take great pleasure in teaching their parents in the foreign language. On the following page you will find a photocopiable master for an OHP slide that explains foreign-language learning with *Playway to English 2 Second edition* in more detail. You can use this OHP slide for parents' evenings.
  - Parents can do the exercises on the CD-ROM with their children.

Photocopiable master:

Characteristics of early foreign language learning

This is how children learn in practice:

- They grasp the meaning of new words with the aid of flashcards.

- They learn to recognise the written form of the language with the aid of word cards.

- They learn correct pronunciation by imitating English native speakers on the CD and DVD.

- They extend their vocabulary through play with the aid of targeted exercises.

- They learn to understand and carry out short action stories.

- They learn songs, rhymes and rhythmic chants.

- They watch short DVD sequences with simple storylines (cartoon stories) and humorous stories (Mr Matt).

- They learn to perform simple dialogues/role plays in class.

- They learn to assess their learning/progress/knowledge/ vocabulary and their ability themselves by means of regular self-assessment activities.

- They also gradually learn to understand about other topics on the curriculum in the foreign language (CLIL).

II.
Lesson plans

 Unit 1
Hello again

 Unit 2
Shopping

 Units 1–2
Show what you can do

 Unit 3
In my house

 Unit 4
My body

 Units 3–4
Show what you can do

 Unit 5
Clothes

 Unit 6
Let's count

 Units 5–6
Show what you can do

 Unit 7
Family

 Unit 8
On the farm

 Units 7–8
Show what you can do

 Unit 9
Travelling

 Unit 10
Holidays

 Units 9–10
Show what you can do

Playway to English

Lyrics: Gerngross/Puchta
Music: Lorenz Maierhofer
© Helbling, Rum/Innsbruck

With PLAY - WAY (clap) learning Eng - lish is fun, with

PLAY - WAY, PLAY - WAY, hip, hip, hoo- ray! hip, hip, hoo- ray! (clap)

Learn- ing to list- en is ea - sy, (clap) learn- ing to speak is not hard, (clap)

come on and smile, (clap) com - mu - ni - cate, (clap) learn- ing Eng-lish is great!

PLAYWAY

snap   snap
left   right

Pictograms in the Teacher's Book:

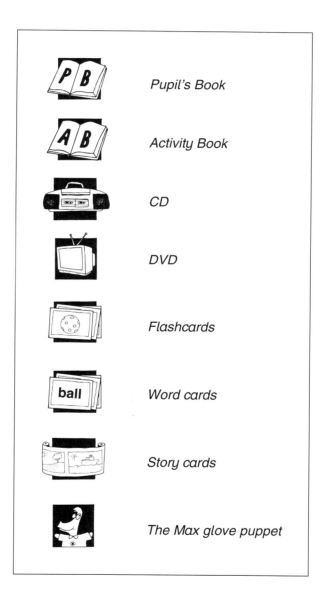

Pupil's Book

Activity Book

CD

DVD

Flashcards

Word cards

Story cards

The Max glove puppet

L E S S O N   1

Vocabulary, phrases and structures:

Hello, nice to see you again; How are you?; I'm fine; Fine, thanks; Hello again; We know lots of words.
Vocabulary revision: colours; toys; school; pets; party; numbers from one to ten

Linguistic skills:

Greeting each other. Asking *how are you?*
Learning the meaning, the pronunciation and the written form of new words.
Singing a song: (*Hello again*).
Learning the lyrics of a song.

Cognitive, motor and social skills:

Maintaining rhythm and melody while speaking in unison, singing and clapping.
Understanding sentences from the CD and connecting them with the corresponding pictures and words in the book.

Cross-curricular integration:

Topic: Speaking motivation 'Meeting and greeting friends'.

Materials:

soft ball; *Flashcards* from *Playway 1:* 1–11, 14, 15, 18, 20, 21, 23–29, 33, 36, 37, 41, 43, 44, 57, 58, 61, 63–64, 67
Word Cards from *Playway 2:* 1–35; 43; CD 1/2–4; *Pupil's Book*, p. 4, ex. 1; *Activity Book*, p. 4, ex. 1–2; glove puppet Max

---

Warm-up

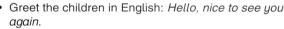

- Greet the children in English: *Hello, nice to see you again.*
- Greet Max in English and change your voice to answer as Max: *Hello, Max. Nice to see you again. How are you? – I'm fine./Fine, thanks.*
- Ask the children to repeat this dialogue a few times.
- Give the glove puppet to individual children. The children greet each other as Max and ask each other: *How are you?*

Revision

- Revise the vocabulary from the first year of the course by giving the children game activities that will allow them to practise the following word groups: school; toys; pets; colours; party; numbers.
- Start drawing the outline of a schoolbag on the board. Stop and ask: *What is it?* Let the children guess before you finish the drawing. Then say: *Tell me some more words for school things.* Make an inviting movement with your hand. The children name the school items they already know.
- Proceed in the same way with the topic areas toys, pets, colours, numbers and party. For revision of these topic areas use the flashcards from the first year of the course.
- Then play the following vocabulary game with the children: Throw a soft ball or a ball of wool to one child. At the same time say one of the words from the topic areas: school, toys, pets, colours, party, numbers.
- Tell the children to throw the ball to each other. The person throwing the ball must at the same time say another word from the same word group.
- Revise the numbers one to ten on the board, saying them at the same time.

Exercises for anchoring the words in the children's productive memory

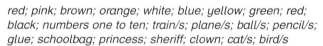

red; pink; brown; orange; white; blue; yellow; green; red; black; numbers one to ten; train/s; plane/s; ball/s; pencil/s; glue; schoolbag; princess; sheriff; clown; cat/s; bird/s

- Hold up the word cards in quick succession. Do not allow the children enough time to read the words letter by letter. They should absorb the written form only as a single entity.
- When the children say the correct word, repeat it. Then get one of them to put the card up on the board next to the corresponding flashcard. Say: *Put it on the board, please.*
- Take down all the flashcards, but leave the word cards on the board. Read them out together with the children several times.
- Tell the children to close their eyes. Turn the word cards face down on the board and tell the children to open their eyes. Point to the word cards in any order and say, each time: *What is it? What do you think?*

Option: An alternative activity is to hold up the word cards one after another, saying the words. Then hand the cards out to individual children. Repeat all the words again. After each word, the child with the correct word card comes out to the board and puts it up next to or below the flashcard.

---

❶ Listen and point. Sing the song.
Song: *Hello again* CD 1/2–3

- Ask the children to open their Pupil's Book at p. 4.

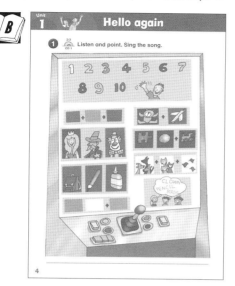

Hello again

Lyrics: Gerngross/Puchta
Music: Lorenz Maierhofer
© Helbling, Rum/Innsbruck

Ref.: One, two, three, four, five, six, se-ven, eight, nine, ten, hel-lo a-gain!

1. Red and pink and brown, prin-cess, she-riff, clown,
2. Ted-dy bear and plane, puz-zle, ball and train,

school-bag, pen-cil, glue, o-range, white and blue. (Come on!)
dogs and cats and birds, we know lots of words. (Oh yes!)

- Play the song CD 1/2. First of all, just sing the chorus of the song with the children.
- Then ask the children to point at the numbers at p. 4 of the Pupil's Book as they sing. They can also clap when they reach ten, and wave when they say: *Hello again.*
- Ask the children to sit in a circle. Lay flashcards for the words of the song face down.
- Say: *Tell me a word. Good.* Turn the card over. Continue until all the flashcards are turned over. Then say: *We know lots of words.* Explain the sentence in L1. Have the children repeat the sentence several times.
- Repeat the vocabulary exercise.
- Play the song *Hello again* CD 1/2 and have the children point to the lyrics in picture form on p. 4 of the Pupil's Book.
- Recite the text several times together with the children.
- Play the song several times. The children sing and point at the respective pictures in the book.
- Reconstruct the lyrics on the board together with the children with the aid of the flashcards and word cards. Stick up the cards corresponding to the sequence of the text. They are allowed to look in their books for this.
- Practise the text by giving instructions such as the following: *(Peter), point to schoolbag, pencil and glue.*

- The child is to point to the pictures of the three things named in rapid succession.
- Ask the children to "read" the text in pair work.
- Sing the song several times with the children. Use the karaoke version of the song on CD1/3.

Option: In very good classes, you can also play a memory game:
Have the children name words that they remember. Then ask them to find the flashcard matching the word named. A child says e.g. *schoolbag*, looks for the right card and turns it over.
Say: *Can you find the card? Let's see. Sorry. Try again. Who can help? Yes, good.*

Tip: Explain the phrase *Hello again* in L1.

Pronunciation tips: Take care with the pronunciation of [θ] in *three*, of [w] in *white* (with rounded lips), of [p] and [b] in *pink* and *brown*.

❶ Listen and write the numbers.
Listening exercise CD 1/4

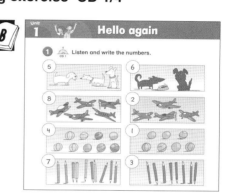

- Ask the children to look at the pictures in ex. 1 on p. 4 in their Activity Book. Say, for example: *Four red planes.* etc. Get the children to point at the respective pictures in their books as you say them.

Tapescript:

One:	Seven orange balls.
One:	Seven orange balls.
Two:	Four red planes.
Two:	Four red planes.
Three:	Eight pink pencils.
Three:	Eight pink pencils.
Four:	Nine green balls.
Four:	Nine green balls.
Five:	Three white dogs.
Five:	Three white dogs.
Six:	Two black dogs.
Six:	Two black dogs.
Seven:	Ten green pencils.
Seven:	Ten green pencils.
Eight:	Five blue planes.
Eight:	Five blue planes.

- Play CD 1/4 and ask the children to number the pictures accordingly from one to ten.
- Play the CD twice.
- Play the CD again and ask the children to check their work.

➋ Match the sentences to the pictures.
Reading exercise

- Write the sentences from ex. 2, p. 4 of the Activity Book on strips of paper and fix them to the board. Point at a sentence and read it out aloud. The children point at the sentences in their books and read along. Next, jumble the order of the sentences.

- Tell the children to match the sentences with the corresponding pictures in ex. 1 by numbering them from one to eight. Do the first sentence together with the children. Say: *Four red planes. What number is it?* Elicit the correct answer: *(Number) two.* From the children. The children go on to number the other sentences in ex. 2.
- To check say: *Three white dogs. What number is it?* The children answer: *(Number) five.*

L E S S O N   2

Vocabulary, phrases and structures:

pound; pence; Here you are; A melon, please; Just a little; Look, there's no mouse; I don't know; Where is it?
Receptive language: *Dad, where's the melon?; I don't know; Look. There's no mouse; Just a little; A melon, please. OK. Here you are; Let's eat the melon; Where are the grapes?; Where's the melon?; £ 2, please.*

Linguistic skills:

Understanding a story (*The mouse in the house*) from the DVD.
Understanding mini-dialogues (scenes from the story) from the CD.

Cognitive, motor and social skills:

Understanding mini-dialogues from the CD, numbering the pictures in the book to correspond.
Understanding sentences from the CD and the written form in the book by colouring the frames accordingly.
Connecting pictures with the corresponding sentences by colouring speech bubbles accordingly.

Cross-curricular integration:

Topic: Speaking motivation 'Buying fruit and vegetables'.

Materials:

CD 1/3; *Pupil's Book*, p. 4, ex. 1; *Flashcards* from *Playway 1*: 30, 32
Flashcards from *Playway 2*: 1–2; DVD *(The mouse in the house)*; CD 1/5–6; *Pupil's Book*, p. 5, ex. 2; *Activity Book*, p. 5, ex. 3–4; coloured pencils (green, blue, yellow, red); paper strips

---

Revision

- Sing the song *Hello again* with the children using CD 1/3. Use p. 4 in the Pupil's Book for this.
- Revise the words *mouse* and *duck* with the flashcards.

Introduction of vocabulary

melon; grapes; pound; pence; two pounds fifty; one pound sixty; fifty-four pence

- Introduce the words *melon* and *grapes* with the aid of the flashcards.

- Introduce the words *pound* and *pence*: Write £ on the board and ask the children whether they know what this sign means. If necessary give the appropriate explanation and also tell the children how much one pound is worth approximately.
- Then explain that *100 pence* make *1 pound*. Write the abbreviation *p* for *pence* (pronounced [piː]) on the board. Practise the words by saying them and having them repeat after you several times.
- Write the following prices on the board:
£2.50
£1.60
54p
- Point to the prices and say at the same time: *Two pounds fifty, one pound sixty, fifty-four pence.* Practise the prices by saying them and having them repeat after you several times.

Note: If you have the appropriate British coins available, allow the children to look at and touch a one pound coin, a two pound coin, a fifty pence, a ten pence and a five pence.

Preparation of key phrases

Just a little.

- Explain the meaning of the phrase *Just a little.* with the aid of corresponding mimes and gestures.

❷ Watch the story.

Mr Matt Story: *The mouse in the house*

- Show the children the DVD story *The mouse in the house* twice (DVD).

DVD script:	**The mouse in the house**
Greengrocer:	Hello. Can I help you?
Danny:	A melon, please.
Greengrocer:	OK. Here you are.
Danny:	Thank you.
Greengrocer:	Two pounds fifty, please.
Daisy:	Here you are.
Greengrocer:	Thank you. Bye!
Daisy:	Bye.
Danny:	Look, Dad. We've got a melon.
Mr Matt:	Mmh. I love melons. Let's eat it.
Daisy:	No! Not now. It's for tomorrow.
Mr Matt:	Just a little. Just one piece!
Danny:	Good morning, Dad.
Mr Matt:	Good morning.
Daisy:	You OK?
Mr Matt:	Yes, I'm fine.
Danny:	Mmh. Let's eat the melon.
Daisy:	Yes. Mmh.
Danny:	Where is it?
Daisy:	I don't know. Dad? Where's the melon?
Mr Matt:	I don't know. I think there's a mouse in the house.
Daisy:	A mouse?
Mr Matt:	Yes, a mouse.
Danny and Daisy:	Oh.
Danny:	A mouse?
Daisy:	There's no mouse. It's Dad.
Greengrocer:	Hello. Can I help you?
Danny:	Some grapes, please.
Greengrocer:	Here you are.
Danny:	Thank you.
Greengrocer:	That's one pound sixty, please.
Daisy:	Here you are.
Greengrocer:	Thank you. Bye!
Danny and Daisy:	Bye!
Daisy:	Look, Dad. We got grapes.
Mr Matt:	Mmh. I love grapes. Let's eat them.
Danny:	Not now, Dad. They're for tomorrow. And this is for the mouse.
Daisy:	Good idea, Danny.
Mr Matt:	Just one. Oh, no! I know.
Daisy:	Good morning, Dad.
Mr Matt:	Good morning, children.
Danny:	You OK?
Mr Matt:	Yeah, I'm fine.
Daisy:	Look. There's no mouse.
Danny:	Great. Let's eat the grapes.
Daisy:	Yes. Mmh. Where are the grapes?
Danny:	I don't know.
Daisy:	Dad? Where are the grapes?
Mr Matt:	I don't know. Look! It's not a mouse. There's a duck in the house.
Danny:	A duck?
Mr Matt:	Yes, a duck. Quack! Quack!
Danny:	There's no duck. It's Dad.
Greengrocer:	Hello! Can I help you?
Danny:	Some plums, please.
Greengrocer:	Put them there. That's fifty-four pence, please.
Daisy:	Here you are.
Greengrocer:	Thank you. There you are. Bye!
Danny and Daisy:	Bye!
Danny:	Look, Dad. We've got plums.
Mr Matt:	Mmh. I love plums. Let's eat them.
Daisy:	No. Not now, Dad. They're for tomorrow. Danny?
Danny:	Yes?
Daisy:	Get me some water.
Danny:	What for?
Daisy:	The duck.
Danny:	Oh. Uh huh.
Mr Matt:	Yes … No! Yes … No! Just one. OK? Just one plum.
Danny and Daisy:	Quack! Quack!

❷ Listen and write the numbers.
Listening exercise CD 1/5

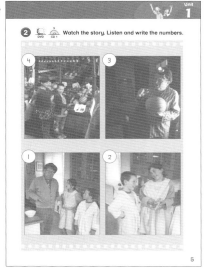

- The children open their Pupil's Book at p. 5, ex. 2 and look at the pictures. Tell the children that they are going to hear individual sentences or short dialogues on the CD. They should match them to the corresponding pictures in the book. Picture 1 has already been numbered.

Tapescript:

Announcer:	*Picture one.*
Daisy:	*Dad, where's the melon?*
Mr Matt:	*I don't know.*
Announcer:	*Once again.*
	Picture one.
Daisy:	*Dad, where's the melon?*
Mr Matt:	*I don't know.*
Announcer:	*Picture two.*
Daisy:	*Look. There's no mouse.*
Announcer:	*Once again.*
	Picture two.
Daisy:	*Look. There's no mouse.*
Announcer:	*Picture three.*
Mr Matt:	*Just a little.*
Announcer:	*Once again.*
	Picture three.
Mr Matt:	*Just a little.*
Announcer:	*Picture four.*
Danny:	*A melon, please.*
Greengrocer:	*OK. Here you are.*
Announcer:	*Once again.*
	Picture four.
Danny:	*A melon, please.*
Greengrocer:	*OK. Here you are.*

- Play the listening exercise twice (CD 1/5). The children number the pictures in the book.
- Then hold your book up so that it can be seen by all. Point to the first picture and ask: *What number is it?* Children: *Four.*

Tip: You can also check the children's answers by saying e.g.: *Just a little. What number is it?* Children: *(It's number) three.*

Preparation of key phrases

Let's eat the melon; Where are the grapes?; Where's the melon?; Two pounds, please.

- Write the four sentences on strips of paper, large enough so that all the children in your class can comfortably read the sentences.
- Hold up one of the paper strips for about half a second only. The children call out the sentence. They should, however, not be able to read the words letter for letter. This helps to avoid interference between the written words and their pronunciation. Carry on as described with the other sentences.

❸ Listen and colour.
Listening exercise CD 1/6

- Ask the children to take out the following coloured pencils: *Green, blue, yellow* and *red.*
- Ask them to look at the sentences in ex. 3 on p. 5 in their Activity Book.

Tapescript:

Blue:	*Where are the grapes?*
Blue:	*Where are the grapes?*
Green:	*Two pounds, please.*
Green:	*Two pounds, please.*
Red:	*Let's eat the melon!*
Red:	*Let's eat the melon!*
Yellow:	*Where's the melon?*
Yellow:	*Where's the melon?*

- Tell the children to listen to the CD and colour the frames around each sentence.
- Play CD 1/6 twice. The children listen and first mark the frames in the corresponding colours. After the track has finished they complete colouring the frames.
- Play the CD again and ask the children to check. Then ask: *Where are the grapes? What colour is it?* The children answer: *It's blue.*

❹ Read, match and colour.
Reading exercise

- Tell the children to colour the empty speech bubbles in ex. 4 on p. 5 in their Activity Book according to ex. 3 above.
- Then ask, for example: *What colour is 'Two pounds, please.'?* The children answer: *Green.*

L E S S O N   3

Vocabulary, phrases and structures:

Receptive language: *Walk to school; Open your schoolbag; Take out a banana; Eat it; Throw the skin away; Walk on; Ouch!; Tom is hungry; He opens his bag; He takes out a pear; Tom eats the pear; Eek!; Tom throws the pear away; Tom walks on; The birds eat the pear.*

Linguistic skills:

Understanding instructions in an action story (*The banana skin*).
Understanding instructions from the CD and matching them with the corresponding pictures.

Cognitive, motor and social skills:

Matching instructions with actions.
Understanding and carrying out jumbled instructions.

Cross-curricular integration:

Topic: Speaking motivation *'The banana skin'.*

Materials:

DVD *(The mouse in the house)*
CD 1/7–8; *Pupil's Book*, p. 6, ex. 3; *Activity Book*, p. 6, ex. 5

Revision

- Revise the Mr Matt story *The mouse in the house* from the previous lesson with the support of the DVD.

Listen and imitate.

Action Story: *The banana skin*

Walk to school; Open your schoolbag; Take out a banana; Eat it; Throw the skin away; Walk on; Ouch!

- Ask the children to stand in a circle or stand up in their places.
- Say the sentences of the action story (above) and at the same time carry them out in mimes/gestures.
- Keep repeating this until you see that the children have a good grasp of the sentences and the actions that go with them.

Carrying out instructions

- Tell the children that you are now going to give the same instructions but not carry them out yourself. Give the same instructions as above in the same order. The children carry out the movements. You do not do any of the movements yourself but give positive feedback (e.g. by nodding your head) when the children carry out the instruction correctly. Continue in this way with the rest of the instructions.
- Keep repeating this until you see that the children can carry out the instructions without difficulty. Gradually increase the pace.

Carrying out the instructions in a jumbled order

- Announce that you are going to give the instructions in a random order and the children must carry them out. Do not join in yourself.
- Keep repeating this until you see that the children can carry out the instructions without difficulty.
- Call on individual children and give each of them one of the instructions to carry out, in any order.

Hello again

**❸ Listen and point.
Write the numbers.**

Action Story: *The banana skin* CD 1/7

- The children open their Pupil's Book at p. 6. The seven pictures are printed in random order. Now give the children sufficient time to look at the pictures.

Tapescript:

*Walk to school.
Open your schoolbag.
Take out a banana.
Eat it.
Throw the skin away.
Walk on.
Ouch!*

- Play the listening exercise (CD 1/7). At first the children just point to the appropriate pictures in the book.
- Explain to the children that they should number the pictures from one to seven.
- Play the listening exercise again and the children number the pictures in the book.
- Go round the class and check the children's work.

Option: Draw a rough page layout on the board to look like Pupil's Book p. 6. Ask the children to dictate the numbers for each box.

**❺ Listen and write the numbers.
Listening exercise CD 1/8**

- Ask the children to look at the pictures in ex. 5 on p. 6 in their Activity Book. The pictures are printed in random order. Tell the children to listen to the CD and to number the pictures accordingly from one to eight.

Tapescript:

One:	Tom is hungry.
Two:	He opens his bag.
Three:	He takes out a pear.
Four:	Tom eats the pear.
Five:	Eek!
Six:	Tom throws the pear away.
Seven:	Tom walks on.
Eight:	The birds eat the pear.

- Play CD 1/8 twice. The children listen and number the pictures in the book.
- Check the children's work: Ask: *What number is 'He opens his bag'?* Children: *Number two.*

Option: With better classes, you can ask: *What's number two?* The children answer with: *He opens his bag.*

LESSON 4

Vocabulary, phrases and structures:

peaches; nuts; kiwis; strawberries; oranges; *Close your eyes; Open your mouth; What is it?; A peach/plum/nut; an orange; That's right.* Receptive language: *What does (Andy) get?; Who gets a (peach)?; I'm hungry, (Mum); Have an apple (Maria); Can I have a banana, (Dad)?; Here you are, (Andy); Give me some plums, please; Thank you.*

Linguistic skills:

Understanding and giving instructions.
Guessing fruits.

Cognitive, motor and social skills:

Understanding dialogues from the CD, drawing and colouring pictures in the book correspondingly. Re-enacting the dialogues in pair work.

Cross-curricular integration:

Topic: Speaking motivation 'Recognising fruit from its taste'.
Art
Drama

Materials:

Flashcards from *Playway 1:* 25–28, 75; fruit you have brought along to the class; knife and plate *Flashcards* from *Playway 2:* 1–6; *Word Cards* from *Playway 2:* 31–41; CD 1/9–10; *Pupil's Book*, p. 7, ex. 4–5; *Activity Book*, p. 7, ex. 6

Revision

- Give the instructions from the action story *The banana skin* from the previous lesson.
- Revise the types of fruit with the aid of the flashcards.
- Revise the phrases *Close your eyes. What is it?* As follows: Take the fruit you have brought along. Ask one child to come out to the front. Say: *Close your eyes.* And put a piece of fruit in his/her hand. The child has to guess what the fruit is:
  Teacher: *(Stefan), feel/smell it. What is it?*
  (Stefan): *A plum./It's a plum.*
  Teacher: *That's right./No, sorry. Try again.*

Introduction of vocabulary

peach/es; nut/s; kiwi/s; strawberry/strawberries; orange/s

- Introduce the new words with the aid of the flashcards and word cards, for example, crack an imaginary nut and take it out of the shell with your thumb and index finger (see also Basic Technology on p. 15 in the introduction to the Teacher's Book).

Exercises for anchoring the vocabulary in the children's recognition memory

- Fix the flashcards to the board.
- Say one new word after the other and get the children to make the corresponding gestures.
- Say one new word after the other and tell one of the children to touch the corresponding flashcard.

Vocabulary exercises with the support of the written forms

peach/es; plum/s; orange/s; kiwi/s; strawberry/strawberries; apple/s; banana/s; pear/s

- Hold up the word cards in quick succession. Do not allow the children enough time to read the words letter by letter. They should absorb the written form only as a single entity.

- When the children say the correct word, repeat it. Then get one of them to put the card up on the board next to the corresponding flashcard. Say: *Put it on the board, please.*
- Take down all the flashcards, but leave the word cards on the board. Read them out together with the children several times.
- Tell the children to close their eyes. Turn the word cards face down on the board and tell the children to open their eyes. Point to the word cards in any order and say, each time: *What is it? What do you think?*
- Turn the cards over when children guess correctly.

Option: An alternative activity is for you to hold up the word cards one after another, saying the words. Then hand the cards out to individual children. Say the words in turn. After each word, the child with the corresponding card comes out to the board and puts it up next to the flashcard.

❹ **Listen and draw.**
Listening exercise CD 1/9

- Ask the children to open their Pupil's Book at p. 7. Give them time to look at the pictures in ex. 4. Explain the exercise: The children are going to hear three dialogues, draw and then colour the missing two fruits in the respective bubbles.

Tapescript:

Announcer:	*One.*
Boy:	*Close your eyes.*
Girl:	*OK.*
Boy:	*Open your mouth.*
Girl:	*Mmh.*
Boy:	*What is it?*
Girl:	*A peach.*
Boy:	*That's right.*
Announcer:	*Two.*
Boy:	*Close your eyes.*
Girl:	*OK.*
Boy:	*Open your mouth.*
Girl:	*Mmh.*
Boy:	*What is it?*
Girl:	*A plum.*
Boy:	*That's right.*
Announcer:	*Three.*
Girl:	*Close your eyes.*
Boy:	*OK.*
Girl:	*Open your mouth.*
Boy:	*Mmh.*
Girl:	*What is it?*
Boy:	*An orange.*
Girl:	*That's right.*

- Now play the listening exercise (CD 1/9). Give the children enough time to draw the missing fruit in dialogues two and three.
- Play the listening exercise again and stop after each dialogue. Ask the children: *What is it?* The children answer with: *(It's) a plum,* after the second dialogue or: *(It's) an orange,* after the third one. Then they colour in the fruit.
- Go round the class and check the children's work.

❺ Say.

Pair work: Multi-sensory vocabulary games

- Cut up some fruit into small pieces and put them on a plate.
- The children open their Pupil's Book at p. 7 and look at ex. 5.
- Sit down with one child in front of the class in such a way that the children can all see. Ask the child to close his/her eyes and open his/her mouth.
- Say: *(Anna), come out, please. Sit down. Close your eyes. Open your mouth.*
- Take a piece of fruit, show it to the children and put it in the child's mouth. Say: *What is it?*
- Let the child guess what it is.
- (Anna): *A plum./It's a plum.*
  Teacher: *Yes, that's right./No, sorry.*
- Demonstrate the dialogue again with a child in front of the whole class.

- Repeat the procedure with other children and practise the expressions thoroughly by getting the children to say and repeat it several times.
- Give each pair a plate with different pieces of fruit to carry out the pair work.
- Then the children re-enact the dialogues of the listening exercise with a partner. It is important that they swap roles in this so that both children can practise all the expressions.
- Go round the class and help if necessary.

❻ Listen and draw.

Listening exercise CD 1/10

- Tell the children to give you some English names. Give them a few examples, e.g. *Benny, Linda*, etc. if necessary.
- The children open their Activity Book at p. 7. Ask: *Who's Karen?* The children point at the appropriate picture in the book. Repeat this several times with the other names, *(Maria, Andy, Tom, Sandra, Karen, Bob, Max, Benny).* Then point at a picture and say: *Who's this?*

Tapescript:

Maria:	*I'm hungry, Mum.*
Mum:	*Have an apple, Maria.*
Andy:	*Can I have a banana, Dad?*
Dad:	*Here you are, Andy.*
Andy:	*Thank you.*
Tom:	*Can I have an orange, Mum?*
Mum:	*Here you are, Tom.*
Tom:	*Thanks, Mum.*
Sandra:	*I'm hungry, Dad.*
Dad:	*Have a pear, Sandra.*
Sandra:	*Thanks. Yummy.*
Karen:	*Can I have a peach, Mum?*
Mum:	*Here you are, Karen.*
Karen:	*Thanks, Mum.*
Bob:	*I'm hungry, Dad.*
Dad:	*Have some nuts, Bob.*
Bob:	*Thanks, Dad.*

Max:	Linda, can I have some grapes?
Linda:	Here you are, Max.
Max:	Thank you, Linda. Grapes, yummy.
Benny:	I'm hungry, Max. Give me some plums, please.
Max:	Here you are, Benny.
Benny:	Thank you.

- Play the first dialogue from CD 1/10.
- Press the pause button and ask: *What does Maria have?* The children answer: *An apple.* Point at the first picture in the book and say: *Right. Let's draw an apple here.* Take a pencil and act as if you were drawing an apple in Mum's hand.
- Play the other dialogues several times if necessary. The children draw the fruits. Then ask questions, e.g.: *What does Andy get? Who gets a peach?*

L E S S O N 5

Vocabulary, phrases and structures:

Vocabulary revision: fruits
Receptive language: *What about pattern number one?*

Linguistic skills:

Consolidating the meanings, the pronunciation and the written form of words.

Cognitive, motor and social skills:

Understanding a combination of words from the CD and associating them with the corresponding pictures in the book.

Understanding numbers from the CD and writing them.
Understanding instructions from the CD and using them to make patterns.

Cross-curricular integration:

Topic: Speaking motivation 'Fruit'.
Maths (numbers 1–10)

Materials:

Flashcards from *Playway 1*: 25–28, 75; *Flashcards from Playway 2*: 1–6; *Word Cards* from *Playway 2*: 31–41
CD 1/11–13; *Pupil's Book*, p. 8, ex. 6–7; *Activity Book*, p. 8, ex. 7–9; (optional) answer key for self-checking

Revision

Vocabulary games with written words

- Put the fruit flashcards up on the board. In good classes, use the word cards from the previous lesson.
- Number the flashcards or word cards from one to ten.
- Give the children about a minute to memorize the words and the corresponding numbers properly. Then tell them to close their eyes.
  Now play a memory game, for example:
  Teacher: *What number is pear/s?*
  Children: *Seven.*
- Alternatively, hand out the flashcards and the word cards to individual children. Name the fruits one after the other and the children with the corresponding cards come out and put them on the board.
- Take down all the flashcards, but leave the word cards on the board. Read out the words with the children, then ask them to close their eyes. Remove one or two cards. Ask the children to open their eyes again. Say: *What's missing?* The children name the missing fruits.

❻ **Listen and write the numbers.**

Listening exercise CD 1/11

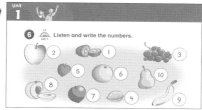

- Ask the children to look at the pictures on p. 8, ex. 6 in their Pupil's Books. Name the fruits and get the children to point at the respective pictures.
- Tell them to listen to the CD and number the pictures accordingly from one to ten.

Tapescript:

One:	Kiwi.
One:	Kiwi.
Two:	Apple.
Two:	Apple.
Three:	Grapes.
Three:	Grapes.
Four:	Nut.
Four:	Nut.
Five:	Strawberry.
Five:	Strawberry.
Six:	Orange.
Six:	Orange.
Seven:	Plum.
Seven:	Plum.
Eight:	Peach.
Eight:	Peach.
Nine:	Banana.
Nine:	Banana.
Ten:	Pear.
Ten:	Pear.

- Play CD 1/11 twice. The children listen and fill in the numbers.
- To check ask, for example: *Number three? What is it?* The children answer accordingly: *Grapes.*

❼ Listen and draw. Find the pattern.

Listening exercise CD 1/12

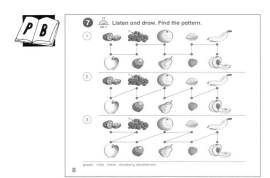

- Tell the children to look at the fruits in ex. 7 on p. 8 in their Pupil's Book. Say the names of the first row of fruit in number one: *Kiwi, grapes, orange, nut, banana.* The children point at the pictures in their books. Then say the second row: *Apple, plum, pear, strawberry, peach.*
- Tell the children that they are going to hear fruits from the CD and that they should draw lines to join the dots underneath and above each fruit. The result should be a pattern.
- Do the first pattern together with the children.
- Hold up your book. Point at number one. Say: *One. Now listen carefully.*
- Play CD 1/12 and stop the CD after number one. While listening pretend to draw lines to join the appropriate dots in your book. The children at first only listen and look. They then listen and draw the lines.

Tapescript:

One: Kiwi, apple, plum, grapes, orange, pear, strawberry, nut, banana, peach.

Two: Kiwi, apple, grapes, plum, orange, pear, nut, strawberry, banana, peach.

Three: Kiwi, grapes, apple, plum, orange, nut, pear, strawberry, banana, peach.

- Play the CD several times more. The children try to find the other two patterns and while listening they draw the lines according to the listening text.
- Check the children's work: Ask individual children to 'read out' their pattern. Say: *Who can read out/What about (pattern) number one/two/three?* Child: *Kiwi – apple – plum – grapes ...*

❼ Listen and match.

Listening exercise CD 1/13

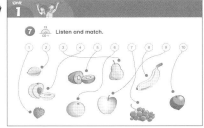

- Ask the children to look at the pictures in ex. 7 on p. 8 in their Activity Book.
- Tell them to listen to the CD and draw lines to match the numbers to the correct fruit.

Tapescript:

One:	Strawberry.
One:	Strawberry.
Two:	Nut.
Two:	Nut.
Three:	Pear.
Three:	Pear.
Four:	Peach.
Four:	Peach.
Five:	Kiwi.
Five:	Kiwi.
Six:	Orange.
Six:	Orange.
Seven:	Grapes.
Seven:	Grapes.
Eight:	Banana.
Eight:	Banana.
Nine:	Apple.
Nine:	Apple.
Ten:	Plum.
Ten:	Plum.

- Play CD 1/13 twice. The children listen and draw the lines.
- Play the CD again and the children check.

❽ Match the words to the pictures.
Reading exercise

- Say the fruits in ex. 7 on p. 8 in the Activity Book in any order. The children point at the appropriate pictures.
- Then read out the fruit words in ex. 8 one after the other and then in any order. The children point at the words in their books.
- Tell them to match the words in ex. 8 with the corresponding pictures in ex. 7 above, by numbering them from one to ten.
- To check say: *Apple. What number is it?* The children answer: *Number nine.*

❾ Find the six words. ↓ →
Word search

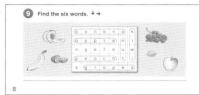

- Hold up the following fruit word cards in quick succession: *Banana, kiwi, apple, nut, grapes, peach* and *pear*. Do not allow the children enough time to read the words letter by letter. They should absorb the written form only as a single entity.
- When the children say the correct word, repeat it. Then put the card up on the board.
- Read them out together with the children several times. Then play *What's missing?* with the cards until all seven fruit word cards are removed from the board.
- Tell the children that there are seven fruit words hidden in the puzzle in Activity Book p. 8, ex. 9. They should try to find the words and circle them. Give them enough time to do this task. Go round the class and help, if necessary.
- Have the fruits read out by the children or put out an answer key in the classroom for the children to check on their own.

Option: This exercise can also be carried out in pair work.

L E S S O N   6

Vocabulary, phrases and structures:

One apple for Benny, … and some grapes for me; …and ten strawberries for me; My favourite colour/ toy/fruit/animal is…; I like plums/bananas; Yummy.

Linguistic skills:

Consolidating the meanings, pronunciation and written form of the words for fruit.
Understanding the meaning of *some (e.g. some grapes)*.
Understanding poems from the CD and while listening reading along in the book.
Learning a poem by heart and reciting your own poem fluently.

Cognitive, motor and social skills:

Drawing a favourite fruit.
Composing one's own poem.
Reciting one's own poem rhythmically.

Cross-curricular integration:

Topic: Speaking motivation 'Creating a poem about fruit'.
Drawing
Creative writing

Materials:

Flashcards from *Playway 1*: 25–28, 75; *Flashcards from Playway 2*: 1–6; *Word Cards* from *Playway 2*: 31–41
CD 1/14–16; *Pupil's Book*, p. 9, ex. 8–9; *Activity Book*, p. 9, ex. 10–11; coloured pencils

Revision

- As revision hand out the fruit flashcards and word cards to individual children. Name the fruits in turn and the children with the appropriate cards come out and put the cards on the board.
- Play *What's wrong?* and *What's missing?* with the cards.

❽ Listen and read.

Listening and reading exercise CD 1/14

- Ask the children to open their Pupil's Book at p. 9 and look at ex. 8.
- Hold up your book. Read out the first poem line by line and point at the respective pictures/words. Point at yourself when reading out the last line: *And some grapes for me.*
- Clarify the meaning of the word *some*. Draw an apple on the board and say: *One*. Draw another apple. Say: *Two*. Then draw five apples and say: *Five*. Then draw some more apples (overlapping) so that it is not clear how many apples exactly there are. Say: *Some apples.*
- Then play the first poem from the CD 1/14. The children listen.
- Play the second poem from the CD and ask the children to listen to it.

Tapescript:

One apple for Benny,
one orange for Linda,
one pear for Li
and some grapes for me.

One orange for Benny,
two kiwis for Linda,
three nuts for Li
and ten strawberries for me.

- Play both poems again and encourage the children to join in.
- Then read the poem line by line with the children several times.
- Get the children to close their books and dictate the (first) poem to you. Write a skeleton version of the poem on the board:

  1 a f B,
  1 o f L,
  1 p f L
  a s g f m.

- Point to the skeleton version of the poem on the board letter by letter and ask the children to 'read' with you.
- Repeat this step two or three times. This gives the children confidence and helps them remember important chunks of language that they will need for the creation of their own poems later.
- Now, delete the quantities and fruit items one after the other. Get the children to read out the complete poem after each deletion. In the end there is only the following structure on the board:

  __ __ f B,
  __ __ f L,
  __ __ f L,
  a __ __ f m.

❾ Create your own poem.
Speaking exercise:
Step to creativity (Word Play) CD 1/15

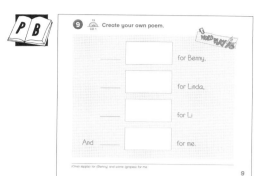

- Tell the children to compose their own poem. In Pupil's Book p. 9, ex. 9, the children write a number from one to ten and draw one fruit item each in one of the three blank spaces provided. They write one number in the last row and draw one fruit item that they like.
- One child might compose this poem, for example:
  1 kiwi for Benny,
  2 apples for Linda,
  3 bananas for Li
  And some plums for me.
- Give the children sufficient time for this work. When they have finished the drawings the children can learn the text of their poems by heart. Show the children the best way to do this. Hold up your book. Recite your poem several times in a low voice and point at the respective words/pictures in the book. Then go round the class and help, if necessary.
- Finally, individual children present their poems to the class. Remember to praise them for their work (*Let's give them a big hand!*).

Note: Give the children the option of presenting their poem just to you on their own first, so that if necessary you can help with the pronunciation.
Individual children may like to say their poems to the karaoke version of CD 1/15.

Preparation of key phrases

My favourite ... is/are ...

- Pre-teach the phrase *My favourite (fruit/...) are (plums/...)* in the following way: Say: *I like plums.* Draw some plums on the board and speak along. Then say, for example: *I like bananas.* Draw some bananas on the board again. Now say: *My favourite fruit are strawberries. Yummy!* Draw some strawberries on the board and draw a heart around your drawing.
- Then ask individual children about their favourite fruit. Say, for example:
  Jason, what's your favourite fruit?

❿ Listen and circle.
Listening exercise CD 1/16

- Hold up your book and name the colours, objects, fruits and animals illustrated in ex. 10 on p. 9 in the Activity Book: *A train, a cat...* The children listen to you and point at the appropriate pictures in their books.
- Tell the children to listen to Max on the CD. He is talking about his favourite colour/toy/fruit and animal. The children circle only his favourite items/colours.

Tapescript:

My favourite colour is blue.
My favourite toy is my train.
My favourite fruit are pears.
My favourite animal is a cat.

- Play CD 1/16 twice.
- The children listen and circle the appropriate pictures.
- Check the children's work: Ask: *What is Max's favourite colour/toy/...?* Children: *Blue/Train/...*

⓫ Draw and say.
Step to creativity (ME-page)
My favourite ...

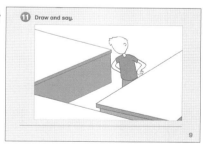

- Tell the children to draw their own face in the outline of the head in ex. 11 on p. 9 in their Activity Book.
- Then they should draw their own favourite toy/fruit/animal and colour. Give the children sufficient time for this. Go round the class and help, if necessary.
- Finally, individual children report to the class.
- One child might say, for example: *My favourite toy is a car. My favourite fruit is bananas.*

L E S S O N   1

Vocabulary, phrases and structures:

potatoes; onions; carrots; green/red peppers; tomatoes; cucumbers
I like (potatoes) …; What about cucumbers?; Yuck! I don't like cucumbers!

Linguistic skills:

Learning the meaning, the pronunciation and the written form of the new words.
Understanding a chant (*I like potatoes*) from the CD.

Cognitive, motor and social skills:

Practising words with a partner.
Hearing a chant from the CD, pointing along in the book and chanting it rhythmically in unison and individually.
Matching words with the appropriate pictures.
Finding words in jumbled letters.

Cross-curricular integration:

Music
Topic: Speaking motivation 'Fruit and vegetables'.

Materials:

Flashcards from *Playway 1*: 25–28, 75; *Flashcards* from *Playway 2*: 1–6; *Word Cards* from *Playway 2*: 31–41
Flashcards from *Playway 2*: 7–12; *Word Cards* from *Playway 2*: 42–47; CD 1/17–18; *Pupil's Book*, p. 10, ex. 1; *Activity Book*, p. 10, ex. 1–2; types of vegetables brought along to the class; bag; glove puppet Max

Revision

- Sit in a circle with the children. Hold up a fruit flashcard just briefly and have the children name the fruit.
- Then put the flashcard face down on the floor. Proceed in the same way with the rest of the flashcards. Then name the fruits one after the other. Individual children turn the relevant flashcard over.
- Hand out the flashcards and word cards to individual children. Say a fruit and the children with the appropriate cards hold them up.

Introduction of vocabulary

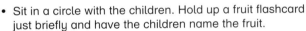

potatoes; carrots; onions; tomatoes; cucumbers; green/red peppers

- Show the flashcards in order and say the corresponding word. Then stick the cards on the board.
- Repeat the words in order at the same time pointing to the corresponding flashcard.

Pronunciation tips: Take care that with the word *onions* that it is pronounced with a [ʌ] as in *but*. The British pronounce *tomato* as follows: [təˈmɑːtəʊ]. The form [təˈmeitəʊ] is found in American English. With *cucumber* the stress is on the first syllable: [ˈkjuːkʌmbə]

Exercises for anchoring the vocabulary in the children's recognition memory

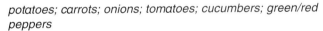

- Call one child to the board, say the words in any order and ask the child to point at the respective words again.
- Call individual children and ask them to take a card from the board and to give it to another child in the class.
  Say: *Peter, take the onions, please. Pass them to Sylvia.*
  Peter: *Here you are.*
  Sylvia: *Thank you.*

- When all the flashcards have been distributed round the class, say e. g.: *Put the onions on the blackboard.* The child with the corresponding flashcard sticks it back on the board. Continue in this way until all the flashcards are back on the board.

Vocabulary game

- Put one of each type of vegetable (*potatoes, carrots, onions, tomatoes, cucumbers, green/red peppers*) into a bag. Ask one child to put his/her hand in the bag (*Feel in the bag.*). He/She is to get hold of one of the vegetables and try to find out by feeling which vegetable it is. After the guess the vegetable in question is shown to the other children for checking.
  Teacher: *Put your hand in the bag. Take something. Feel it. What is it?*
  Child: *A carrot.*
  Teacher: *Take it out. Show it to the others. Yes, you are right.*
- Continue this game with several children.

Vocabulary exercises with the support of the written forms

potatoes; carrots; onions; tomatoes; cucumbers; green/red peppers

- Hold up the word cards in quick succession. Do not allow the children enough time to read the words letter by letter. They should absorb the written form only as a single entity.
- When the children say the correct word, repeat it. Then get one of them to put the card up on the board next to the corresponding flashcard. Say: *Put it on the board, please.*
- Take down all the flashcards, but leave the word cards on the board. Read them out together with the children several times.
- Play *What's missing?* with the cards.

Option: An alternative procedure is for you to hold up the word cards one after another, saying the corresponding words. Then hand the cards out to individual children. Say the words in sequence. After each word, the child with the corresponding card comes out to the board and puts it up next to or below the flashcard.

Sentence building

I like/I don't like (tomatoes).

- Build the phrases *I like …* and *I don't like …* as follows:
- Stick the flashcards on the topic of vegetables on the board. Then draw a heart /smiley face (☺) next to one of the flashcards and say a sentence with *I like* corresponding to this card, e.g.: *I like tomatoes.* Proceed in the same way with some of the other flashcards.
- Ask the children to repeat *I like tomatoes/…* a few times.
- Have individual children draw a smiley face (☺) on the board and say the corresponding sentence: *I like …* and whisper cues to help them.
- Then draw a frowning face (☹) next to one of the flashcards and say a sentence with *I don't like* corresponding to this card, e.g.: *I don't like potatoes.* Proceed in the same way with some of the other flashcards.
- Have the children repeat: *I don't like potatoes/…* a few times.
- Ask individual children to come out to the board. Ask them to draw a frowning face (☹) next to one picture and say the corresponding sentence. *I don't like …*
- Then write the following sentences on the board: *I like tomatoes. – I don't like potatoes.* Get the children to say the sentences after you several times.

❶ Listen and point. Say the chant.
Chant: *I like potatoes* CD 1/17–18

- The children look at the pictures on p. 10 in the Pupil's Book. Name the types of vegetables illustrated. The children point to the appropriate pictures in the book.

Tapescript:

Boy:	I like potatoes, I like tomatoes, I like carrots, yummy, yummy!
Girl:	I like potatoes, I like onions, I like peppers, yummy, yummy!
Group of children:	Potatoes, tomatoes, carrots and peppers. Potatoes, tomatoes, carrots and peppers. Munch, crunch, munch, crunch. Munch, crunch, munch! Yummy, yummy, yummy! Munch, crunch, munch, crunch. Munch, crunch, munch! Yummy, yummy, yummy!
Girl:	What about cucumbers?
Boy:	Cucumbers? Yuck! I don't like cucumbers!

- Then play the chant from CD 1/17.
- Play the chant again. The children point at the corresponding pictures at p. 10, ex. 1 in the Pupil's Book.
- Practise the chant with the children in sections. Say it first, the children repeat. Use the corresponding flashcards (*potatoes, carrots, onions, tomatoes, cucumbers, green/red peppers*) as visual support.
- Recite the text several times together with the children in the prescribed rhythm.
- Play the first part of the CD 1/18 (*And now you!*) The children point along with it in the book and say the missing words.
- Then play the second part of the CD 1/18 (karaoke version) and the children say the chant.
- Again the children point in the book and chant the text in unison in rhythm.
- Now the chant is recited with roles split among two groups. One group (boy) is lead by you, one group (girl) by the glove puppet. The pictures in the book are used as a visual aid. The third verse (group of children) is spoken by everyone together.

❶ Match the words to the pictures.
Reading exercise

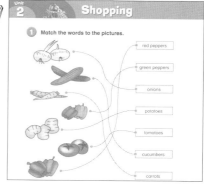

- Ask the children to look at ex. 1 on p. 10 in their Activity Book. Read out the words for vegetables on the left of the page first one after the other, then in any order. The children point at the corresponding words.
- Name the vegetables again and the children point at the corresponding pictures.
- Tell them to match the words with the corresponding pictures by drawing lines. The first word *red peppers* is already done.
- Go round the class and check the children's work.

❷ Write.
Jumbled letters

- Write the following letters on the board: *p l e p a*
- Look at the children and say: *It's a fruit. What is it?* The children try to find the hidden word. Elicit the correct answer: *Apple.*
- Tell the children to find the six vegetable words in ex. 2 on p. 10 in their Activity Book.
- Check the childrens work: Get individual children to read out the words in order. Write them on the board and the children check.

Option: This task can be carried out in pair work.

L E S S O N   2

Vocabulary, phrases and structures:

Good morning; Four (carrots), please.
Receptive language: *How many … are there? There are …*

Linguistic skills:

Understanding and being able to say plural forms of fruit and vegetables.
Understanding short shopping dialogues from the CD.

Cognitive, motor and social skills:

Understanding shopping dialogues from the CD, identifying quantities and numbering the pictures in the book.

Cross-curricular integration:

Mathematics: Counting from one to six.
Topic: Speaking motivation 'Asking and answering about quantities of fruit'.

Materials:

CD 1/18; *Pupil's Book*, p. 10, ex. 1
CD 1/19; *Pupil's Book*, p. 11, ex. 2; *Activity Book*, p. 11, ex. 3

Revision

- Say the chant *I like potatoes* from the previous lesson together with the children to the karaoke version CD 1/18. Use p. 10 in the Pupil's Book as visual support.

Pre-teaching key phrases

How many … are there?; There are …

- Start to draw a carrot. Stop your drawing and get the children to guess. Ask: *What is it? What do you think? Guess.* Continue your drawing until the children name the respective vegetable. Say: *Right. A carrot.*
- Now get the children to close their eyes or turn around. Draw, for example, another three carrots on the board. Cover the board. Get the children to open their eyes or turn around. Say: *How many carrots are there now? What do you think?* Let the children guess. Then open the board and say: *There are four carrots.*
- Continue in this way with two other types of vegetables.

❷ Listen and write the numbers.

Listening exercise CD 1/19

- Hold up the Pupil's Book briefly and point to the first illustration on p. 11. The children open their book at p. 11. Now point to the first picture and say: *How many tomatoes are there?* Count together with the children: *One, two, three, four, five. Five tomatoes. Right.* Proceed in the same way with the remaining types of vegetables in the pictures.
- Tell the children that they are going to hear shopping dialogues. They should number the respective pictures in the book from one to six.

Tapescript:

Announcer:	One.
Girl:	Good morning.
Man:	Good morning.
Girl:	Three red peppers, two onions, six potatoes and five cucumbers, please.
Man:	OK. Three red peppers, two onions, six potatoes and five cucumbers.
Announcer:	Two.
Boy:	Good morning.
Woman:	Good morning.
Boy:	Three green peppers, two carrots, six potatoes, five cucumbers, please.
Woman:	OK. Three green peppers, two carrots, six potatoes, five cucumbers.
Announcer:	Three.
Girl:	Good morning.
Man:	Good morning.
Girl:	Four carrots, five tomatoes, three cucumbers and one onion, please.
Man:	Four carrots, five tomatoes, three cucumbers and one onion.
Announcer:	Four.
Boy:	Good morning.
Woman:	Good morning.
Boy:	Five red peppers, four green peppers, two carrots and six cucumbers, please.
Woman:	OK. Five red peppers, four green peppers, two carrots and six cucumbers.
Announcer:	Five.
Girl:	Good morning.
Man:	Good morning.
Girl:	Four carrots, five tomatoes and three onions, please.
Man:	OK. Four carrots, five tomatoes and three onions.
Announcer:	Six.
Boy:	Good morning.
Woman:	Good morning.
Boy:	Five red peppers, four green peppers, two onions and six cucumbers, please.
Woman:	OK. Five red peppers, four green peppers, two onions and six cucumbers.

- Now play the listening exercise from CD 1/19. Stop the CD after each dialogue so that the children have sufficient time to find the correct picture.
- Draw a grid with six boxes on the board. This grid represents p. 11 in the Pupil's book. Have the children dictate the numbers for the corresponding box. *What number is it?*
- If the children do not agree on answers, play the listening exercise several times.

❸ **Look, read and write the numbers.**
Reading exercise

- Hold your Activity Book up just briefly and point to the first illustration on p. 11. The children open their book at p. 11. Now point to the first picture and say: *How many cucumbers are there?* Count together with the children: *One, two, three. Three cucumbers. Right.* Proceed in the same manner with the remaining types of vegetables and pictures.
- Then read out the first paragraph underneath the pictures. The children read along. Say: *It's number ….* Look at the children and get them to give you the right answer. Children: *… three.* Say: *Right. It's number three.*
- Proceed in the same manner with the remaining texts.

L E S S O N   3

Vocabulary, phrases and structures:

(Maria) likes/doesn't like; I like/don't like...
Receptive vocabulary: *What do you like?; What don't you like?; What about you?*

Linguistic skills:

Expressing likes or dislikes.
Listening to a partner in a conversation and giving information.
Understanding what someone likes and doesn't like on the CD.

Cognitive, motor and social skills:

Thinking about your own likes and dislikes.
Recording the results by sticking in pictures.

Cross-curricular integration:

Topic: Speaking motivation 'Discussing what fruit you like/dislike'.

Materials:

Flashcards from *Playway 1*: 25–28, 75; *Flashcards* from *Playway 2*: 1–12; *Word Cards* from *Playway 2*: 31–47
Pupil's Book, p. 12, ex. 3; CD 1/20; *Activity Book*, p. 12, ex. 4–5; stick-in pictures from the appendix in the *Pupil's Book;* glove puppet Max

Revision

- Revise the words for types of fruit and vegetables already learnt with the aid of the flashcards and word cards.

Exercises for anchoring the vocabulary in the children's recognition memory

- Play a guessing game with the children: Take the glove puppet in one hand and a flashcard in the other. Hold the flashcard so that it can't be seen.
- Change your voice to speak as Max.
  Mmmh, I like ... and rub your stomach at the same time. Have the children guess what Max likes.
  Max: *What is it? What do you think?*
  Children: *Apples?*
  Max*: No, sorry.*
  Children: *Bananas?*
  Max: *Yes, that's right. I like bananas.*
- Max can also say: *Yuck! I don't like ...*
  Pull a face at the same time. Have the children guess.
- When the children have guessed correctly, e.g. *Green peppers?*, say as Max: *Yes, that's right. I don't like green peppers.*

❸ Stick and say.

Sticker activity

- Show the children the page in the appendix of the Pupil's Book with the stick-in pictures for p. 12, ex. 3.
- Name the types of fruit and vegetables illustrated in random order and the children point at the respective pictures in the appendix of the book.
- Explain to the children that they are only to stick the fruit and vegetables that they like in the box in the top half of p. 12 in the Pupil's Book. They stick the types of fruit and vegetables that they don't like in the bottom box on p. 12.
- Give the children sufficient time for this work. Go round the class and help if necessary.
- Then ask the children, e.g.: *What do you like, Maria? –* Maria: *(I like) apples, pears, nuts ...*
  What don't you like, Tom? – Plums, cucumbers ...
  What about you, Sandra? – I like .../I don't like ...

- In addition in able groups you can ask the children what they have noticed about the likes and dislikes of the other children in the class:
  Say: *Maria likes ...* Have the children complete the sentence.
  Say: *Maria doesn't like ...* Get the children to name the types of fruit and vegetables that Maria doesn't like.

Pair work: Speaking exercise

- The children should tell at least three different partners which types of fruit and vegetables they like or don't like.
- Practise the expression for this pair work (*I like ...; I don't like ...*) by saying and repeating several times before the children carry out the pair work. You could mix the pairs by playing music. The children go round the class as the music plays. When the music stops the children work with the person who is standing closest to them. They tell each other what they like and what they don't like.

❹ Listen and write the names.
Listening exercise CD 1/20

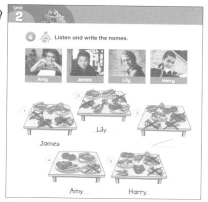

- The children open their Activity Book at p. 12 and look at the photos and pictures in ex. 4. Say the names of the children in the book: *Amy, James, Lily* and *Harry*. The children look at the respective names.
- Then explain the listening task: The children are going to hear what *Amy, James, Lily* and *Harry* like and what they don't like. They should find out which tables belong to whom and write the corresponding names below the tables on the lines provided in the book. Tell the children that one table is left.
- Play CD 1/20. Press the pause button after the first child, Amy. Give the children sufficient time to find her table and write the name below.
- Continue with the remaining children in the same manner. Go round the class and check.

Tapescript:

Speaker:	What do you like, Amy?
Amy:	I like potatoes, tomatoes, red and green peppers. I don't like cucumbers.
Speaker:	James, what about you? What do you like?
James:	I like potatoes, cucumbers and carrots. I don't like tomatoes, red and green peppers and onions.
Speaker:	What about you, Lily?
Lily:	I like cucumbers, potatoes, carrots, red and green peppers. I don't like onions and tomatoes.
Speaker:	Harry. What do you like?
Harry:	I like tomatoes, cucumbers, carrots and red and green peppers. I don't like onions and potatoes.

❺ Say.
Speaking exercise

- Get the children to look at ex 5 on p. 12 in their Activity Book. Point to the speech bubble. Say: *Amy's table is number ...* Elicit the correct answer: *Four.* Repeat the whole sentence: *Amy's table is number four.* Get the children to repeat several times.
- Then go on asking: *What about James?* Child: *James' table is number one.*

L E S S O N   4

Vocabulary, phrases and structures:
Receptive language: *Good morning; Six tomatoes..., please; Linda, the flowers, please; No, Max; How much is it?; Here you are; Goodbye; Yummy; Two pounds, please.*

Linguistic skills:
Understanding a story (*At a shop*) from the DVD and the CD and from narration by the teacher. Joining in with story-telling. Carrying out role plays.

Cognitive, motor and social skills:
Following the narrative structure of a story on DVD and CD.

Presenting a time sequence visually.
Putting pictures in the right order in a picture story and sticking them in.
Role playing different characters.
Matching pictures with the corresponding texts (speech bubbles).

Cross-curricular integration:
Topic: Speaking motivation 'Buying fruit'.

Materials:
DVD (*At a shop*); CD 1/21–22; *Story Cards* from *Playway 2*: 1–8; *Pupil's Book*, pp. 13–14, ex. 4–5; stick-in pictures from the appendix of the *Pupil's Book*; *Activity Book*, p. 13, ex. 6; glove puppet Max; answer key; paper strips

Revision
- Ask the children what they can remember about the likes and dislikes of classmates from the previous lesson: *What does Lorenz like?/What about Laura?* The children answer, for example: *Bananas, nuts, pears ...*

❹ Watch the story.

Cartoon Story: *At a shop*

- Show the children the video sequence *At a shop* twice (DVD).

DVD script: *At a shop*

Linda, Benny, Max:	Good, morning.
Shop assistant:	Good morning.
Linda:	Six tomatoes, four green peppers and three cucumbers, please.
Shop assistant:	Six tomatoes, four green peppers and three cucumbers.
Max:	Linda, the flowers, please.
Linda:	No, Max.
Max:	Oh!
Benny:	How much is it?
Shop assistant:	Two pounds.
Benny:	Oh, two pounds. Here you are.
Linda, Benny:	Goodbye.
Shop assistant:	Goodbye.
Max:	Goodbye. Flowers, yummy.

Note: Not all the language in the DVD sequences or CD versions of the stories are presented in the cartoon story in the Pupil's Book. This is mainly because of the length of the stories but also this serves to encourage the children to listen for the necessary information in order to complete the gap fill in the Pupil's Book.

❹ Listen and stick.

Listening exercise: Sticker activity CD 1/21

- Play the listening version of the story twice (CD 1/21). The children stick the stick-in pictures from the appendix in the corresponding blank spaces in the Pupil's Book on p. 13 while they are listening.
- Check the children's work.

Option: To promote self-checking put out a completed picture story in the classroom. The children go and check their own work themselves.

Telling the story.

- Now tell the story with the aid of the story cards (see the tips on Basic Technology in the Introduction).

Option: In high-ability groups, the story can also be performed as a role play after appropriate intensive practice. Proceed as follows: Re-enact the story *At the shop*. You take on the part of the shop assistant with the glove puppet playing the part of Max. Two children take the parts of Linda and Benny. Help the children by whispering cues.
Later individual children also play the parts of the shop assistant and of Max.

Pre-teaching key written phrases

£2, please; Mum, the cucumbers, please; Goodbye; Good morning; Three onions, please; Thank you

- Write the six sentences on strips of paper, large enough so that all the children in your class can comfortably read the sentences.
- Hold up one of the paper strips for about half a second only. The children call out the sentence. They should, however, not be able to read the words letter for letter. This helps to avoid interference between the written words and their pronunciation. Carry on as described with the other sentences.

❺ Listen and point.

Listening exercise CD 1/22

- Ask the children to open their Pupil's Book at p. 14 and look at the pictures in ex. 5.
- Tell them that they are going to listen to a shopping dialogue and they should point at the respective pictures in the book.

Tapescript:

Tom/Sue:	*Good morning.*
Greengrocer:	*Good morning.*
Sue:	*Three apples and two tomatoes, please.*
Greengrocer:	*Here you are. £2, please.*
Tom:	*Here you are.*
Greengrocer:	*Thank you.*
Tom/Sue:	*Goodbye.*
Greengrocer:	*Goodbye.*

- Play CD 1/22 twice. The children listen and point.
- Read out the texts in the speech bubbles in jumbled order. The children point at the respective texts in their books.

❺ Act out.
Mini-dialogue

Use the paper strips to work on the dialogue in the following way:

- Hand out the paper strips to individual children. Say the sentences in any order. The children with the respective paper strips hold them up.
- Then re-enact the dialogue with the help of the hand puppet. Adjust your voice and say: *Good morning! Three apples and two tomatoes, please.* Answer as the greengrocer and say: *Two pounds, please.* Swap places while acting. Get the children to hold up the corresponding sentences, while speaking the dialogue.
- Then get the children to come out and put the paper strips in the correct order on the board. In case of misunderstandings, also ask the other children in class to help. Say: *What do you think? What comes next/ here?* etc.
- Read out the whole dialogue together with the children pointing at the respective sentences on the board several times.
- Encourage children to take over the roles of the children in the story. You act as the greengrocer. Later, children also take over the role of the greengrocer.
- Divide the children in groups of three and get them to practise the dialogue. Go round the class and help, if necessary.
- Volunteers act out the dialogue in front of the class.
- Get the other children to applaud *(Let's give them a big hand)*.

❻ Look and write the numbers.
Reading exercise

- The children open their Activity Book and look at the pictures at the upper half of p. 13.
- Ask them to match the pictures/situations with the speech bubbles below by writing the corresponding numbers in the circles provided in the book.
- Check the children's work: Ask: *Good morning. What number is it?* Children: *Three.*

L E S S O N   5

Vocabulary, phrases and structures:

Receptive language: *You need; Cut the apple; Cut the banana and some grapes; Cut the kiwi and the strawberries; Add some yoghurt; Mix everything; Yummy; In my favourite fruit salad there are …*

Linguistic skills:

Saying *how many.*
Understanding the ingredients of Max's favourite fruit salad from the CD.
Talking about one's own favourite fruit salad.

Cognitive, motor and social skills:

Discovering various vegetables in a picture puzzle and saying how many there are of each.
Understanding the ingredients of Max's favourite fruit salad from the CD and ticking the corresponding pictures in the book.
Drawing, talking and writing about one's own favourite fruit salad.

Cross-curricular integration:

Topic: Speaking motivation 'Discussing quantities of fruit and how to make a fruit salad'.
Mathematics: Counting from one to ten.

Materials:

DVD (*At a shop*); *Story Cards* from *Playwag 2:* 1–8; glove puppet Max
Flashcards from *Playway 1:* 25–28, 75; *Flashcards* from *Playway 2:* 1–12; *Word Cards* from *Playway 2:* 10–19, 31–47; CD 1/23; *Activity Book*, pp. 14–15, ex. 7–9

Revision

- Revise the story *At a shop* from the previous lesson. Use the DVD and the story cards for this.

Mini-dialogues

- Then get volunteers to act out short shopping dialogues. Put the flashcards of fruit and vegetables up on the board. Take the glove puppet and say the following shopping dialogue several times:

Max:	*Good morning.*
Max:	*Two bananas and three cucumbers, please.*
Teacher:	*£3, please.*
Max:	*Here you are.*
Teacher:	*Thank you.*
Teacher:	*Goodbye.*

- Individual children play the part of Max and later both parts.
- Revise numbers from one to ten with the help of the word cards. Hold up the word cards in quick succession and in any order. The children indicate the appropriate number with their fingers.

❼ Look, count and write.
Picture puzzle

- Ask the children to look at the picture on p. 14 in their Activity Book for about ten seconds only. They then close their books. Ask: *How many cucumbers are there?* Write the children's guesses on the board. Continue in the same way with the other vegetables. Then say: *Let's check.* The children open their books and count. They fill in the numbers in the boxes at the bottom of the page.
- Tell the children to close their books. Play a *Call my bluff game* with them.
- Say, for example: *There are eight onions.* If the children think this is the wrong number, they stand up. If they think the number you have given is right, they remain seated.

Vocabulary revision with the help of the written forms

- Revise all the fruits with the aid of the flashcards and word cards in the usual manner. Stick them on the board.

❽ Listen and circle.

Listening exercise CD 1/23

- Ask the children to look at the picture in ex. 8 on p. 15 in the Activity Book. Name the illustrated fruits and get the children to point at the corresponding pictures in the book.

- Tell the children that they are going to listen to the CD and that they should circle only the fruits Max mentions.

Tapescript:

In my favourite fruit salad there are grapes, peaches, kiwis, pears and nuts.

- Play CD 1/23 twice. Now the children circle the corresponding pictures in the book.
- The children then listen again and check. Ask: *What's in Max's favourite fruit salad?* Children: *(There are) nuts, pears, grapes.*

❾ Draw and say.

Step to creativity (ME-page)

My favourite fruit salad

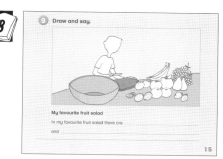

- Ask the children to look at ex. 9 in their Activity Book on p. 15. Tell them to draw their own face in the outline of the head.
- They then colour only the fruits they want to put into their own favourite fruit salad.
  Make sure the children understand that they should not colour all the fruits.
  Give the children sufficient time for this. Go round the class to help, if necessary.
- When all the children have finished with their drawings write the following sentence starter on the board:
  In my favourite fruit salad there are _____ and _____.
- Ask the children to guess your favourite fruit salad. When the children have guessed the ingredients, stick the respective word cards on the board to complete the sentence.
- Practise the phrase: *In my favourite fruit salad there are … thoroughly* by getting the children to say and repeat it several times.
- Then the children complete the sentence in ex. 9 on p. 15 in the Activity Book according to their own drawings.
- Get individual children to read out their sentences.

C L I L:
Content and Language Integrated Learning

Objectives:

Following instructions.
Learning to make healthy food.
What is healthy food?

Materials:

Pupil's Book, p. 15, ex. 6; a bowl, a knife, a spoon, a cutting board, an apple, a banana, some grapes, a kiwi, some strawberries and some yoghurt

6 How to make a fruit salad.
Following the instructions of a recipe

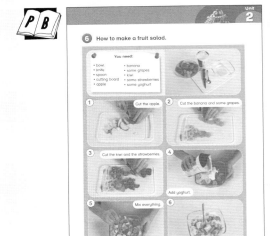

- Work on the new words with the aid of the food and objects you have brought to class.
- Ask the children to open their Pupil's Books at p. 15 and look at the pictures in ex. 6.

- Read out the note *You need:* at the top. The children read along.
- Then read out the instructions of the recipe one after the other (steps from one to six). The children read and look along in their books.
- Now prepare the fruit salad and speak along:

Note: This is a good opportunity for children to experience step-by-step English instructions.

Expressions:

Cut the apple.
Cut the banana and some grapes.
Cut the kiwi and the strawberries.
Add yoghurt.
Mix everything.
Yummy!

- Finally, give all the children a taste of the fruit salad and ask them, for example: *Simon, do you like it?*
Simon: *Yes./Yummy./No./It's ok./…*

L E S S O N 1

Vocabulary, phrases and structures:
Checking of vocabulary acquisition in Units 1–2.

Linguistic skills:
Understanding and saying the important words and sentences from Units 1–2 on the topic areas 'fruit and vegetables'.

Cognitive, motor and social skills:
Matching words and phrases from the CD to the corresponding pictures and situations.
Matching words and sentences from the CD with the corresponding written form.
Checking the results with the aid of an answer key.
Self-evaluation

Materials:
CD 1/24–25; *Pupil's Book*, pp. 16–17, ex. 1–4; coloured pencils; answer key

---

Self-evaluation

Option: Divide *Show what you can do* into two lessons.

Note: For notes on the basic methodology of this section, see *Show what you can do* on p. 18 of the introduction in the Teacher's Book.

❶ Listen and write the numbers.
Listening exercise CD 1/24

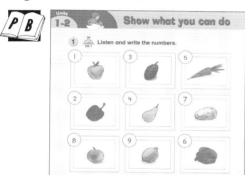

- Tell the children to find out by themselves which food words in the Pupil's Book on p. 16, ex. 1 they already know.
- The children check independently whether they can match the words they hear to the corresponding pictures.

Tapescript:

Number one:	*Apple.*
Number one:	*Apple.*
Number two:	*Red pepper.*
Number two:	*Red pepper.*
Number three:	*Plum.*
Number three:	*Plum.*
Number four:	*Pear.*
Number four:	*Pear.*
Number five:	*Carrot.*
Number five:	*Carrot.*
Number six:	*Green pepper.*
Number six:	*Green pepper.*

Number seven:	*Potato.*
Number seven:	*Potato.*
Number eight:	*Peach.*
Number eight:	*Peach.*
Number nine:	*Onion.*
Number nine:	*Onion.*

- Now play the listening exercise (CD 1/24).
- The children number the pictures in the book accordingly. The first picture has already been numbered.
- Go round the class and help the children, if necessary.
- Set out a completed sheet and let the children check their results independently.

❷ Match the words to the pictures.
Reading exercise

- Tell the children that they are now to find out by themselves which words in the Pupil's Book on p. 16, ex. 2 they can already read well.
- The children now check independently whether they can match the written words in ex. 2 to the corresponding pictures in ex. 1.
- Set out a completed sheet and let the children check their results independently.

---

❸ **Listen and write the numbers.**

Listening exercise CD 1/25

- Ask the children to find out by themselves which sentences in the Pupil's Book on p. 17, ex. 3 they can already guess and say.

```
Tapescript:

Number one:     Close your eyes.
Number one:     Close your eyes.

Number two:     I like carrots.
Number two:     I like carrots.

Number three:   I don't like peppers.
Number three:   I don't like peppers.

Number four:    Here you are.
Number four:    Here you are.
```

- Now play the listening exercise from CD 1/25.
- The children number the pictures in the book accordingly. The first picture has already been numbered.
- Go round the class and help, if necessary.
- Set out a completed sheet and let the children check their results independently.

❹ **Match the sentences to the pictures.**

Reading exercise

- Tell the children that they are now to find out themselves which sentences in the Pupil's Book on p. 17, ex. 4, they can already read well.
- The children now check independently whether they can match the written sentences to the corresponding pictures in ex. 3.
- Set out a completed sheet and let the children check their results independently.

L E S S O N   1

Vocabulary, phrases and structures:

table; lamp; curtains; sofa; chair; mat; telephone; TV; cupboard
Receptive language: *There's a green sofa; There are yellow curtains; What colour is your (sofa)?; What colour are your (curtains)?*

Linguistic skills:

Learning the meaning, the pronunciation and the written form of the new words.
Understanding new words from the CD.
Asking and answering questions.
Exchanging information.

Cognitive, motor and social skills:

Matching words with the corresponding pictures and the corresponding actions.
Colouring in objects.
Asking about the colour of objects on a partner's picture and colouring in objects accordingly.

Cross-curricular integration:

Topic: Speaking motivation 'Describing furniture in a home'.

Materials:

soft ball
Flashcards from *Playway 1:* 5–11; *Flashcards* from *Playway 2:* 13–21; *Word Cards* from *Playway 2:* 48–56; CD 1/26; *Pupil's Book*, p. 18, ex. 1; *Activity Book*, p. 16, ex. 1; coloured pencils

Revision

- Stand in a circle with the children. Name a word from the word group colours, e.g. *yellow* and throw a soft ball to one child. The child who catches the ball names another colour and throws the ball to another child and so on. In this way revise the word groups vegetables, fruit, pets, numbers and school things.

Introduction of vocabulary

table; lamp; curtains; sofa; chair; mat; telephone; TV; cupboard

- Show each flashcard, say the English word and do a corresponding action to it, e.g.:
  sofa – Lean back on an imaginary sofa.
  lamp – Switch an imaginary lamp on.
  table – Show the outline of a table etc.
- Stick the flashcards to the board when the children have repeated the word.

Vocabulary exercises with the support of the written forms

table; lamp; curtains; sofa; chair; mat; telephone; TV; cupboard

- Hold up the word cards in quick succession. Do not allow the children enough time to read the words letter by letter. They should absorb the written form only as a single entity.
- When the children say the correct word, repeat it. Then get one of them to put the card up on the board next to the corresponding flashcard. Say: *Put it on the board, please.*
- Take down all the flashcards, but leave the word cards on the board. Read them out together with the children several times.
- Tell the children to close their eyes. Turn the word cards face down on the board and tell the children to open their eyes. Turn over the word cards in any order and say, each time: *What is it? What do you think?*

Option: An alternative procedure is for you to hold up the word cards one after another, saying the corresponding words. Then hand the cards out to individual children. Say the words in sequence. After each word, the child with the corresponding card comes out to the board and puts it up next to or below the picture (flashcard).

❶ Listen and point.
Listening exercise CD 1/26

Tapescript:

sofa	telephone
chair	TV
lamp	curtains
table	mat
cupboard	

- Play the listening exercise (CD 1/26) a few times. The children listen and point at the respective pictures on p. 18, ex. 1 in the Pupil's Book.
- Then hold your book up. Point to the individual items of furniture. Practise the words by saying and repeating several times. Then point faster and faster to the individual items of furniture in your book. The children name the corresponding words.

Pronunciation tips: Take care that the [æ] in *lamp* is pronounced as open as possible. Pay attention to the clear diphthongisation in *table* ['teɪbl]. Make sure in the pronunciation of *cupboard* ['kʌbəd] that only the [b] is audible.

Pair work

- The children work in pairs with one book. Child A points to an item of furniture and child B names the word. Then they swap roles.

Vocabulary revision and reinforcement of key phrases

What colour is the (sofa) …?

- Repeat the colours with the aid of the flashcards from Playway to English 1.
- Hold the flashcard of the sofa so that the children cannot see it. Ask: *What colour is the sofa?* The children guess. Proceed in the same way with the other items of furniture.

❶ Colour and say.

Pair work: Speaking exercise

- Ask the children to open their Activity Book at p. 16.
- Work with the drawing of the living room on the top half of the page. Say the words one after the other. The children point to the corresponding picture in each case.

- Divide the children into pairs. Child A colours the items in picture A in the colours of his/her choice. Child B does the same with picture B.
- Tell the children that they should set up a schoolbag or a book between their books so that their partners cannot see how the drawings are coloured. Give the children sufficient time for this.
- Demonstrate the game with one child in front of the class. Ask: *What colour is your sofa, Christine?* Christine says, for example: *Orange.* Pretend to colour the sofa in your book orange. Then Christine asks you, for example: *What colour is your table?* etc.
- Practise the expression: *What colour is your…?* thoroughly by getting the children to say and repeat it several times.
- Then ask one child: *What colour are the curtains?* Practise this question in the same way.
  Now the children carry out the pair work.
  Child A asks child B what colours the items in child B's picture are, for example: *What colour is your table?* Child B e.g.: *Blue.*
  Child A colours the table in picture B in his book blue. Child A continues with the remaining items in the same way. Go round the class and help, if necessary.
- When child A has coloured all the items of furniture it is child B's turn to ask.
- When both children have finished colouring the items of furniture they compare their pictures.
- If the questions *What colour is your …?/What colour are your …?* are too difficult for your class, then it is recommended that the children ask as follows: Child A: *Table. What colour?* Child B: *Green.*

L E S S O N 2

Vocabulary, phrases and structures:

mice; floor; door; on; family
Receptive language: *The family; the family's not here; The mice are having fun; What's happening?; Oh dear!; Mice, mice, mice everywhere; on the sofa/chair/cupboard/floor/curtains/door.*

Linguistic skills:

Learning the meaning, the pronunciation and the written form of the words.
Singing a song (*The mice are having fun*).
Understanding poems from the CD and while listening, reading along in the book.
Learning by heart and reciting fluently one's own poem.

Cognitive, motor and social skills:

Learning the words of a song with the aid of actions and pictures.
Maintaining the rhythm and melody while speaking in unison and singing.
Drawing items of furniture and composing one's own poem.
Reciting one's own poem rhythmically.

Cross-curricular integration:

Music
Topic: Speaking motivation 'Describing furniture in a room'.

Materials:

Flashcards from *Playway 2*: 13–23; *Word Cards* from *Playway 2*: 48–58
CD 1/27–30; *Pupil's Book*, pp. 18–19, ex. 2–4

Revision

- Revise the words from the previous lesson with the aid of the flashcards and word cards in the usual manner.

Introduction of vocabulary

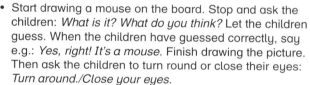

mice; floor; door; on; family

- Start drawing a mouse on the board. Stop and ask the children: *What is it? What do you think?* Let the children guess. When the children have guessed correctly, say e.g.: *Yes, right! It's a mouse.* Finish drawing the picture. Then ask the children to turn round or close their eyes: *Turn around./Close your eyes.*
- Add two or three mice to the drawing. Cover the board. The children turn round again or open their eyes. Ask: *How many mice are there? Guess.* Let the children guess. When the children have guessed the correct number open the board. Write the word mice on the board. Say the word several times and get the children to repeat it.
- Introduce the words *floor* and *door* with the aid of the flashcards and word cards. Say the words several times and have the children repeat them.
- Introduce the preposition *on* in the following way: Place a pencil case on a desk and a pencil on the pencil case. Say: *Look, the pencil is on the pencil case. And the pencil case is on the desk.* Support your words by the corresponding gestures.
- Introduce the word *family* with the sentence *Mr Matt, Danny and Daisy are a family.*

❷ Listen and point. Sing the song.

Song: *The mice are having fun*

CD 1/27–28

- The children open their Pupil's Book at p. 18 and look at the pictures on the bottom half of the page (ex. 2) for about five seconds.

- Then the children close their books and try to remember the words.
  Say: *Tell me some words.*
- Also ask the children, for example: *Where are the mice?* Elicit the answer: *On the sofa/floor …*
- Explain the phrase: *The mice are having fun!* in L1.

The mice are having fun

Lyrics: Gerngross/Puchta
Music: Lorenz Maierhofer
© Helbling, Rum/Innsbruck

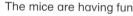

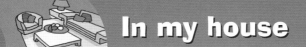
• Play the song (CD 1/27). At first the children just listen and follow in the book.
• Then say the words of the song line by line.
  The children point at the pictures in the book.
• Play the song several times.
• Say the words with the children in the rhythm of the song with the children pointing at the respective pictures in the book again.
• Stand in a circle with the children. Play the song again and all sing it together. Do the corresponding actions to jog their memory.
• Finally, sing the song to the karaoke version (CD 1/28).

❸ **Listen and read.**
  Listening and reading exercise CD 1/29

• Ask the children to open their Pupil's Book at p. 19 and look at ex. 3.
• Hold up your book. Read out the first poem line by line and point along.

Tapescript:

In my room
There's a pink sofa,
There's a blue TV,
There are green curtains,
And there's a little house.
For Freddie the mouse.

In my room
There's a white chair,
There's a green bed,
There are red curtains,
And there's a pink mat.
For Tiger my cat.

• Then play the first poem from the CD (CD 1/29). The children listen.
• Play the second poem from the CD and get the children listen to it.
• Play both poems again and encourage the children to speak along.
• Then read the poems line by line with the children several times.
• Get the children to close their books and dictate the (first) poem to you. Write a skeleton version of the poem on the board:

> *I m r t's a ___,*
> *T's a __,*
> *T a __,*
> *....*

• Point to the skeleton version of the poem on the board letter by letter and ask the children to 'read' with you.
• Repeat this step two or three times. This gives the children confidence and helps them remember important chunks of language that they will need for the creation of their own poems later.

❹ **Create your own poem.**

Speaking exercise:
Step to creativity (Word Play) CD 1/30

• Tell the children to compose their own poem. Hold your Pupil's Book up and point along in your book with your explanation. The children draw one item of furniture each in one of the first three lines on p. 19.
• Tell them that in the last two lines the choice is between *house/mouse* and a name or *mat/cat* and a name. Help the children with names for mice or cats. Say: *Give me names for mice.* Write them on the board. Do the same with names for cats.

One child might compose the following poem for example:
In my room there's a pink chair,
There's a yellow table,
There are blue and red curtains,
And there's a green mat.
For Kitty the cat.

• Give the children sufficient time for this work. When they have finished the drawings the children learn the text of their poems by heart. Show the children the best way to do this. Hold your Pupil's Book up and point along in your book with your own example. Then go round the class and help if necessary.
• Finally, individual children present their poems to the class. Remember to praise them for their work: *(Let's give them a big hand).*
• Individual children may like to say their poems to the karaoke version (CD 1/30).

Note: Give the children the option of presenting their poem just to you on their own first, so that, if necessary, you can help with the pronunciation.

L E S S O N   3

Vocabulary, phrases and structures:	**Cross-curricular integration:**

Vocabulary, phrases and structures:
There is a pink sofa, there are two yellow chairs, …

Linguistic skills:
Understanding the new words from the CD.

Cognitive, motor and social skills:
Understanding descriptions of rooms from the CD and matching them to the corresponding pictures. Describing a room.

Cross-curricular integration:
Topic: Speaking motivation 'Describing furniture in a room'.

Materials:
CD 2/28; *Flashcards* from *Playway 2:* 13–23; *Word Cards* from *Playway 2:* 48–58
CD 1/31; *Activity Book*, pp. 17–18, ex. 2–3; coloured pencils

Revision

- Together with the children sing the song *The mice are having fun!* from the previous lesson to the karaoke version (CD 1/28).
- Ask individual children to present their self-composed poem from the previous lesson.
- Revise the items of furniture with the aid of the flashcards and word cards in the usual manner.

❷ Listen and say.
Listening exercise   CD 1/31

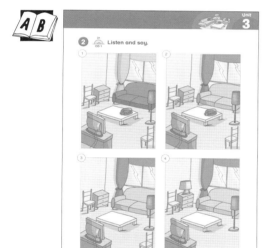

- Ask the children to look at the rooms in ex. 2 on p. 17 in their Activity Book. Tell them that they are going to hear descriptions of the rooms. The children should identify the rooms and say which number they are.

Tapescript:

There's a pink sofa, there are two yellow chairs, there are blue curtains, there's a white table, a telephone, a TV, a cupboard and a pink lamp.
What number is it?

There's a pink sofa, there's one yellow chair, there are blue curtains, there's a white table, a TV, a cupboard and there are two pink lamps.
What number is it?

There's a pink sofa, there are two yellow chairs, there are blue curtains, there's a white table, a TV, a cupboard and a pink lamp.
What number is it?

There's a blue sofa, there are two yellow chairs, there are pink curtains, there's a white table, a TV, a telephone, a cupboard and a pink lamp.
What number is it?

- Play CD 1/31. Stop the CD after the first description. Give the children sufficient time to identify the room. Ask: *What number is it?* Children: *(It's) number one.*
- Proceed in this way with the other three descriptions.

❸ Match the sentences to the pictures.
Reading exercise

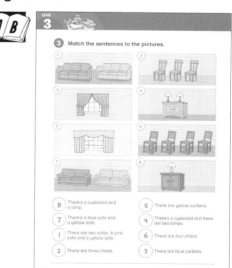

- Before you ask the children to open their books and look at the sentences in ex. 3, p. 18 you may prefer to write the sentences on strips of paper and fix them on the board. Point at the sentences and read them aloud one after the other. The children point at the sentences in their book and read along.
- Tell the children to match the sentences to the corresponding pictures above by numbering them from one to eight.
- To check say: *There's a cupboard and a lamp. What number is it?* The children answer: *Number eight.*

L E S S O N   4

Vocabulary, phrases and structures:

Let's watch TV!; Listen! A car; Oh no! They've got a cat! A cat! Let's run; The TV's on! That's strange; I can smell mice!; It's time for fun.
Receptive language: *Come on!; Hooray; The sofa's for me and Fred; All right; The curtains are for me and Billy!; The lamp and the cupboard are for Mike and me; Hey, come here!; Open the cupboard; Ah. A chocolate bar!; Climb onto a chair; Take the chocolate bar; Jump down; Ouch! Your foot!; You drop the chocolate bar; Your dog grabs the chocolate bar; Shout: 'Give it back!'*

Linguistic skills:

Understanding a story (*Time for fun!*) from the DVD and the CD and from narration by the teacher.
Joining in with story-telling.
Acting out a role play.
Understanding sentences from the CD.
Understanding a chain of instructions in an action story (*The chocolate bar*).
Understanding instructions from the CD and matching with the corresponding pictures.

Cognitive, motor and social skills:

Representing a time sequence visually.
Following the narrative structure of a story on DVD and CD.
Sticking the stick-in pictures correctly in the picture story.
(Optional) comparing the answers of one's own work independently with an answer sheet.
Understanding characters through role play.
Understanding sentences from the CD and matching them to the corresponding pictures in the book.
Matching instructions with actions.
Understanding and carrying out jumbled instructions.

Cross-curricular integration:

Topic: Speaking motivation *'Time for fun'* and *'The chocolate bar'*.

Materials:

soft ball
Flashcards 13–23; DVD (*Time for fun*); CD 1/32–34; *Pupil's Book,* pp. 20–22, ex. 5–6; *Activity Book,* p. 19, ex. 4; stick-in pictures from the appendix of the *Pupil's Book*; answer key; paper strips

Revision

- Play the following *Word ping-pong* game with the children. Divide the children up into two teams. Start with the words for items of furniture. Throw a soft ball to team A and say, for example: *Lamps.* The one who catches the ball says a different (plural) word for an item of furniture and throws the ball to team B. The teams throw the ball back and forth until one of them can't think of a word. The last team to say a word scores a point.
- Proceed in this way with the words for colours/animals/…

Preparation of key phrases

Time for fun!; That's strange!

- Explain the phrases *Time for fun!* and *That's strange!* in L1.

❺ **Watch the story.**

Cartoon Story: *Time for fun!*

DVD script: *Time for fun!*

Mouse 1:	Come on! It's time for fun!
Other mice:	Hooray!
Mouse 2:	The sofa's for me and Fred!
Other mice:	All right.
Mouse 3:	The curtains are for me and Billy!
Other mice:	All right.

Mouse 4:	The lamp and the cupboard are for Mike and me!
Other mice:	All right.
Mouse 1:	Hey, come here! Let's watch TV! Listen! A car. Oh no! They've got a cat!
Other mice:	A cat! Let's run!
Dad:	The TV's on! That's strange.
Cat:	Mmmmmmmh! I can smell mice!

Note: Not all the language in the DVD sequences or CD versions of the stories are presented in the cartoon story in the Pupil's Book. This is mainly because of the length of the stories but also this serves to encourage the children to listen for the necessary information in order to complete the gap fill in the Pupil's Book.

- Show the children the video sequence *Time for fun!* twice (DVD).

Preparation of key written phrases

Let's watch TV; Listen! A car; They've got a cat!; Let's run!; The TV's on; That's strange; I can smell mice.

- Write the sentences on strips of paper, large enough so that all the children in your class can comfortably read the sentences.

- Hold up one of the paper strips for about half a second only. The children call out the sentence. They should, however, not be able to read the words letter for letter. This helps to avoid interference between the written words and their pronunciation. Carry on as described with the other sentences.

Option: You can also read out the sentences in the speech bubbles in the Pupil's Book at pp. 20–21. The children point at the corresponding sentences.

❺ Listen and stick.

Listening exercise: Sticker activity CD 1/32

- Play the listening version of the story twice from CD 1/32. The children stick the stick-in pictures from the appendix in the Pupil's Book in the corresponding blank spaces in the book (pp. 20 and 21) while they are listening.
- Check the children's work.

Option: To promote self-checking it is recommended that you put out a completed picture story in the classroom. The children go and check their own work themselves.

Additional task for high-ability groups
Role play

- In high-ability groups the story can also be performed as a role play after appropriate intensive practice. Proceed as follows:
- Play the listening version of the story again (CD 1/32). The children close their eyes and see the story in their imagination.
- Play the story with the roles distributed among the children. The children play the parts of the mice and that of the cat. Play the part of the father. Help the children by whispering cues. Afterwards the children can play all the parts.

❹ Listen and write the numbers.
Listening exercise CD 1/33

- The children open their Activity Book at p. 19 and look at the pictures. Tell the children that they are going to hear individual sentences on CD. They should match them to the corresponding pictures in the book.

Tapescript:

Speaker:	One.
Boy:	A dog! Let's run.
Speaker:	Two.
Girl:	The TV is on. That's strange.
Speaker:	Three.
Boy:	Let's watch TV.
Speaker:	Four.
Girl:	Listen! A car.
Speaker:	Five.
Boy:	They've got two rabbits.
Speaker:	Six.
Girl:	I can smell oranges.

- Play the listening exercise from the CD 1/33 twice. The children listen and write the corresponding numbers in the circles provided in the book.
- Check the children's work: Hold your book up. Point to the first picture and ask: *What number is it?* Children: *(Number) three.*

Note: You can also check the children's answers by saying e.g.:
Let's watch TV. What number is it?
Children: *(It's number) three.*

Vocabulary extension

drop; grab; chocolate bar

- Clarify the meaning of the words *drop* and *grab* through appropriate mimes and gestures.
- Ask the children: *What's chocolate bar in L1?*

Action Story: *The chocolate bar*

Listen and imitate.

- Ask the children to stand in a circle or stand up in their places.
- Say the sentences of the action story and at the same time carry them out in mimes/gestures:

Open the cupboard.
Ah. A chocolate bar!
Climb onto a chair.
Take the chocolate bar.
Jump down.
Ouch! Your foot!
You drop the chocolate bar.
Your dog grabs the chocolate bar.
Shout: 'Give it back!'

- Keep repeating this until you see that the children have a good grasp of the sentences and the actions that go with them.
- Tell the children that you are now going to give the same instructions but they will do the actions. Give the same instructions as above in the same order. The children carry out the action. Don't do the actions yourself but give positive feedback (e.g. by nodding your head) when the children carry out the instruction correctly. Continue with the rest of the instructions in the same way.
- Keep repeating this until you see that the children can carry out the instructions without difficulty. Gradually increase the pace.
- Announce that you are going to give the instructions jumbled up. (*Now in any order.*) The children carry them out. You, however, do not do any of the actions.

❻ Listen and point.
   Write the numbers.

Action Story: *The chocolate bar* **CD 1/34**

- The children open their Pupil's Book at p. 22. The nine pictures are printed in random order. Now give the children sufficient time to look at the pictures.

Tapescript:

Open the cupboard.
Ah. A chocolate bar!
Climb onto a chair.
Take the chocolate bar.
Jump down.
Ouch! Your foot!
You drop the chocolate bar.
Your dog grabs the chocolate bar.
Shout: "Give it back!"

- Play the listening exercise from CD 1/34. At first the children just point to the appropriate pictures in the book.
- Tell the children that they are now to number the pictures from one to nine.
- Play the listening exercise again. The children number the pictures in the book.
- Go round the class and check the children's work.

Check: Draw a grid with nine boxes on the board. This grid represents p. 22 in the book. Have the children dictate the numbers for the corresponding box *(What number is it?)*.

L E S S O N   5

Vocabulary, phrases and structures:

Vocabulary revision: numbers from one to ten
eleven; twelve; thirteen; fourteen; fifteen; sixteen; seventeen; eighteen; nineteen; twenty; fifteen minus/plus two is …; It's my turn; It's your turn.
Receptive language: *Start; Finish.*

Linguistic skills:

Learning the meaning, the pronunciation and the written form of the new numbers.
Using the expressions necessary for a game.

Cognitive, motor and social skills:

Playing a game in pairs.
Understanding and following the rules of a game.

Cross-curricular integration:

Mathematics: Adding and subtracting with numbers from one to twenty.
Topic: Speaking motivation 'Designing and describing a room'.

Materials:

CD 1/32; *Pupil's Book*, pp. 20–21, ex. 5
Pupil's Book, p. 23, ex. 7; CD 1/35; *Activity Book*, pp. 20–21, ex. 5–8; paper strips; dice for the children; tokens

Revision

- Revise the cartoon story *Time for fun!* with the aid of the listening version from the CD 1/32 and the pictures in the Pupil's Book (pp. 20–21).
- Play the game *Max says...* with the instructions of the action story *The Chocolate bar* from the previous lesson:
Tell the children to perform the various actions. For example, say: *Max says, 'Open the cupboard.'* The children obey your instructions, but only when you begin them with *Max says...* If you give an instruction without saying *Max says...* the children must not carry it out. Anyone who does it is 'out'.

Vocabulary revision and extension

one; two; three; … twenty

- Revise or reinforce the numbers one to twenty by writing the numbers on the board and saying them at the same time. First point to the numbers in order, then in random order and have the children repeat several times.
- Count from one to twenty. While doing this vary the volume of your voice and the speaking pace (start counting slowly and then faster and faster and the other way round). The children speak along with you.

- Ask individual children to come out to the board and touch a number, e.g. *Jenny, come out and touch number fifteen.*
- Pair work (back writing): Ask the children to work in pairs. Child A turns round and child B writes a number from one to twenty with his/her finger on child A's back. Child A has to guess the number. Then they swap roles. Then write some simple additions and subtractions on the board, e.g,
8 + 10 =
19 – 7 =
- Read the sample sum out, say: *Eight plus ten is …* and look at the children. Elicit the correct answer: *Eighteen.*
- Then say: *Nineteen minus seven is …* and have the children carry out the calculation and give the answer.

Pronunciation tip: Be careful that with the numbers *thirteen, fourteen* to *nineteen* the second syllable is more heavily stressed than the first: [ˌθɜːˈtiːn], [ˌfɔːˈtiːn] etc.

Preparation of written forms of numbers

eleven; twelve; thirteen; fourteen; fifteen; sixteen; seventeen; eighteen; nineteen; twenty

- Write the numbers from eleven to twenty in written form on strips of paper, large enough so that all the children in your class can comfortably read them.
- Hold up one of the paper strips for about half a second only. The children call out the number. They should, however, not be able to read the words letter for letter. This helps to avoid interference between the written words and their pronunciation. Carry on as described with the other sentences.

❼ Do sums.
Pair work: Arithmetic game

- The children open their Pupil's Book at p. 23 and look at the game.
- Say: *Find the start/finish.* Hold up your book so that you can point at the sums and the children can see.
- Then read out the calculations in order: *Four plus three is ...* The children point at the sums in their books and give you the answers. Afterwards have individual children read out the sums and others say the results.
- Reinforce *It's my/your turn*, and *Throw the dice*, with appropriate gestures. Practise the new phrases with the children by having them repeat after you several times.
- Then demonstrate the game with one child. Let the others watch until they are all sure about the rules of the game.
- Say: *Throw the dice.* Ask the child to throw the dice. The child throws e.g. three. Say: *Three.* Point to the spaces in the book and say: *Move to three.* On space three is the following sum: *Eleven plus five is ...* Read out the sum and ask the child playing with you to give the answer to the sum. If the child cannot solve the sum she/he misses a go. Now it is your turn etc. The first person to reach *Finish* is the winner.
- If necessary explain the game in L1.
- Distribute the dice and the tokens. Now have the children play in pairs or in small groups. Go round the class and help if necessary.

❺ Do sums and write.
Arithmetic

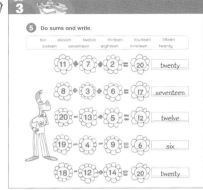

- Count from ten to twenty and ask the children to repeat the numbers several times. Then say a number from ten to twenty and ask a child to come to the front and write the number on the board above the respective strip of paper.
- Ask the children to look at the written numbers in the box in ex. 5 on p. 20 in their Activity Book. Read out the numbers in jumbled order. The children point at the corresponding numbers.
- Do one sum together with the children. Then get them to first write the answer in figures and then the answer in written form into the book.
- Check the children's work: Write the sums on the board. Get the children to give you the correct results. Record the answers on the board (in numbers and in written form).

❻ Write.
Step to creativity

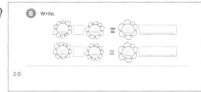

- Focus the children on the empty flowers in ex 6, p. 20 of the Activity Book. Ask them to make their own sums using the numbers from one to twenty. They should write the sum but leave the answer flower empty. When they have finished, the children can change books with a partner and try to answer their sums by writing in the last flower. Once they have completed the sums, ask some of the children to come up to the board and to write one of their sums. Ask children in the class to give an answer.

❼ Listen and match.
Listening exercise CD 1/35

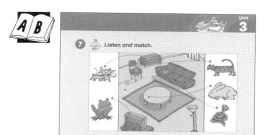

- Ask the children to look at the picture of Max's room in ex. 7 on p. 21 in their Activity Book only for about five seconds. Then the children close their books and give you words they remember. Write the words on the board. Get the children to look again very briefly at p. 21 and give you more words. Write them on the board again.
- Then tell them that they are going to hear Max on the CD talking about his crazy room.
- Explain the word *crazy* as something strange or unusual if necessary, translate it in L1.
- The children should listen and point at the items of furniture and animals Max mentions.
- Play CD 1/35 twice. The children first point at the respective place and animal in the book. Then they first draw lines from the animal to the corresponding piece of furniture.

Tapescript:

Max: Look at my crazy room.
           There's a snake on the sofa.
           There's a frog on the TV.
           A cat on the chair.
           A rabbit on the table.
           And there are three mice on the cupboard.

---

❽ Draw and say.
Step to creativity (ME-page)
My crazy room

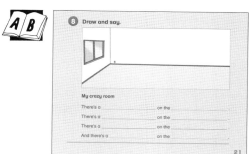

- Ask the children to draw their own crazy room in ex. 8 at p. 21 in their Activity Book.
- Tell them to compose their own text: *My crazy room.* Give the children sufficient time for this work. When they have finished the children practise reading their texts so they remember them well.
- Go round the class and help with the pronunciation, if necessary.
- Finally, individual children read out their texts.

L E S S O N 1

Vocabulary, phrases and structures:

Vocabulary revision: numbers one to twenty;
tooth/teeth; knee/s
eye/s; mouth; nose; hand/s; head; ear/s; hair;
shoulder/s; arm/s; finger/s; toe/s; leg/s; foot/feet

Linguistic skills:

Learning the meaning, the pronunciation and the
written form of the new words.

Cognitive, motor and social skills:

Understanding words from the CD and matching
them to pictures and words.

Reacting to words and instructions with appropriate
actions.
Matching words with numbers.
Carrying out pair work.

Cross-curricular integration:

Topic: Speaking motivation 'Naming parts of the
body'.

Materials:

Flashcards from *Playway 1:* 72–73
Flashcards from *Playway 2:* 24–36; *Word Cards*
from *Playway 2:* 59–73; CD 2/1–3; *Pupil's Book*,
p. 24, ex. 1–2

Vocabulary revision

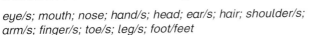

numbers from one to twenty; tooth/teeth; knee/s

- Revise the numbers one to twenty.
- Revise the words *tooth/teeth* and *knee/s* with the aid of
  the flashcards and stick them on the board.

Introduction of vocabulary

eye/s; mouth; nose; hand/s; head; ear/s; hair; shoulder/s;
arm/s; finger/s; toe/s; leg/s; foot/feet

- Introduce new words with the aid of the flashcards in the
  usual manner.

Vocabulary exercises with the support of the written forms

- Hold up the word cards in quick succession. Do not
  allow the children enough time to read the words letter
  by letter. They should absorb the written form only as a
  single entity.
- When the children say the correct word, repeat it. Then
  get one of them to put the card up on the board next to
  the corresponding flashcard. Say: *Put it on the board,*
  please.
- Take down all the flashcards, but leave the word cards
  on the board. Read them out together with the children
  several times.
- Tell the children to close their eyes. Change the
  positions of the word cards. Say: *Open your eyes.*
  What's wrong? Ask individual children to put the cards
  back in their correct places.

Exercises for anchoring the vocabulary in the children's recognition memory

- Name the individual parts of the body, at first in order
  and then jumbled up. Ask the children to touch the
  corresponding part of the body.
- Say, for example: *Touch your teeth. Touch your arms.*

❶ Listen and write the numbers.

Listening exercise CD 2/1

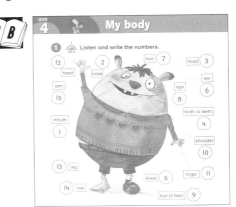

- The children look at the illustration on p. 24, ex. 1 in their
  Pupil's Book.
- Name the parts of the body in any order. The children
  point to the pictures and then to the words.
- Explain the listening exercise: Tell the children to match
  the numbers to the corresponding parts of the body in
  the Pupil's Book and write them in the spaces.

Tapescript:

One:	Mouth.	Nine:	Foot.
Two:	Nose.	Ten:	Shoulder.
Three:	Head.	Eleven:	Finger.
Four:	Tooth.	Twelve:	Hand.
Five:	Knee.	Thirteen:	Leg.
Six:	Ear.	Fourteen:	Toe.
Seven:	Hair.	Fifteen:	Arm.
Eight:	Eye.		

- Play the listening exercise twice (CD 2/1).
- Check the results of the listening exercise in the following way: Name a part of the body and ask one child to say the number written next to that body part.

Exercises for anchoring the vocabulary in the children's productive memory

- Take the body part flashcards and put them in a pile on your desk. Take a flashcard from the pack, look at it and ask: *What is it?* The child who guesses the flashcard can ask another question.

Pronunciation tip: Pay attention with teeth [ti:θ] to the correct pronunciation of the [θ]. It is not to be spoken as an [s]. Have the children say the correct sound several times.

❷ Play the game. Point and say.
Pair work: Speaking exercise

- The children work in pairs (see Pupil's Book, p. 24, ex. 2). Child A points to a part of the body and child B names it. Then they swap roles.

Vocabulary game: *Max says ...*

- Practise following instructions together with the children by saying the sentences and doing the matching actions. The children imitate your actions:

  Touch your toes/nose/eyes/head/feet/face ...!
  Shake your arms/hands/fingers ...!
  Clap your hands!
  Open your mouth!
  Close your eyes!
  Sit down!
  Stand up!

- Ask the children to carry out various activities.
- Say, for example: *Max says, 'Open your mouth.'* The children only carry out your instructions if they are introduced *by Max says ...* If an instruction is given without being introduced by *Max says ...* this must not be carried out. Whoever still does it is out.

Tip: If the game is played a lot, the result is often that the children hardly make any "mistakes" after a while. To increase the degree of difficulty, proceed as follows: You say e.g.: *Max says, 'Touch your teeth'.*, but you carry out a different action. You touch your ears for example.

L E S S O N   2

Vocabulary, phrases and structures:
Bend your knees; Touch your toes/hair/chair/the sky; Clap your hands; Shake your fingers/head; Stamp your feet; Jump up high.
Receptive language: *OK now. Close your eyes; Monster one has got four orange eyes ...*

Linguistic skills:
Understanding the new words and a chant (*Bend your knees*) from the CD.

Cognitive, motor and social skills:
Pointing to the right pictures or doing the right actions while listening and speaking rhythmically. Understanding a description, recognising and numbering the corresponding illustration in the book.

Cross-curricular integration:
Music

Materials:
Flashcards from *Playway 2: 24–36; Word Cards* from *Playway 2: 59–73*
Pupil's Book, p. 25, ex. 3; CD 2/4–5; *Activity Book*, pp. 22–23, ex. 1–3

Vocabulary revision
- Revise the body words with the help of the flashcards and word cards in there usual manner.
- Then play the game on Pupil's Book p. 24, ex 2.

❸ **Listen and point. Say the chant.**

Chant: *Bend your knees* **CD 2/2–3**

Tapescript:

Speaker 1:	*Bend your knees.*
	Touch your toes.
	Clap your hands.
	Touch your nose.
Speaker 2:	*Bend your knees.*
	Touch your toes.
	Clap your hands.
	Touch your nose.
Speaker 1:	*Shake your fingers.*
	Touch your hair.
	Stamp your feet.
	Touch your chair.
Speaker 2:	*Shake your fingers.*
	Touch your hair.
	Stamp your feet.
	Touch your chair.
Speaker 1:	*Shake your head.*
	Jump up high.
	Grow and grow.
	Touch the sky.
Speaker 2:	*Shake your head.*
	Jump up high.
	Grow and grow.
	Touch the sky.

- Play the chant (CD 2/2) and carry out the actions named.
- Play the chant again and have the children point at the respective pictures in the Pupil's Book on p. 25. Clarify the meaning of the words *grow* and *sky* through appropriate gesture/mime.
- Say the text while the children do the actions.
- Practise the chant with the children by giving two instructions and carrying them out. The children imitate your actions and repeat after you.
- Get the children to repeat the verses rhythmically and carry them out.

- Play the chant (CD 2/2). The children point to the corresponding pictures in the book and join in the repeat verses.
- Also say the chant to the first part of the karaoke version CD 2/3. The children point at the respective pictures in the book and say first of all the missing parts of the text. Then play the second part of the CD 2/3 (karaoke version) and the children say the whole text in two groups.

❶ **Listen and write the numbers.**

Listening exercise CD 2/4

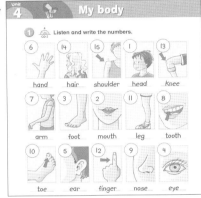

- Ask the children to look at the pictures in ex. 1 at p. 22 in their Activity Book.
  Tell them to listen to the CD and number the pictures accordingly from 1 to 15.

Tapescript:

One:	*Head.*		*Nine:*	*Nose.*
Two:	*Mouth.*		*Ten:*	*Toe.*
Three:	*Foot.*		*Eleven:*	*Leg.*
Four:	*Eye.*		*Twelve:*	*Finger.*
Five:	*Ear.*		*Thirteen:*	*Knee.*
Six:	*Hand.*		*Fourteen:*	*Hair.*
Seven:	*Arm.*		*Fifteen:*	*Shoulder.*
Eight:	*Tooth.*			

- Play CD 2/4 twice. The children listen and fill in the numbers.
- Play the CD again and the children check.
- Check the children's work by touching, for example your head. Ask: *What number is it?* The children answer: *(Number) one.*

❷ **Look at the pictures in ❶ and write.**
  Writing exercise

- Ask the children to look at ex. 2 at p. 22 in their Activity Book. Read out the body words in jumbled order. Then tell the children to match the words in the box in ex. 2

to the pictures in ex. 1. The children write the words underneath the corresponding pictures in ex. 1.

- Check the children's work by holding up a body flashcard, for example *knee*.
  Ask the children: *What number is it?*
  Children: *(Number) fourteen.*

❸ Listen and write the numbers.
Listening exercise CD 2/5

- Draw a monster on the board similar to the monsters in the Activity Book on p. 23. Use coloured chalks. Have the children watch while you are drawing. Speak while you are drawing. Say e.g.: *My monster has got three big ears …two pink teeth …* etc. Then say: *Nice, isn't it?* Cover the drawing or fold up the board. Ask: *What has my monster got? Can you remember?*
- Get the children to reconstruct it from memory, e.g.: *(It has got) three legs, yellow hair …* Afterwards have the children compare their statements with the drawing on the board.
- Ask the children to open their Activity Book at p. 23. The children look at the monsters in ex. 3 for about fifteen seconds, place a pencil in the book and close it.
- Say: *Tell me about the monsters.* The children say e.g.: *Two yellow ears, ….*
- Explain the listening exercise to the children: They should close their eyes, listen carefully and imagine the monster that is being described.

Tapescript:

Speaker 1:   OK now. Close your eyes.
Monster one has got four orange eyes,
six green teeth, two big yellow ears,
four arms and three legs.
Once more:
Monster one has got four orange eyes,
six green teeth, two big yellow ears,
four arms and three legs.
Now open your eyes.

Speaker 2:   Close your eyes again.
Monster two has got three green eyes,
six yellow teeth, four yellow ears, six
arms and two legs.
Once more:
Monster two has got three green eyes,
six yellow teeth, four yellow ears, six
arms and two legs.
Now open your eyes.

Speaker 3:   Close your eyes.
Monster three has got one big red eye,
four orange teeth, four pink ears, four
arms and three legs.
Once more:
Monster three has got one big red eye,
four orange teeth, four pink ears, four
arms and three legs.
Now open your eyes.

Speaker 4:   Close your eyes again.
Monster four has got two yellow eyes,
eight orange teeth, six pink ears, two
arms and six legs.
Once more:
Monster four has got two yellow eyes,
eight orange teeth, six pink ears, two
arms and six legs.
Now open your eyes.

Speaker 5:   Monster five has got three
yellow eyes, two pink ears,
six arms, one leg and five green teeth.
Once more:
Monster five has got three
yellow eyes, two pink ears,
six arms, one leg and five green teeth.
Now open your eyes.

Speaker 6:   Close your eyes.
Monster six has got four yellow ears,
two green eyes, two arms,
two red teeth and four legs.
Once more:
Monster six has got four yellow ears,
two green eyes, two arms,
two red teeth and four legs.
Now open your eyes.

- Play the first picture description of the listening exercise from CD 2/5.
- Stop the CD after the first description and ask the children to open their books and number monster one. Proceed in the same manner with the remaining five picture descriptions.
- Check the answers to the listening exercise together with the children. Hold up the page so the children can see and point to the corresponding picture. Say: *Number one. What has the monster/it got? The monster/It has got four orange eyes, six green teeth, two big yellow ears, four arms and three legs.*
- Continue in this way with the other pictures.

Unit 4 — My body

L E S S O N 3

Vocabulary, phrases and structures:

Receptive language: *Wilbur gets out of bed; He shakes his arms; He shakes his legs; He bends his knees; He says hello to his dog; Oh, no!; Wilbur runs into the bathroom; He cleans his teeth; Joe runs into the kitchen; He brings his dog some water; Joe and his dog are happy.*

Linguistic skills:

Understanding instructions in an action story (*Wilbur*).
Understanding instructions from the CD and matching with the corresponding pictures.
Understanding sentences from the CD.

Cognitive, motor and social skills:

Matching instructions with actions.
Understanding sentences from the CD and matching them to the corresponding pictures in the book.
Completing a text.

Cross-curricular integration:

Topic: Speaking motivation *'Wilbur'.*

Materials:

CD 2/3
CD 2/6–8; *Pupil's Book*, p. 26, ex. 4; *Activity Book*, p. 24, ex. 4–5

Revision

- Speak the chant *Bend your knees* from the previous lesson together with the children in two groups to the karaoke version CD 2/3.

Action Story: *Wilbur*

- For reinforcement of the action story carry out the following steps in the usual manner (see also Introduction of the Teacher's Book, p. 16):
  – Listen and imitate
  – Carry out instructions
  – Carry out the instructions jumbled up

❹ Listen and point. Write the numbers.

Action Story: *Wilbur* CD 2/6

- The children open their Pupil's Book at p. 26. The eight pictures are printed in random order. Give the children sufficient time to look at the pictures.

Tapescript:

Wilbur gets out of bed.
He shakes his arms.
He shakes his legs.
He bends his knees.
He says hello to his dog.
Oh, no!
Wilbur runs into the bathroom.
He cleans his teeth.

- Play the listening exercise CD 2/6.
- The children listen and point at the respective pictures in the book.
- Then play the listening exercise again. This time the children number the pictures.
- Go round the class and check the children's work.

❹ Listen and point.

Listening exercise CD 2/7

- Ask the children to look at ex. 4 on p. 24 in their Activity Book. Tell them to listen to the CD and point at the pictures in the book.

Tapescript:

Sam gets out of bed.
He says hello to his dog.
Oh, no!
Sam runs into the kitchen.
He brings his dog some water.
Sam and his dog are happy.

- Play CD 2/7 twice. The children point at the respective pictures in their books.

❺ Listen again and write.
Writing exercise CD 2/8

- The children look at the words in the box in ex. 5 on p. 24 in their Activity Book. Read out the words in order, then jumbled up. The children read along.
- Then read the text line by line.
- Say: *Sam gets out of ...* Pause and look at the children. The children say: *... bed.* Proceed in this way with the rest of the text.
- Play CD 2/8 several times, if necessary. The children fill in the missing words from the box while listening.
- Check the childrens work: Get individual children to read out the whole sentences.

L E S S O N   4

Vocabulary, phrases and structures:

Receptive language: *Bend your knees; Shake your arms, one, two, three!; Now jump; What are you doing?; Shhh! Look!; What?; Come with me; Look at this; This is great! Give it to me!; Stamp your feet; Stretch; And now touch your toes; My back/ shoulders/knees; My arms/legs; My goodness; Danny! Daisy!; What is it, Dad?; Look; Come with me; To the doctor's; No!; What's that?; Aaaaaah!; Here you are, Dad; Very funny! Watch this; Next, please!; Come on, lazy! Off the sofa and join in too.*

Linguistic skills:

Understanding a story (*Mr Matt keeps fit*) from the DVD.
Understanding mini-dialogues (scenes from the sketch) from the CD.
Being able to read and understand written sentences.

Cognitive, motor and social skills:

Understanding mini-dialogues from the CD and numbering the pictures in the book to correspond.

Cross-curricular integration:

Topic: Speaking motivation *'Mr Matt keeps fit'.*
Art

Materials:

DVD (*Mr Matt keeps fit*); CD 2/9–10; *Pupil's Book*, p. 27, ex. 5; *Activity Book*, p. 25, ex. 6–7; coloured pencils

Revision

- Play the game *Max says...* with the instructions from the action story *Wilbur* from the previous lesson.

❺ Watch the story.

Mr Matt Story: *Mr Matt keeps fit*

- Show the children the DVD scene *Mr Matt keeps fit.*

DVD script: *Mr Matt keeps fit*

Fitness trainer:	Bend your knees, one, two!
	Shake your arms, three, four!
	Now jump. One, two, three!
	Shake your fingers!
	Stamp your feet!
	Stretch and stretch and stretch!
	Now touch your toes, three, four!
	Come on lazy!
	Yes, you!
	Off the sofa and join in, too!
	Here we go!
Danny:	What are you doing?
Daisy:	Shhh! Look!
Danny:	I've got an idea!
Daisy:	What?
Danny:	Come with me.
Danny:	Look at this!
Daisy:	This is great! Give it to me!
Mr Matt:	My back!
	My shoulders!
	My knees!
	My arms!
	My legs!
	My goodness!
	Danny! Daisy!
	Daisy and Danny: What is it, Dad?
Mr Matt:	Look!
Mr Matt:	My arms!
	My legs!
	My back!
Daisy and Danny:	My goodness!
Mr Matt:	Come with me.
Daisy:	Where are we going?
Mr Matt:	To the doctor's!
Daisy:	Dad?
Mr Matt:	What?
Daisy:	Look!
Mr Matt:	No!
Daisy:	Look, Dad!
Mr Matt:	What's that?
Danny:	Watch me, Dad!
Mr Matt:	Aaaaah!
Danny:	Here you are, Dad!
Mr Matt:	Hahahaha!
	Very funny!
	Watch this!
	My arm!
	My knees!
	My back!
Doctor:	Next, please!
Mr Matt:	My nose!
Daisy and Danny:	My goodness!

❺ Listen and write the numbers.
Listening exercise CD 2/9

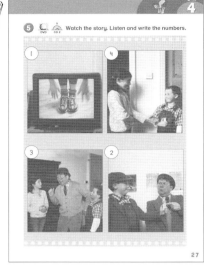

- The children open their Pupil's Book at p. 27 and look at the pictures. Tell them that they are going to hear individual sentences or short dialogues on the CD. They should match them to the corresponding pictures in the book. Picture one has already been numbered.

Tapescript:

Announcer:	Picture one.
Fitness instructor:	Now touch your toes.
Announcer:	Once again.
	Picture one.
Fitness instructor:	Now touch your toes.
Announcer:	Picture two.
Mr Matt:	What's that?
Danny:	Watch me, Dad!
Announcer:	Once again.
	Picture two.
Mr Matt:	What's that?
Danny:	Watch me, Dad!
Announcer:	Picture three.
Mr Matt:	Come with me.
Daisy:	Where are we going?
Mr Matt:	To the doctor's.
Announcer:	Once again.
	Picture three.
Mr Matt:	Come with me.
Daisy:	Where are we going?
Mr Matt:	To the doctor's.
Announcer:	Picture four.
Danny:	Look at this.
Daisy:	This is great! Give it to me.
Announcer:	Once again.
	Picture four.
Danny:	Look at this.
Daisy:	This is great! Give it to me.

- Play the listening exercise twice (CD 2/9). The children listen and number the pictures in the book.
- Then hold your book up so that it can be seen by all. Point to the fourth picture in the book and ask: *What number is it?* Children: *(It's number) two.*

Option: Ask, for example: *What's that? – Watch me, Dad!* Children: *(It's number) two.*

Preparation of key written phrases

I've got an idea; Where are we going?; Look at my tooth; Ouch, my back!; Next, please; Watch me, Megan.

- Write the six sentences on strips of paper, large enough so that all the children in your class can comfortably read the sentences.
- Hold up one of the paper strips for about half a second only. The children call out the sentence. They should, however, not be able to read the words letter for letter. This helps to avoid interference between the written words and their pronunciation. Carry on as described with the other sentences.

❻ Listen and colour.
Listening exercise CD 2/10

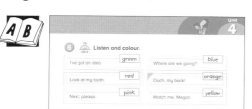

- Ask the children to take out the following coloured pencils: *Orange, blue, pink, green, red* and *yellow.*
- Ask the children to look at the sentences in ex. 6 on p. 25 in their Activity Book.

Tapescript:

Orange:	*Ouch, my back!*
Orange:	*Ouch, my back!*
Blue:	*Where are we going?*
Blue:	*Where are we going?*
Pink:	*Next, please.*
Pink:	*Next, please.*
Green:	*I've got an idea.*
Green:	*I've got an idea.*
Red:	*Look at my tooth.*
Red:	*Look at my tooth.*
Yellow:	*Watch me, Megan.*
Yellow:	*Watch me, Megan.*

- Tell them to listen to the CD and to colour the frames around each sentence according to what they hear.
- Play CD 2/10 twice. The children listen and first mark the frames in the corresponding colours. Later they complete colouring the frames.
- Play the CD again and ask the children to check their answers.
- To check ask: *Where are the grapes. What colour is it?* The children answer: *It's blue.*

❼ Read, match and colour.
Reading exercise.

- Tell the children to colour the empty speech bubbles in ex. 7 on p. 25 in their Activity Book according to ex. 6 above.
- To check ask, for example: *What colour is 'Look at my tooth.'?* The children answer: *Red.*

L E S S O N   5

Vocabulary, phrases and structures:

My tummy/knee/nose/arm/shoulder... hurts; My/eyes/feet hurt.

Linguistic skills:

Understanding statements from the CD.
Differentiating between words in the singular and the plural.
Making statements about how people feel.

Cognitive, motor and social skills:

Matching statements with actions.
Understanding statements from the CD and numbering pictures accordingly.
Working in pairs.
Finding body words in a word snake.
Circling the body parts that hurt according to the CD.

Cross-curricular integration:

Topic: Speaking motivation 'Health and your body'.

Materials:

DVD (*Mr Matt keeps fit*)
CD 2/11–12; *Pupil's Book*, p. 28, ex. 6–7; *Activity Book*, p. 26, ex. 8–9; (optional) answer key for self-checking

Revision

- Revise the Mr Matt story *Mr Matt keeps fit* from the previous lesson with the support of the DVD.

Game to prepare key phrases

- Play *Call my bluff* with the class. Explain the phrase *It hurts*. (Translate – if necessary – into L1).
- Say e.g.: *My tummy hurts*, but hold your hands over your ears as if you had earache. In this case the children have to stand up. If however you say the sentence and at the same time act as if you had tummy ache the children stay sitting down. After a while one child takes over your role.

❻ Listen and write the numbers.
Listening exercise CD 2/11

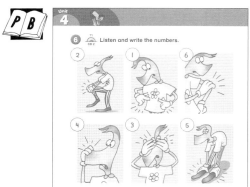

- The children open their Pupil's Book at p. 28 and look at the pictures in ex. 6.
- Play the listening exercise (CD 2/11). The children number the pictures in the book correspondingly from one to six.
- Check the children's work in the following way:

- Draw a grid with six boxes on the board that represents the boxes in ex. 6.
  Point to the first box on the board.
  Ask: *What number is it?*
  Children: *Two.*
  Write the corresponding number in the first box.

Tapescript:

Announcer:	One.
Max:	*My tummy hurts.*
Announcer:	Two.
Max:	*My knee hurts.*
Announcer:	Three.
Max:	*My eyes hurt.*
Announcer:	Four.
Max:	*My nose hurts.*
Announcer:	Five.
Max:	*My feet hurt.*
Announcer:	Six.
Max:	*My arm hurts.*

- Continue in this way with the remaining boxes in the grid.
- Say the sentences in order: *My knee hurts. My tummy hurts.* etc. The children point at the respective pictures in the book.

❼ Say.
Pair work: Speaking exercise

- Ask one child to come out in front of the class and show by gestures and mimes where it hurts.

- Then say: *Your ... hurt/hurts.* Repeat this exercise with several children.
- Get other children to come out in front of the class and indicate where they have a pain. Now the class must say: *Your ... hurt/hurts.*
- Tell the children in L1 when they should say *hurt* and when they should say *hurts. (i.e. plural = hurt: My toes hurt).*
- The children look at ex. 7 on p. 28 in the Pupil's Book. Practise the expressions thoroughly beforehand with the children: *Your tummy hurts/Your shoulder hurts ...* Write some of these expressions on the board and read them out. Get the children to repeat several times.
- Tell them that they are now to work in pairs.
- Child A imitates pain and child B names it. Then they swap roles.
- Go round the class and help if necessary.

8 Circle the words.
Search game

- The children look at ex. 8 on p. 26 in their Activity Book. Tell them to find the hidden words in the word snake and circle them. Hold your book up and demonstrate this task. Point at the word *head* and say it. Then pretend to circle the word in your book.
- The children then try to find the remaining fourteen words and circle them.
- Alternatively, this exercise can be carried out in pair work.
- To check the children's work get individual children to read out the words one after the other. The others listen and check.

Option: You can also place an answer key for self-checking out in the classroom. The children go and check themselves.

9 Listen and circle.
Listening exercise CD 2/12

- Ask the children to look at ex. 9 on p. 26 in their Activity Book. There are six pictures of children numbered from one to six.
- Tell the children to listen to the CD and to circle the body parts that hurt in the pictures.

Tapescript:	
Speaker:	*One.*
Boy:	*My tummy hurts.*
Speaker:	*Two.*
Girl:	*My knee hurts.*
Speaker:	*Three.*
Boy:	*My eyes hurt.*
Speaker:	*Four.*
Girl:	*My nose hurts.*
Speaker:	*Five.*
Boy:	*My feet hurt.*
Speaker:	*Six.*
Girl:	*My arm hurts.*

- Play the CD 2/12 several times.
- To check the children's work ask: *My nose hurts. What number is it?* Children: (*Number*) *four.*

L E S S O N 6

Vocabulary, structures and phrases

My monster has got blue hair/one red eye/etc…;
What has the monster got?; The monster has got…

Linguistic skills:

Understanding the description of a monster from the CD.
Describing one's own monster.

Cognitive, motor and social skills:

Training of sensory perception.
Drawing one's own monster and describing it.
Naming the five senses (touch, hearing, sight, taste and smell).

Matching the pictures in the book to the senses.
Making a body dice.
Playing a game with others and keeping to rules.

Cross-curricular integration:

Topic: Speaking motivation 'Creating and describing a new character'.
Art
Science – senses

Materials:

CD 2/13; *Activity Book*, p. 27, ex. 10–11; coloured pencils; body dice (photocopiable master from the appendix in the *Teacher's Book,* p. 158)

---

⑩ Listen and draw.

Listening exercise CD 2/13

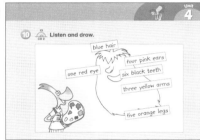

- The children look at ex. 10 on p. 27 in their Activity Book. Tell them to listen to Max on CD 2/13 describing his monster. The children should listen carefully and draw the monster according to the listening text.

Tapescript:

Max: *My monster has got blue hair, one red eye, four pink ears, six black teeth, three yellow arms and five orange legs.*

- Play CD 2/13 twice. The children draw while listening to the CD.
- To check the children's work ask: *What has the monster got? The monster has got …* Look at the children. Get them to describe the monster: … *Blue hair, one red eye,* etc.

---

⑪ Draw and say.

Step to creativity (ME-page)
My monster has got …

- Ask the children to draw a monster of their own choice into the space provided in ex. 11 on p. 27 in their Activity Book.
- Give the children sufficient time to do this.
- Ask individual children to describe their monster. Help through whispering cues, if necessary. The other children should close their eyes and try to imagine the monster being described.

Option: This exercise can also be carried out in pair work: The children get together with a partner and describe their monsters to each other. Child A says, for example: *My monster has got three pink eyes, four green ears, six black teeth, one red arm and three yellow legs.* Child B has to close his/her eyes and tries to imagine the monster. Then child A shows his/her drawing to child B. Then they swap roles.

A game: the body dice

- Each child makes a copy of the body dice (see photocopiable master in appendix of the *Teacher's Book*, p. 158). Distribute photocopies and get the children to make the body dice together with you.
- Demonstrate the individual steps and accompany your activities with the corresponding English instructions. Keep to the right pace so that each child can follow your instructions easily.
- Keep repeating your instructions and praise the children when they get it right.

Instructions and expressions:

Cut the dice out. Cut along the dotted lines. Like this. Yes, very good.
Now, fold it along the lines. Like this.
Well done.
Put some glue here and here and put the dice together. Like this. Be careful. OK.
That's right. Good!

- Go round the class and help, if necessary.
- The children get together with a partner or a small group. They take it in turns to roll one dice and say which of the five senses each picture represents.
- Demonstrate the game with a child in front of the class. Roll the dice.
- If the dice shows the hand, say, for example: *To feel (a ball of wool/etc.)*. If you can give a description of what the sense shown is used for, you get a point.
- If the dice shows *Roll again*, you may take another turn. The person with the most points is the winner.

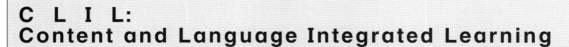

C L I L:
Content and Language Integrated Learning

Objectives:
To find out about the five senses.
To train the senses.

Materials:
Pupil's Book, p. 29, ex. 8; some things that make interesting noises, e.g. zips, keys; some things with interesting flavours, e.g. jam, honey, crisps, vinegar; some things that smell strong, e.g. Coffee, perfume, soap, and some small items for a feeling bag, e.g. a coin, a pencil sharpener, a feather. (If possible, some binoculars and a microscope.)

Revision.

• Write a few sentences on the board, for example: *My tummy hurts. My feet hurt.* etc. Point to one sentence after the other and the children do the corresponding gestures.

❽ Look and tick (✓).

Thinking exercise

• The children look at ex. 8 on p. 29 of their Pupil's Book.
• Tell them that they are now to find out which sense is involved in which picture. The children should tick the appropriate box in the picture bar (*mouth, eye, ear, hand, nose*). Go through the situations with the children in order and speak as you do so.
• If necessary translate difficult words in L1.

Expressions:

Look at the pictures. Tick one of the five boxes.

Picture number one. The girl is eating an ice cream.
Mmmh! She likes the taste a lot!
Tick the correct box.
Which one is it? Correct! It's the mouth.

Picture number four. What a lovely smell!
The flower smells nice.
Do you use your mouth, eye, ear, hand or nose?
Tick one of the five boxes.
Which one is it? Correct! It's your nose.

Picture number two. The boy touches the horse.
It's soft!
Tick one of the five boxes.
Which one is it? Correct! It's the hand.

Picture number three. The boy is looking at something.
Tick the correct box.
Which one is it? Correct! It's the eye.

Picture number five. The boy is listening to the music.
He likes the sound.
Again, tick one of the five boxes.
Which one is it? Correct! It's the ear.

Exercises on the five senses
Guess the sounds

• Practise with the children the names for various noisy objects e.g.: *Zip, tap, key.* Ask the children to turn round. Then make different sounds with one of the objects mentioned or stamp your foot on the floor, snap your fingers, clap your hands etc. Ask the children what each sound is.

Expressions:

Turn round/Close your eyes and listen carefully.
What is it?
A zip(per), stamping feet, clicking fingers, clapping hands, the water tap, keys, paper etc.

Taste food

- Bring items of food that the children know and practise the English terms for them. Reinforce words such as *sweet, sour, salty, bitter*. Blindfold some of the children and get them to taste small pieces of these food items.
- The children will answer the question *What is it?* in L1. Translate the answers into English.

Expressions:

Let me blindfold you. Open your mouth.
Is it sour/salty/sweet/bitter? What is it?
A lemon, a gherkin, jam, honey, salty crackers etc.

Smell it

- Bring objects that the children know and practise the English terms for them. Then blindfold some of the children and get them to smell them.

Expressions:

Smell it. What is it?
Garlic, onion, a rose, a lemon, an orange, coffee, pepper, soap, perfume etc.

A feeling bag

- Reinforce with the children the words for various small objects such as *pencil sharpener, paperclip, coin, feather* etc.
- Put all the objects into a pillowcase. Get one child to feel an object with his/her eyes closed first of all from the outside. Then he/she can put his/her hand in the pillowcase.

Expressions:

I have got a pillowcase and some objects:
A coin, a feather, a pen, a button, a ball of wool, a key, a paperclip etc.
Let's put all these things into the pillowcase. Tom, come out, please. Close your eyes. Feel one object from the outside, through the pillowcase. What is it? Now put your hand inside. Touch one object. What is it?

Look at it

- If you have a microscope and specimens available, have the children look through the device and guess what the specimen is. Practise beforehand the relevant English terms for the objects (specimens, e. g. *water drop from a pond, flower, hair from a cat*).
- You can also have the children look through the window using binoculars and ask what they can see.
- Then ask them what the difference is between a microscope and binoculars. The children answer in L1. Objects are enlarged through a microscope. Distant objects appear nearer through binoculars.

Expressions:

Look through the microscope/binoculars.
What can you see?
What is the difference between a microscope and binoculars?

L E S S O N   1

Vocabulary, phrases and structures:	**Cognitive, motor and social skills:**
Checking of vocabulary acquisition in Units 3–4.	Matching words and sentences from the CD to the corresponding pictures.
Linguistic skills:	Numbering these words and sentences according to the CD.
Understanding and being able to say and read important words and sentences from Units 3 and 4 on the topic areas 'furniture' and 'body'.	Checking the results with the aid of an answer key. Self-evaluation
	Materials:
	CD 2/14–15; *Pupil's Book,* pp. 30–31, ex. 1–4; coloured pencils; answer key

Self-evaluation

Option: Divide *Show what you can do* into two lessons.

Note: For notes on the basic methodology of this section, see *Show what you can do* on p. 18 of the introduction in the Teacher's Book.

❶ Listen and write the numbers.

Listening exercise CD 2/14

- Tell the children that they are going to find out which words in the Pupil's Book on p. 30, ex. 1 they can already understand well.

Tapescript:

Number one:	Lamp.
Number one:	Lamp.
Number two:	Chair.
Number two:	Chair.
Number three:	Hair.
Number three:	Hair.
Number four:	Tooth.
Number four:	Tooth.
Number five:	Mouth.
Number five:	Mouth.
Number six:	Curtains.

Number seven:	Hands.
Number seven:	Hands.
Number eight:	Table.
Number eight:	Table.
Number nine:	Feet.
Number nine:	Feet.
Number ten:	Ear.
Number ten:	Ear.
Number eleven:	Nose.
Number eleven:	Nose.
Number twelve:	Cupboard.
Number twelve:	Cupboard.

- Play the listening exercise CD 2/14.
- The children number the pictures in the book accordingly. The first picture has already been numbered.
- Go round the class and help the children, if necessary.
- Set out a completed sheet and let the children check their results independently.

❷ Match the words to the pictures.

Reading exercise

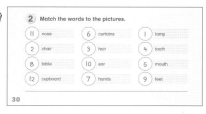

- Tell the children that they are going to find out which words in the Pupil's Book on p. 30, ex. 2 they can already read.
- The children match the written words to the corresponding pictures in ex. 1.
- Set out a completed sheet and let the children check their results independently.

❸ Listen and write the numbers.
Listening exercise CD 2/15

- Tell the children they are going to find out which sentences in the Pupil's Book on p. 31, ex. 3 they can already understand.

Tapescript:

Number one:	*My tummy hurts.*
Number one:	*My tummy hurts.*
Number two:	*Let's watch TV.*
Number two:	*Let's watch TV.*
Number three:	*Let's run!*
Number three:	*Let's run!*
Number four:	*I can smell onions.*
Number four:	*I can smell onions.*

- Now play the listening exercise CD 2/15.
- The children number the pictures in the book accordingly. The first picture has already been numbered.
- Go round the class and help the children, if necessary.
- Set out a completed sheet and let the children check their results independently.

❹ Match the sentences to the pictures.
Reading exercise

- Tell the children that they are going to find out which sentences in the Pupil's Book on p. 31, ex. 4 they can already read.
- The children now check independently whether they can match the written sentences to the corresponding pictures in ex. 3.
- Set out a completed sheet and let the children check their results independently.

L E S S O N   1

Vocabulary, phrases and structures:

Vocabulary revision: colours; numbers from one to twenty
cap; woolly hat; dress; trainers; pullover; jacket; skirt; shoes; socks; T-shirt; hat; Three red woolly hats plus two blue woolly hats plus four green woolly hats are nine woolly hats.
Receptive language: *How many (blue)... (woolly hats)... are there?; Susan is wearing a (white) T-shirt,...*

Linguistic skills:

Learning the meaning, the pronunciation and written form of the new words.
Understanding new words and descriptions from the CD.
Asking questions about the number of articles of clothing.
Formulating addition sums.

Cognitive, motor and social skills:

Understanding the new words from the CD and pointing to the appropriate pictures.
Matching words to the corresponding *flashcards.*
Working in pairs.
Recognising a number of articles and carrying out addition sums.
Understanding descriptions from the CD and matching them to the pictures in the book.

Cross-curricular integration:

Topic: Speaking motivation 'Using clothing to describe someone's appearance'.
Mathematics: Identifying and adding quantities.

Materials:

Flashcards from *Playway 1*: 5–11
Flashcards from *Playway 2*: 37–48; *Word Cards* from *Playway 2*: 74–85; CD 2/16–17; *Pupil's Book*, p. 32, ex. 1–2; *Activity Book*, p. 28, ex. 1–2; (optional) articles of clothing, washing line and clothes pegs; answer key

Revision

• Revise the colours already learnt with the aid of the flashcards.

Vocabulary revision and introduction

cap; woolly hat; dress; trainers; pullover; jacket; skirt; shoes; socks; T-shirt; jeans; hat

• Show the flashcards for articles of clothing and give the English term at the same time:
  a woolly hat, a dress ...
• Stick all the flashcards on the board. Say the words in order and point to the corresponding picture.
• If you have spare articles of clothing at hand, put the articles of clothing on as you name them. Then call out individual children. Say e.g.: *Michelle, touch the T-shirt/ the shoes/the dress/the jeans...*
• Put up a washing line in the classroom and say e.g.: *Tom, give me the socks/the dress/..., please.* Hang the article of clothing up with the clothes pegs.

Tip: The English distinguish between *hat* and *cap* in the following way: *Cap* always has a peak; *hat* not only means a hat with a brim but also a *woolly hat.*

Exercises for anchoring the vocabulary in the children's recognition memory

• Say the clothes words in order and ask individual children to point to the pictures on the board.
• Say the words in random order and ask a child to point at the respective words on the board.
• Ask the children to close their eyes and say the words at different volumes and pitches several times. At first the children just listen.

Vocabulary exercises with the support of the written forms

• Hold up the word cards in quick succession. Do not allow the children enough time to read the words letter by letter. They should absorb the written form only as a single entity.
• When the children say the correct word, repeat it. Then get one of them to put the card up on the board next to the corresponding flashcard. Say: *Put it on the board, please.*
• Take down all the flashcards, but leave the word cards on the board. Read them out together with the children several times.
• Tell the children to close their eyes. Turn the word cards face to the board and tell the children to open their eyes. Point to the word cards in any order and say, each time: *What is it? What do you think?* Turn the cards over as children guess the words.
• Tell the children to close their eyes. Change the positions of the word cards. Say: *Open your eyes. What's wrong?* Ask individual children to put the cards back in their correct places.

Option: An alternative procedure is for you to hold up the word cards one after another, saying the corresponding words. Then hand the cards out to individual children. Say the words in sequence. After each word, the child with the corresponding card comes out to the board and puts it up next to or below the flashcard.

❶ Listen and point.
Listening exercise CD 2/16

- Ask the children to open their Pupil's Book at p. 32 and to look at ex.1.
- Explain the listening exercise: The children should listen and point to the correct articles of clothing which are arranged round the edge of the picture.

Tapescript:

A woolly hat.
A dress.
A cap.
Jeans.
A T-shirt.
Shoes.
Trainers.
Socks.
A pullover.
A jacket.
A hat.
And a skirt.

- Play the listening exercise twice (CD 2/16). The children point along in the Pupil's Book first at the pictures and then at the words.

Pair work: Speaking exercise

- The children work in pairs with p. 32 ex. 1 of the Pupil's Book: Child A covers the word underneath an item of clothing. Child B says what item of clothing they think it is. Child A reveals the word to show whether child B is right or not.

Game: Perception

- Play the following guessing game: Tell the children that they are only allowed to look very briefly for approx. five seconds at the articles of clothing inside the frame in the Pupil's Book on p. 32. Then ask: *How many woolly hats are there?*
- The children guess, e.g.: *Five/Three/...* Say: *That's wrong./Yes, that's right.*
- Proceed likewise with the remaining articles of clothing.

❷ Do the sums.
Pair work: Arithmetic examples

- Demonstrate the first calculation exercise on the lower half of p. 32 in the Pupil's Book.
- Do the first sum on the board. Draw one red, one blue and one green woolly hat on the board. Speak as you do it. Underneath write the following arithmetical signs:
  + + =
- Say the terms several times and have the children repeat them: *Plus … plus … is …*
- Then point to the red woolly hat. Say: *How many red woolly hats are there?* The children count the red woolly hats inside the frame at the top of p. 32 in the Pupil's Book and say: *Three.*
  Say: *Yes, good.* Enter the number three on the board under the red woolly hat and say: *Three plus …*
  Point to the blue woolly hat and say: *Now, how many blue woolly hats are there? etc.*
- Highlight the final result on the board correspondingly and say it at the same time. Practise the expressions for this arithmetic operation thoroughly by getting the children to say and repeat it several times.
- The children do the remaining three sums as individual work. Go round the class and help if necessary.
- To check ask: *How many blue/... skirts/pullovers/jackets are there?* Record the arithmetic operations on the board and say at the same time: *One (skirt) plus two (skirts) plus five (skirts) is eight skirts.*
- The children check their answers by means of the picture on the board.

❶ Find the ten words. ↓ →
Word search

- Ask the children to open their books at p. 28 in their Activity Book and look at ex. 1. There are ten words for clothes hidden in the word search. Tell the children to find the words and circle them.
- Allow the children to do this exercise together with a partner. When the children have finished, ask: *Who's got seven words?* The children who have found seven words raise their arms. Say: *Good.* Ask: *Who's got eight words or more? – Great! Well done!*
- Get the children that have found all ten words to read them out.

Option: To promote self-checking it is recommended that you put out an answer key in the classroom. The children go and check their own work themselves.

❷ Listen and write the names.

Listening exercise CD 2/17

- Write the following names on the board: *Susan, Debra, Frank, Mike*. Read out the names and point at the respective names on the board. Get the children to repeat several times. Then point at the names and get the children to call them out.

- Now ask the children to open their Activity Book at p. 28 and look at ex. 2. Tell them to listen to the CD and find Susan, Debra, Frank and Mike. Ask them to write the names on the on the lines provided in the book.

Tapescript:

Susan is wearing a white T-shirt, a red pullover, a blue skirt, blue socks and yellow trainers.

Mike is wearing an orange cap, a green T-shirt, blue jeans, green socks and blue trainers.

Frank is wearing a green cap, a green T-shirt, blue jeans, black socks and white trainers.

Debra is wearing a white T-shirt, a yellow pullover, a green skirt, yellow socks and white trainers.

- Play CD 2/17. Stop after the first description and give the children sufficient time to find Susan.
- Proceed with the remaining descriptions in the same way as described above.
- Check the children's work: Hold your book up, so that all the children can see it well. Point to a child in the book and the children give you the corresponding name.

L E S S O N   2

Vocabulary, phrases and structures:

Receptive language: *You're in the swimming pool; Get out of the water; Dry yourself; Put on your jeans; Put on your shoes and socks; Put on your T-shirt; Put on your jacket; Walk out; Oh, no! You're wearing your swimming goggles; Walk away; Get your swimming goggles; The boy's foot hurts.*

Linguistic skills:

Understanding the chain of instructions of an action story (*Oh, no!*).
Understanding instructions from the CD and matching with the corresponding pictures.

Cognitive, motor and social skills:

Matching instructions with actions.
Understanding and carrying out jumbled instructions.

Cross-curricular integration:

Topic: Speaking motivation *'Oh, no!'*.

Materials:

Flashcards from *Playway 2:* 37–48; *Word Cards* from *Playway 2:* 74–85
CD 2/18; *Pupil's Book*, p. 33, ex. 3; CD 2/19;
Activity Book, p. 29, ex. 3

Revision

- Revise the articles of clothing with the aid of the flashcards and the word cards in the usual manner.
- Stand in a circle. Get individual children to act out the following instructions: *Mark, touch a red pullover/blue dress/green shirt/... Point to socks/trainers/...*

Vocabulary extension

swimming goggles

- Clarify the meaning of the word *swimming goggles* through appropriate gestures or use the illustration on p. 33 in the Pupil's Book.

Action Story: *Oh, no!*

- Work on the action story in the usual manner (see also Introduction of the Teacher's Book, p. 16):
  - Children listen and imitate your actions
  - They carry out instructions
  - They carry out instructions in a jumbled order

**❸ Listen and point.
Write the numbers.**

Action Story: *Oh, no!* CD 2/18

- The children open their Pupil's Book at p. 33. The nine pictures are printed in random order. Give the children sufficient time to look at the pictures.
- Now play the listening exercise twice (CD 2/18). At first the children just point to the appropriate pictures in the book.

Tapescript:

*You're in the swimming pool.
Get out of the water.
Dry yourself.
Put on your jeans.
Put on your shoes and socks.
Put on your T-shirt.
Put on your jacket.
Walk out.
Oh, no! You're wearing your swimming goggles!*

- Play the listening exercise again and now the children number the pictures in the book.
- Go round the class and check the children's work.
- Check the children's work: Draw a grid with nine boxes on the board. This grid represents p. 33 in the book. Have the children dictate the numbers for the corresponding box (*What number is it?*)

❸ Listen and write the numbers.

Listening exercise CD 2/19

- Ask the children to look at the pictures in ex. 3 at p. 29 in their Activity Book. The eight pictures are printed in random order. Give the children sufficient time to look at the pictures.

Tapescript:

One:	*Get out of the swimming pool.*
One:	*Get out of the swimming pool.*
Two:	*Put your swimming goggles on a chair.*
Two:	*Put your swimming goggles on a chair.*
Three:	*Dry yourself.*
Three:	*Dry yourself.*
Four:	*Put on your shoes.*
Four:	*Put on your shoes.*
Five:	*A boy throws your swimming goggles into the water.*
Five:	*A boy throws your swimming goggles into the water.*
Six:	*The boy falls into the swimming pool.*
Six:	*The boy falls into the swimming pool.*
Seven:	*Get your swimming goggles.*
Seven:	*Get your swimming goggles.*
Eight:	*Walk away.*
Eight:	*Walk away.*

- Play the listening exercise from CD 2/19 twice. The children listen and write the corresponding numbers in the circles provided in the book.
- Check the children's work: Hold your book up. Point to the first picture and ask: *What number is it?* Children: *(Number) six.*

Note: You can also check the children's answers by saying, for example: *Get your swimming goggles. What number is it?* Children: *(It's number) six.*

L E S S O N 3

Vocabulary, phrases and structures:

He is wearing; She is wearing.
Receptive language: Father Bear has a hobby; He makes woolly hats; Joe, this hat is for you; Joe is not happy; I hate it. Aaaargh!; It's time for school; Bye, Dad; It's Fred, the fox; Oh, what a lovely hat; Fred puts the hat on; Joe is in the classroom; Wonderful; Stupid me; We're going shopping; I don't know what to wear; Put on your... Take the jacket off; Yeah, you look great.

Linguistic skills:

Understanding a text *(The woolly hat)* from the DVD and the CD and from being narrated by the teacher.
Joining in with story-telling.
Carrying out role plays.

Cognitive, motor and social skills:

Following the narrative structure of a story on DVD and CD.
Representing a time sequence visually.
Sticking the stick-in pictures correctly in a picture story.
Joining in with role play.
Understanding a text from the CD and circling clothes accordingly.
Carrying out an information-gap activity in pair work.

Cross-curricular integration:

Topic: Speaking motivation 'Using clothing to describe someone's appearance'.
Art

Materials:

DVD *(The woolly hat)*; CD 2/20–23; *Story Cards* from *Playway 2:* 9–17; *Pupil's Book,* pp. 34–35, ex. 4–5; *Activity Book,* p. 30, ex. 4–5; glove puppet Max; stick-in pictures from the appendix of the *Pupil's Book*; answer key; coloured pencils

Revision

- Revise the instructions of the action story *Oh no!* from the previous lesson.

Note: Not all the language in the DVD sequences or CD versions of the stories are presented in the cartoon story in the Pupil's Book. This is mainly because of the length of the stories but also this serves to encourage the children to listen for the necessary information in order to complete the gap fill in the Pupil's Book.

❹ Watch the story.

Cartoon Story: *The woolly hat*

- Show the children the DVD story *The woolly hat* (DVD).

DVD script:	*The woolly hat*
Storyteller:	Father Bear has a hobby. He makes woolly hats.
Father Bear:	Joe, this hat is for you.
Joe:	Oh! Thank you.
Storyteller:	Joe is not happy.
Joe:	I hate it. Aaargh!
Storyteller:	It's time for school.
Joe:	Bye, Dad.
Father Bear:	Bye-bye, Joe.
Joe:	Bye-bye, woolly hat!
Storyteller:	Ah! It's Fred, the fox.
Fred:	Oh, what a lovely hat.
Storyteller:	Fred puts the hat on. Joe is in the classroom.
Other animals:	Ah! What a lovely hat! Wonderful!
Joe:	Stupid me!

❹ Listen and stick.

Listening exercise:
Sticker activity CD 2/20

- Play the listening version of the story twice (CD 2/20).

- The children stick the stick-in pictures from the appendix in the corresponding blank spaces in the Pupil's Book at pp. 34–35, ex. 4 while they are listening.
- Check the children's work.

Option: To promote self-checking it is recommended that you put out a completed picture story. The children go and check their own work themselves.

Telling the story

- Now tell the story with the aid of the story cards.
- Distribute the story cards to individual children. Tell the story again. The children with the corresponding pictures come out to the front. Finally all the children who were given the story cards are standing in the order of the sequence of the story in front of the class. The pictures are held up so that they can be seen well by all.

Story reconstruction game

- Tell the children that you are tired and you may get some of the facts wrong while telling the story. The children should listen particularly carefully and correct the mistakes.
- Say e.g.: *Father Bear has a hobby. He makes jeans.* The children correct the mistake: *No. Woolly hats.* Repeat the sentence with the right wording: *He makes woolly hats.*
- Continue in this way.

Tip: The children put their hands up or say stop when they discover a mistake. The mistakes are "corrected" by the children if possible. Then the story is continued.

Additional task for high-ability groups
Role play

- In high-ability groups the story can also be performed as a role play after appropriate practice.
- Play the listening version of the story again (CD 2/20). The children close their eyes and see the story in their imaginations.
- Re-enact the story. You play the part of the storyteller. The children play the other parts. Help the children by whispering cues.
- After several practises one child can also take on the role of the storyteller.

Tip: Use certain articles of clothing to identify the parts, for example a woolly hat for Joe.

⑤ Listen and colour.
Listening activity CD 2/21

- The children open their Pupil's Books at p. 35 and look at ex. 5. Tell them that they are going to hear a CD and should colour the boy and the girl according to the listening text.
- Play CD 2/21 twice.
- Tell the children to mark the clothes in the corresponding colours according to the instructions in the listening exercise and afterwards colour them.

Tapescript:

Speaker 1:   *His hat is blue.*
His jacket is red.
He's wearing a yellow pullover.
He's wearing blue jeans.
His trainers are red.

Speaker 2:   *She's wearing a pink cap.*
Her pullover is grey.
Her skirt is pink.
She's wearing white socks and black shoes.

- Go round the class and check the children's work. Ask: *What colour's the boy's/girl's pullover/…?*

Preparation of key phrases

Hurry up; I don't know what to wear; put on; take off

- Introduce the new phrases by saying the following dialogue with the glove puppet Max.
- Say: *Hurry up, Max!* Make an inviting gesture.
- Answer as Max: *I don't know what to wear.* Explain the meaning by an appropriate action (e.g.: Max shakes his head and points to his clothing).
- Say to Max: *Put on your blue T-shirt/red shoes …* Pretend that Max is going to put on a T-shirt, his shoes.
- Say: *Take off your shoes, put on your green trainers.* etc. Pretend that Max is taking his shoes off and putting others on, etc.

④ Listen and circle.
Listening exercise CD 2/22

- The children open their Activity Book at p. 30 and look at the illustration in ex. 4 for about five seconds.
- Have them close their books and say: *Give me words.* The children name the articles of clothing and their colours: *A red jacket, yellow socks*, etc.
- Then name all the articles of clothing and colours again and the children point at the respective pictures in the book. Introduce the colour *purple* by saying: *Yellow and purple trainers.* Have the children point to the corresponding trainers in the book and repeat several times.
- Tell the children that they will hear a dialogue from the CD. First, they should circle the articles of clothing that Max puts on.

Tapescript:

Linda: Max, hurry up, we're going shopping.
Max: I don't know what to wear.
Linda: Put on your black T-shirt, your green jeans, your red socks, your white trainers, and your blue jacket.
Max: OK, my black T-shirt, my green jeans, my red socks, my white trainers and my blue jacket.
Linda: Take the jacket off. Put on your orange jacket. Yeah, you look great. A black T-shirt, green jeans, red socks, white trainers and an orange jacket.

- Play the listening exercise (CD 2/22).
- Next ask the children what Max now has on: *What is Max wearing?*
- If there are any uncertainties play the CD again and say: *Listen again. Listen very carefully.*
- If there is time the children draw Max.

Preparation of key phrases

What colour is the jacket? What colour are the shoes? It's blue/...; They're brown/...

- Practise the phrases by asking one boy and one girl to come out to the board. The other children have time briefly to look at both children.
- Go to the back wall of the classroom. The children turn round to you so that they cannot see the two children at the board.
- Ask e.g.: *What's Michael wearing?* The children say, for example: *Black jeans.*
- Then ask: *What's Marie-Louise wearing?* The children say, for example: *A T-shirt.*

- Say: *Right. She's wearing a T-shirt. What colour is it?* Children: *Red.*
- In this way ask further questions about the clothing of the two children at the board. Repeat the children's answers in full sentences and have the children repeat them.

⑤ Colour and say.
Pair work: Speaking Exercise

- The children look at ex. 5 on p. 30 of their Activity Book.
- Tell the children to colour the boy's clothing. They must use only one colour for each article of clothing and set up a schoolbag between the books so that their partner cannot see the drawing.
- Two children then demonstrate the following pair work with your help:
- Child A tells child B how s/he has coloured the clothing of the boy in the book: *A blue woolly hat ...* etc.
- Child B colours the second boy in his/her book according to this description. Then the children swap roles and child B says how he/she has coloured the boy. Child A now colours the second boy in his/her book according to this description.
- Give the children sufficient time for this pair work. Go round the class and help if necessary.

Note: Constantly introduce phrases that enable the children to carry out the course of the lesson or their pair work in English. *Can you say it again, please? Can you help me, please?*

L E S S O N 4

Vocabulary, phrases and structures:

my T-shirt's red; my jeans are blue; like a parrot in a zoo
Receptive language: *Joe is at home; He's sad; Stupid me; My lovely hat; I've got an idea; I can make a woolly hat; What a lovely colour.*

Linguistic skills:

Consolidating the meanings, pronunciation and written form of the clothes words.
Understanding a poem from the CD and following in the book.
Learning by heart and fluently reciting one's own poem.

Cognitive, motor and social skills:

Drawing fruit.
Composing one's own poem.
Reading rhythmically.
Understanding a story from the CD and putting pictures in the correct order.

Cross-curricular integration:

Topic: Speaking motivation 'Using clothes to describe your own appearance'

Materials:

CD 2/20; *Pupil's Book*, pp. 34–35, ex. 4
CD 2/23–25; *Activity Book*, p. 31, ex. 6; *Pupil's Book*, p. 36, ex. 6–7

Revision

- Play the listening version of the story *The woolly hat* again (CD 2/20). The children follow it in the Pupil's Book at pp. 34–35.
- Then have the children perform the story as a role play.
- Also revise the articles of clothing with the aid of the flashcards.

❻ Listen and write the numbers.
Listening exercise CD 2/23

- Ask the children to look at p. 31 in their Activity Book.

Tapescript:

Storyteller:	*Joe is at home. He's sad.*
Joe:	*Stupid me. My lovely hat.*
	Ah. I've got an idea. I can make a woolly hat.
	Oh, no!
Joe's dad:	*Let me help you, Joe.*
Joe:	*Yes, please.*
	Thank you, Dad.
Fred:	*Hello, Joe.*
Joe:	*Hello, Fred.*
Fred:	*What a lovely colour.*
Joe:	*Thanks, Fred.*

- Play CD 2/23. The children listen and put the pictures in the correct order by filling in the numbers.
- Check the children's work: Hold your book up, so that all the children can see. Point at the pictures and the children say the correct number.

Option: Say, for example: *Joe is at home. He's sad. What number is it?*

Introduction of new vocabulary

zoo; parrot

- Introduce the word *zoo* by asking the children: *What animals can you see in a zoo?* Children: *Elephants, hippos, …* Get them to repeat the new word *zoo* several times.
- Start to draw a parrot on the board. Use coloured chalk for this, if available. Stop the drawing and get the children to guess what it is. Say: *What is it? What do you think?* Continue with the drawing. When finished elicit the word *parrot* from the children and get them to repeat several times.

Vocabulary games with the support of the written words

colours

- Write the colours that the children have learned so far on strips of paper. Introduce the written form of the colours in the usual manner (also see the introduction p. 15). Stick them on the board and number them.
- Give the children about a minute to enable them to memorize the words and the corresponding numbers properly. Then tell them to close their eyes.
- Now play a memory game, for example:
  Teacher: *What number is blue?*
  Children: *Three.*

❻ Listen and read.

Listening and reading exercise CD 2/24

- Ask the children to open their Pupil's Book at p. 36 and look at ex. 6.
- Read out the first poem line by line and point along. When reading out the last line point to the drawing of the parrot on the board.

Tapescript:

Look at me.
My T-shirt's red.
My jacket's green.
My jeans are blue.
Like a parrot in a zoo.

- Then play the poem from CD 2/24. The children listen.
- Play the poem again and encourage the children to join in.
- Read the poem line by line with the children several times.
- Get them to close their books and dictate the poem to you. Write a skeleton version of it on the board:

  L a m
  M T's r.
  M j's g.
  M j a b.
  L a p i a z.

- Point to the skeleton version of the poem on the board letter by letter and ask the children to 'read' with you.
- Repeat this step two or three times. This gives the children confidence and helps them remember important chunks of language that they will need for the creation of their own poems later.

❼ Draw, write and say.

Speaking exercise:
Step to creativity (Word Play) CD 2/25

- Tell the children to compose their own poem. The children draw an item of clothing in each one of the three blank spaces provided on p. 36. Next to the drawing of the clothes they write a colour.
- Give the children sufficient time for this work. Go round the class to check and help, if needed. When they have finished the drawings and writing the children learn the text of their poems by heart. Show the children the best way to do this. Hold up your book. Recite your own poem several times in a low voice and point at the respective lines in the book.
- Finally, individual children present their poems to the class. Remember to praise them for their work (*Let's give them a big hand!*).
- Individual children may like to say their poems to the karaoke version of track 2/25 on the CD.

Note: Give the children the option of presenting their poem just to you on their own first, so that if necessary you can help with the pronunciation.

L E S S O N 5

Vocabulary, phrases and structures:

My favourite T-shirt is...
Receptive language: *I don't like it; Can I try the T-shirt on?; Can I help you?; I'll take the blue jacket; That's nice.*

Linguistic skills:

Understanding a story *(The T-shirt)* from the DVD.
Understanding mini-dialogues (scenes from the sketch) from the CD.
Completing a text.

Cognitive, motor and social skills:

Understanding mini-dialogues from the CD and numbering the pictures in the book to match.
Matching sentences to pictures.
Drawing one's own favourite clothes.

Cross-curricular integration:

Topic: Speaking motivation *'The T-shirt.'*
Art

Materials:

DVD *(The T-shirt)*; CD 2/26–28; *Pupil's Book*, p. 37, ex. 8; *Activity Book*, pp. 32–33, ex. 7–10; coloured pencils, soft ball; paper strips

Revision

- For revision ask individual children to read their self-composed poem from the previous lesson.

Word ping-pong

- Play *Word ping-pong* with the children. Divide the children up into two teams. Start with the words for clothes. Throw a soft ball to team A and say, for example: *Jeans.* The one who catches the ball says a different (plural) word for clothes and throws the ball to team B. The teams throw the ball back and forth until one of them can't think of a word. The last team to say a word scores a point.
- Proceed in this way with the words for body parts/colours/…

Option: This game can also be played in pairs.

❽ Watch the story.

Mr Matt Story: *The T-shirt*

- Show the children the video sequence *The T-shirt* twice (DVD).

DVD script: *The T-shirt*

Shop assistant:	Good morning.
Mr Matt and Daisy:	Good morning.
Shop assistant:	Can I help you?
Mr Matt:	A T-shirt, please.
Shop assistant:	For you, sir?
	Mr Matt: Yes.
Shop assistant:	What colour?
Mr Matt:	I love all colours.
Shop assistant:	Red?
Daisy:	I like it.
Mr Matt:	I don't like it.
Shop assistant:	Green?
Daisy:	I like it.
Mr Matt:	I don't like it.
Shop assistant:	Blue
Daisy:	I like it.

Mr Matt:	I don't like it.
Shop assistant:	Yellow?
Daisy:	I like it.
Mr Matt:	I don't like it.
	Aaaaaah! That's nice!
Daisy:	No, Dad! Pleeeeeeease!
Mr Matt:	I like it!
Daisy:	I don't like it!
Mr Matt:	Can I try it on?
Shop assistant:	Yes, here you are.
Daisy:	Dad. Is it OK?
Dad:	No.
Daisy:	Take it off!
Dad:	Help me!
Mr Matt:	I'll take it!

❽ Listen and write the numbers.

Listening exercise CD 2/26

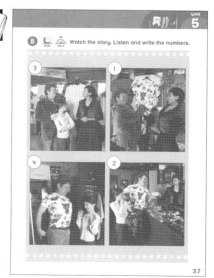

- The children open their Pupil's Book at p. 37, ex. 8 and look at the pictures. Tell the children that they are going to hear individual sentences on the CD. They should match them to the corresponding pictures in the book. Picture number one has already been numbered.

Tapescript:

Announcer:	Picture one.
Mr Matt:	Can I try it on?
Announcer:	Once again.
	Picture one.
Mr Matt:	Can I try it on?
Announcer:	Picture two.
Mr Matt:	I'll take it.
Announcer:	Once again.
	Picture two.
Mr Matt:	I'll take it.
Announcer:	Picture three.
Shop assistant:	Good morning. Can I help you?
Announcer:	Once again.
	Picture three.
Shop assistant:	Good morning. Can I help you?
Announcer:	Picture four.
Daisy:	Take it off!
Announcer:	Once again.
	Picture four.
Daisy:	Take it off!

- Play the listening version of the story (CD 2/26). The children listen and number the pictures in the book.
- Then hold your book up. Point to the first picture and ask: *What number is it?* Children: *Three.*

Option: Say, for example: *Good morning. Can I help you?* Children: *(It's number) three.*

Preparation of key phrases

I don't like it; Can I try the T-shirt on?; Can I help you?; I'll take the blue jacket; That's nice.

- Write the sentences on strips of paper, each large enough so that all the children in your class can comfortably read the sentences.
- Hold up one of the paper strips for about half a second only. The children call out the sentence. They should, however, not be able to read the words letter for letter. This helps to avoid interference between the written words and their pronunciation. Carry on as described with the other sentences.

Option: You can also write the sentences on the board and point along. The children say the respective sentences.

❼ Listen and colour.
Listening exercise CD 2/27

- Ask the children to take out the following coloured pencils: *Orange, blue, pink, yellow, green* and *red.*
- Ask the children to look at the sentences in ex. 7 on p. 32 in their Activity Book.

Tapescript:

Pink:	I don't like it.
Pink:	I don't like it.
Yellow:	I'll take the blue jacket.
Yellow:	I'll take the blue jacket.
Green:	Can I try the T-shirt on?
Green:	Can I try the T-shirt on?
Red:	Yellow?
Red:	Yellow?
Orange:	Can I help you?
Orange:	Can I help you?
Blue:	That's nice.
Blue:	That's nice.

- Tell them to listen to the CD and colour the frames around each sentence according to what they hear.
- Play CD 2/27 twice. The children listen and first mark the frames in the correct colours. Later they complete colouring them in.
- Play the CD again and the children check.
- To check say: *I don't like it. What colour is it?* The children answer: *It's pink.*

❽ Read, match and colour.
Reading exercise

- Tell the children to colour the empty speech bubbles in ex. 8 on p. 32 in their Activity Book according to ex. 7 above.
- Then ask, for example: *What colour is 'I'll take the blue jacket'?* The children answer: *Yellow.*

❾ Listen and colour.
Listening exercise CD 2/28

- Ask the children to look at the picture in ex. 9 on p. 33 in the Activity Book. Name the illustrated clothes and get the children to point at the corresponding pictures in the book.
- Tell them to listen to the CD and to colour the clothes according to the listening text.

Tapescript:

Max: My favourite T-shirt is yellow, my favourite cap is pink, my favourite jacket is blue, my favourite jeans are black and my favourite trainers are black and white.
Once again.
My favourite T-shirt is yellow, my favourite cap is pink, my favourite jacket is blue, my favourite jeans are black and my favourite trainers are black and white.

- Play CD 2/28. The children first only mark the clothes in the colour according to the CD. Later they finish colouring them.
- The children then listen again and check. Ask: *What colour is Max's favourite T-shirt/his favourite cap/...?* Children: *(It's) yellow/pink.*

❾ Draw, write and say.
Step to creativity (ME-page)
My favourite clothes

- Ask the children to look at ex. 10 in their Activity Book at p. 33. Tell them to draw their own clothes in their favourite colours.
- Give the children sufficient time for this. Go round the class to help, if necessary.
- When all the children have finished with their drawings write the following sentence starter on the board:

  My favourite _____ is _____.
  My favourite _____ are ___.

- Look at the children and get them to guess. When the children have guessed your favourite clothes they complete the sentences below.
- Practise the phrases *My favourite (cap) is ... My favourite (jeans) are ...* thoroughly by getting the children say and repeat it several times.
- Then the children complete the sentences in ex. 10 on p. 33 in their Activity Book according to their own drawings.
- Finally, get individual children to read out their texts.

L E S S O N   1

Vocabulary, phrases and structures:

ten; twenty; thirty; forty; fifty; sixty; seventy; eighty; ninety, a hundred; Twenty plus ... forty is ninety; What's missing?; Yes, right; No, sorry.

Linguistic skills:

Understanding numbers from 0 to 100 from the CD.
Learning the meanings, the pronunciation and the written form of the new numbers in tens from 0 to 100.
Using arithmetical language.

Cognitive, motor and social skills:

Understanding numbers from 0 to 100.
Colouring circles to match numbers.
Carrying out simple calculations in pair work.

Cross-curricular integration:

Topic: Speaking motivation 'Recognising numbers'.
Mathematics: numbers from 0 to 100.
Art

Materials:

DVD *(The T-shirt)*
strips of paper with numbers ten to one hundred written in words; CD 1/29–31; *Pupil's Book*, p. 38, ex. 1–2; *Activity Book*, p. 34, ex. 1–2; coloured pencils

Revision

- Revise the Mr Matt story *The T-shirt* from the previous lesson. Use the DVD for this.

Revision and introduction of vocabulary

ten; twenty; thirty; forty; fifty; sixty; seventy; eighty; ninety; a hundred

- Introduce the numbers from thirty to a hundred in tens by writing them in figures on the board and saying them at the same time.
- Also revise ten and twenty and write the numbers 10 and 20 in front of the number 30 on the board. Point to each of the numbers in turn and say them several times.

Exercises for anchoring the vocabulary in the children's recognition memory

- Say the numbers in random order. Ask one child to point at the respective numbers on the board.
- Then name the tens in random order. The children write the numbers with their finger in the air.

Exercises for anchoring the vocabulary in the children's productive memory

- Say the tens from 10 to 100 several times. Ask the children to say them with you.
- Now point in random order at the numbers on the board. The children name the number in question. Help if necessary.
- Say one of the 'tens'. Individual children say the two on either side.
  Say e.g.: *Forty.*
  One child says: *Thirty and fifty.*
- If necessary for explanation point to the two numbers on either side on the board.
- Pair work (back writing): The children "write" numbers from 10 to 100 with their finger on their partner's back: Child A writes on child B's back. Child B tries to guess the number. Then they swap roles.

Introduction of the written form of the numbers

- Hold up pieces of paper with the whole tens from ten to a hundred in quick succession. Do not allow the children enough time to read the words letter by letter. They should absorb the written form only as a single entity.
- Stick the pieces of paper next to the numbers in figures written on the board.
- Remove all the numbers, but leave the strips of paper on the board. Read out the numbers together with the children several times.

❶ **Listen and point.**
Listening exercise CD 2/29

- Ask the children to look at ex. 1 on p. 38 in their Pupil's Books. Tell them to listen to the CD and point at the respective numbers in the book.

Tapescript:

Ninety.	*Sixty.*
Twenty.	*Ten.*
Seventy.	*Fifty.*
Thirty.	*Eighty.*
A hundred.	*Forty.*

- Play CD 2/29 twice. The children listen and point at the numbers.

Vocabulary extension

zero

- Write the numbers from one to nine before the tens to 100 on the board. Write a zero before one and say the number several times.
- The children speak after you. Call out one child to the board and say e.g.: *Forty*. The child points to the number. Carry out the exercise with several children. Increase the difficulty by naming two numbers, e.g.: *Zero and twenty*. The child points to both numbers.

Pronunciation tip: Pay attention with zero ['ziərou] to the voiced [z]. Practise it with the children by having them hum like a bee.

❷ Listen and colour. Say.
Listening exercise CD 2/30

- The children open their Pupil's Book at p. 38 and look at ex. 2. for about five seconds. Get the children to close their books and name the numbers. *Give me the numbers*. Write the numbers said by the children on the board. If the children have not named all the numbers depicted, say: *Open your book again and check. What's missing?* The children are allowed to have another brief look in the book and tell you the missing numbers.
- Tell the children that they are now to mark the number circles in the corresponding colours according to the instructions in the listening exercise, and afterwards colour them (see example: *a hundred – blue*).

Tapescript:

A hundred – blue.
Nine – red and yellow.
Ninety – orange.
Seven – pink and green.
Eighty – brown.
Seventy – yellow.
Two – orange and blue.
Five – brown and pink.
Sixty – red.
Six – green and red.
Fifty – pink.
Three – brown and orange.
Forty – grey.
Eight – grey and blue.
Thirty – green.
Four – blue and pink.
Twenty – red and blue.
Ten – orange and green.
Zero – yellow and pink.
One – brown and grey.

- Play the listening exercise several times (CD 2/30). The children mark the number circles.
- Check the children's answers by asking: *Number eight. What colour is it?* The children name the corresponding colours: *Grey and blue.*
- When they have checked all the numbers the children complete colouring the circles.

❷ Say.
Pair work: Speaking exercise

- Child A has the Pupil's Book closed. Child B asks: *What colour is nine?* Child A: *Red and yellow.*
- Child B asks ten questions. For every correct answer child A gets one point. Then they swap roles. The winner is the one who has collected more points.

❶ Listen and write the numbers.
Listening exercise CD 2/31

Tapescript:

Orange – seventy.
Orange – seventy.
Blue – ninety.
Blue – ninety.
Brown – eighty.
Brown – eighty.
Yellow – a hundred.
Yellow – a hundred.
Red – sixty.
Red – sixty.
Pink – fifty.
Pink – fifty.
Grey – forty.
Grey – forty.
Green – thirty.
Green – thirty.
Red and blue – twenty.
Red and blue – twenty.
Orange and green – ten.
Orange and green – ten.

- Play CD 2/31 and get the children to write the numbers in the corresponding coloured balloons in the Activity Book on p. 34, ex. 1.
- Play the CD again. The children check their answers.

❷ Match the numbers with the words. Colour.

Reading exercise

Match the numbers with the words. Colour.

| pink | red and blue | green |
| fifty | twenty | thirty |

| orange | orange and green | yellow |
| seventy | ten | a hundred |

| red | grey | blue | brown |
| sixty | forty | ninety | eighty |

34

- Tell the class to take out the following coloured pencils: *Pink, orange, brown, blue, yellow, red, grey,* and *green.*
- Then the children colour the frames around the written numbers below in the same colours as the circles above, e.g. the frame around *ten* in orange and green, and so on.
- When the children have finished, ask them to look at the page for five seconds. Then tell them to close their books. Say: e.g. *Orange and green.* The children call out the number marked in those colours.

L E S S O N   2

Vocabulary, phrases and structures:

Vocabulary revision: round tens from ten to a hundred
piggy bank; camera; skateboard; football; hammer; pounds; I've got ten/…/a hundred pounds in my piggy bank; Now where's the hammer?; I've got a football and a camera/a boat, a skateboard and a car!; Can you give me a pound, please?; What for?; I want a new piggy bank!

Linguistic skills:

Practising the meaning, the pronunciation and the spelling of numbers from 30 to 100 (in tens).
Saying mental arithmetic additions with tens.
Singing a song (*Pounds in my piggy bank*).

Cognitive, motor and social skills:

Pair work: practising numbers in tens.
Maintaining the rhythm and melody while speaking in unison and singing.
Pointing to the right pictures in the book while speaking and singing.
Listening to the CD and drawing lines to connect numbers accordingly.
Doing a word search.
Writing numbers in tens from ten to one hundred.

Cross-curricular integration:

Music
Topic: Speaking motivation 'Dealing with different amounts of money'.
Mathematics

Materials:

Strips of paper saying ten to one hundred from previous lesson
Flashcards from *Playway 2*: 49–50; *Word Cards* from *Playway 2*: 85–87; CD 2/32–34; *Pupil's Book*, p. 39, ex. 3; *Activity Book*, p. 35, ex. 3–5; paper strips; (optional) answer key for self-checking

---

Revision

- Revise the whole tens from ten to a hundred with the aid of the strips of paper from the previous lesson in the usual manner.
- Alternatively, write the words on the board.

Introduction of vocabulary with the support of the written form

piggy bank; camera; skateboard; football; hammer

- Introduce the new words *piggy bank* and *camera* with the aid of the flashcards and the word cards.
- Introduce the word *hammer* with the aid of corresponding gestures or a drawing on the board.
- It can be assumed that the children know the words *skateboard* and *football*. However, for these words too, practise the correct English pronunciation by saying and having them repeat several times.

❸ Listen and point. Sing the song.
Song: *Pounds in my piggy bank* CD 2/32–33

- The children open their Pupil's Book at p. 39 and look at the numbers in ex. 3. Name the numbers first of all in order and then in random order. The children point at the respective numbers/pictures in the book.
- Now name the objects depicted on the bottom left of p. 39: *Football, camera, boat, skateboard* and *car*. Again the children point at the respective numbers/pictures.
- Play the song twice (CD 2/32). The children point to the pictures in the book.
- Stand in a circle. Go round the inside of the circle and hum the tune. The children you go past pick up the tune and begin to hum along. Go round in the circle several times until in the end all the children are humming the tune with you.
- Then start to sing the words and the children gradually sing with you.
- Finally, sing the song again to the karaoke version (CD 2/33).

❸ Listen and draw lines.
Listening exercise CD 2/34

- Ask the children to look at ex. 3 on p. 35 in their Activity Book. Name the numbers in any order. The children point along in their books.
- Ask them to guess what is hidden in the picture. Say: *What is it? What do you think?* The children try to guess: *It's a dog/cat/*etc.

Tapescript:

Draw a line from number eighty to number sixty. Number eighty to number sixty.

Draw a line from number thirty to number forty. Number thirty to number forty.

Draw a line from number ninety to number twenty. Number ninety to number twenty.

Draw a line from number ten to number fifty. Number ten to number fifty.

Draw a line from number seventy to number twenty. Number seventy to number twenty.

What is it? – It's Clever Joe at the circus.

- Play CD 2/34. The children draw lines connecting the numbers in the picture as given on the CD.
- Play the CD a second or third time, if necessary. The children listen and check. Ask: *What is it?* Children: *A bear.* Say: *Right! A bear. What's his name? What do you think?* Get the children to give you names. Elicit the name: *Joe.* Say: *It's (Clever) Joe.* Tell them that next lesson, they are going to watch a DVD about *Clever Joe.*

Pounds in my piggy bank

Lyrics: Gerngross/Puchta
Music: Lorenz Maierhofer
© Helbling, Rum/Innsbruck

*) Clever Joe: Now where's the hammer? *(spoken)*

Speaking: Clever Joe: Dad?
Father Bear: Yes?
Clever Joe: Can you give me a pound, please?
Father Bear: What for?
Clever Joe: I want a new piggy bank!
Father Bear: Here you are.
Clever Joe: Thank you!

❹ Find the ten numbers. ↓ →

Word search

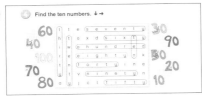

- Ask the children to open their Activity Book at p. 35 and look at ex. 4. There are tens from one to one hundred hidden in the word search. Tell the children to find the numbers and circle them.
- Allow the children to do this exercise together with a partner. When the children have finished, ask: *Who's got seven numbers/words?* The children who have found seven words raise their arms. Say: *Good.* Ask: *Who's got eight or more? – Great! Well done!*
- Get the children that have found all ten numbers to name them.

Option: To promote self-checking it is recommended that you put out an answer key in the classroom. The children go and check their own work themselves.

❺ Write the words.

Writing exercise

- Hold up one of the paper strips with the written numbers from ten to one hundred for about a second. The children call out the numbers.
- Hand out the paper strips to individual children. Write the tens from 10 to 100 in figures in jumbled order on the board.
- Point to the numbers in any order. The children call out the numbers and the ones with the corresponding written numbers come out and stick the paper strips on the board next to the numbers in figures.
- Then get the children to close their eyes and delete the numbers in figures, but leave the paper strips with the written numbers on the board. Jumble them up. The children open their eyes again and say the numbers as you point along.
- Tell the children to write the words next to the numbers in ex. 5 on p. 35 in their Activity Book.
- Check the children's work by getting the children to order the paper strips on the board from 10 to 100 and writing the numbers in front of them again. The children check their work against the numbers on the board.

L E S S O N   3

Vocabulary, phrases and structures:

circus; the maths test; I can't do it; Can I try?

Linguistic skills:

Understanding a story (*Clever Joe*) from the DVD and the CD and from narration by the teacher.
Joining in with the story-telling.
Acting out a role play.

Cognitive, motor and social skills:

Following the narrative structure of a story.
Representing a time sequence visually.
Putting stick-in pictures in the right order in a picture story.
Understanding sentences from the CD and numbering pictures in the book accordingly.

Cross-curricular integration:

Topic: Speaking motivation *'Clever Joe'*.

Materials:

Story Cards from *Playway 2*: 18–29; DVD (*Clever Joe*); *Flashcard* from *Playway 2*: 51; *Word Card* from *Playway 2*: 88; CD 2/35–36; *Pupil's Book*, pp. 40–41, ex. 4; *Activity Book*, p. 36, ex. 6; stick-in pictures from the appendix of the *Pupil's Book*; answer key

---

Vocabulary revision

- Say the tens from ten to one hundred several times with the children and at the same time write them on the board.
- Point to the tens. Ask one of the children to name the 'ten' with the numbers on either side of it.
- Write a zero on the board and say *zero* several times.

- Have the children repeat it after you several times in unison.
- Together with the children do a countdown in tens.
- Start with a hundred. Go back to zero. Start standing up and as you count, crouch further and further down. At zero jump up in the air with your arms outstretched and shout out loud: *Zero.*
- Repeat the countdown.

Vocabulary extension, preparation of important words and phrases

clever; circus; The maths test; I can't do it; Can I try?

- Clarify the meaning of the word *clever* through appropriate gesture and mime: for example, tap on your forehead.
- Introduce the word *circus* with the aid of the flashcard that illustrates the word. Also introduce the written form with the aid of the word card.
- Clarify the meaning of the phrases *The maths test.* and *I can't do it.* with the aid of the story card that illustrates these two sentences.
- Translate *Can I try?* into L1, if necessary.

❹ Watch the story.

Cartoon Story: *Clever Joe*

- Show the children the video sequence *Clever Joe* twice (DVD).

DVD script: *Clever Joe*

Teacher:	OK, children. Tomorrow there's a maths test.
Animals:	OK, sir.
Storyteller:	All the animals are doing maths. But Joe isn't. He's doing crazy things. It's the next day. The maths test.
Joe:	I can't do it!
Teacher:	OK, children. Tomorrow there's an English test.
Animals:	OK, sir.
Storyteller:	All the animals are doing English. But Joe isn't doing English. He's doing crazy things. It's the next day. The English test.
Joe:	I can't do it!
Badger:	Let's go to the circus.
Animals:	Great! Fantastic! Yes, let's!
Circus director:	Ladies and gentlemen! I'm so sorry. Our acrobat's ill! I'm sorry!
Animals:	Oooooh!
Joe:	Can I try?
Circus director:	Sure. Come here. Fantastic. Ladies and gentleman, give Joe a big hand!
Teacher:	OK, children. Tomorrow there's a maths test.
Animals:	OK, sir.
Storyteller:	All the animals are doing maths. Joe is not. He's thinking.
Joe:	Aaaah. I know! Practice!
Storyteller:	It's the next day. The maths test. The next day.
Teacher:	Joe?
Joe:	Yes, sir?
Teacher:	Come here, please. You can do it! Well done!
Animals:	Yeah!

Note: Not all the language in the DVD sequences or CD versions of the stories are presented in the cartoon story in the Pupil's Book. This is mainly because of the length of the stories but also this serves to encourage the children to listen for the necessary information in order to complete the gap fill in the Pupil's Book.

❹ Listen and stick.

Listening exercise:

Sticker activity CD 2/35

- Play the listening version of the story twice (CD 2/35). The children stick the stick-in pictures from the appendix in the corresponding blank spaces in the Pupil's Book, pp. 40–41 while they are listening.
- Check the children's work.

Telling the story

- Now tell the story with the aid of the story cards in the usual manner.

Story reconstruction game

- Tell the children that you want to tell the story but need help. Start telling the story slowly and point at the same time to the corresponding picture. Stop suddenly and ask the children to help.
  Teacher: *OK, children. Tomorrow there's a ...*
  Children: *... maths test.*
  Teacher: *OK, ...*
  Children: *... sir ...*
  Continue in this way.

Teacher's Book • Playway to English 2 Second edition   **101**

Additional task for high-ability groups: Role play

- In high-ability groups the story can also be performed as a role play after intensive practice.
- Play the listening version of the story again (CD 2/35). The children close their eyes and see the story in their imaginations.
- Re-enact the story. You play the part of the storyteller. The children play the other parts. Help the children by whispering cues.
- After several practices one child can also take on the role of the storyteller.

❻ Listen and write the numbers.

Listening exercise CD 2/36

- The children open their Activity Book at p. 36 and look at the pictures in ex. 6. Tell them that they are going to hear individual sentences on the CD. They should match them to the corresponding pictures in the book.

> **Tapescript:**
>
> One: She's doing crazy things.
> Two: I can't do it!
> Three: Aaaaah! I know. I can do it.
> Four: Well done!
> Five: The children are doing maths.
> Six: Tomorrow there's an English test.

- Play the listening exercise from CD 2/36 twice. The children listen and number the pictures in the book according to the listening text.
- Check the children's work: Hold your book up. Point to the first picture and ask: *What number is it?* Children: *(Number) five.*

Note: You can also check the children's answers by saying e.g.: *The children are doing maths. What number is it?* Children: *(It's number) five.*

L E S S O N   4

Vocabulary, phrases and structures:

Vocabulary revision: numbers from 0 to 100
I'm so sorry; Let's go to the swimming pool; Tim is ill; Ben is thinking; Anne come here, Can I try?; It's my turn; It's your turn; I don't know; What is it?; Throw the dice; Start; Finish; I'm/You're the winner.

Linguistic skills:

Understanding and using some expressions necessary to play a game.

Cognitive, motor and social skills:

Playing a game in pairs.
Understanding and following the rules of a game.

Matching written sentences to the appropriate pictures in the book by colouring the respective speech bubbles.
Categorizing words and copying them.

Cross-curricular integration:

Topic: Speaking motivation 'Following the rules of a game'.

Materials:

CD 2/35; *Pupil's Book*, pp. 40–41, ex. 4
Flashcards from *Playway 2*: 1–48; *Word Cards* from *Playway 2*: 31–85; *Pupil's Book*, p. 42, ex. 5; CD 2/37; *Activity Book*, pp. 37–38, ex. 7–9; paper strips; dice for half the class; tokens for all the children

Revision

- Revise the cartoon story *(Clever Joe)* from the previous lesson. For this use the listening version (CD 2/35) and pp. 40 and 41 in the Pupil's Book.
- To revise the numbers play the following game with the children: The children stand next to each other in a line. Name one 'ten' number. Then name the next highest ten

number. The children go one small step forwards. Then name the next highest ten number. The children again take one step forwards etc. If you name a lower ten number the children go one step back. Count forwards and backwards and get the children to convert this into steps.

Preparation of written phrases

I'm so sorry; Let's go to the swimming pool; Tim is ill; Ben is thinking; Anne, come here; Can I try?

- Write the six sentences on strips of paper, large enough so that all the children in your class can comfortably read the sentences.
- Hold up one of the paper strips for about half a second only. The children call out the sentence. They should, however, not be able to read the words letter for letter. This helps to avoid interference between the written words and their pronunciation. Carry on as described with the other sentences.

Option: Write the sentences on the board. Point at the sentences in quick succession and the children call them out. Cover the board and get the children to say the sentences.

❼ Listen and colour.
Listening exercise CD 2/37

- The children take out the following coloured pencils: *Orange, blue, pink, yellow, green* and *red*.
- Ask the children to look at the sentences in ex. 7 on p. 37 in their Activity Book.

Tapescript:

Yellow:	Can I try?
Yellow:	Can I try?
Red:	Anne, come here.
Red:	Anne, come here.
Blue:	Tim is ill.
Blue:	Tim is ill.
Orange:	Let's go to the swimming pool.
Orange:	Let's go to the swimming pool.
Pink:	Ben is thinking.
Pink:	Ben is thinking.
Green:	I'm so sorry.
Green:	I'm so sorry.

- Play CD 2/37 twice. The children listen and first mark the frames in the corresponding colours. When the CD has stopped they complete colouring the frames.
- Play the CD again and the children check.
- To check say: *Ben is thinking. What colour is it?* The children answer: *(It's) pink.*

❽ Read, match and colour.
Reading exercise

- Tell the children to colour the empty speech bubbles in ex. 8 on p. 37 in their Activity Book according to ex. 7 above. Then ask, for example: *What colour is 'I'm so sorry'?* The children answer: *Green.*

Vocabulary revision and pair work

- Revise the words for body parts, clothes, fruit, vegetables and items of furniture with the aid of the flashcards and word cards. Play a memory game with the cards.
- Then ask the children to look at the board game in their Pupil's Book on p. 42 for about 30 seconds and to try to remember as many words as possible.
- Say: *'Stop!'* and have them close their books. Ask the children to say words to you that they remember. Have them open their books again and say all the words in order together with the children. Start at *START, potatoes – plum – rain – …* etc.
- Demonstrate the following pair work with one child in front of the whole class:
  Child A takes a piece of paper, covers one of the pictures in the first line and asks: *What is it?* Child B now tries to guess which picture is covered. He/She has three goes. Then child B covers one of the next five pictures and child A tries to guess the hidden picture.
- Now the children carry out this pair work.

Practising expressions for a game

- Practise and reinforce the following expressions. Say each sentence and do the corresponding actions to it. The children imitate your actions:
  – *It's my turn.* Point to yourself.
  – *It's your turn.* Point to one of the children.
  – *Throw the dice.* Throw an imaginary dice.
  – *What is it?* Draw a question mark on the board.
  – *I don't know.* Shrug your shoulders.
- Now say the sentences several times. The children do the corresponding actions.

❺ Play the game. Say.
Game: Snakes and Ladders

❾ Match and write.
Forming categories

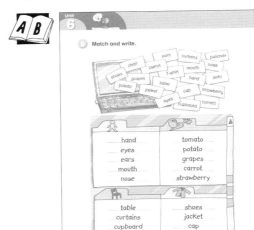

- Explain the rules for the board game in the Pupil's Book on p. 42 in L1. The game is played with one book in pairs. Child A and child B put their tokens on the start. Child A throws the dice and moves his/her token on the board the number he/she has thrown. If the token lands on e.g. the picture for *plum*, child A says *plum*. Then it is child B's turn. If child A does not know the word *plum* child B may say it and then throw the dice twice. The number of spots on the dice are added together and child B may move forwards that number of squares with his/her token.
- If the token lands on a square that has the start of a ladder (e.g. *sun*) then the token can climb the ladder and be placed on the square at the end of the ladder (in this case *trainers*).
- If the token lands on the tail of a snake (e.g. *green pepper*) the token has to be put back on the square where the head of the snake is (in this case *plum*).
- The first person to reach FINISH is the winner.
- Have the children play in twos and go from pair to pair. Help, if necessary. Try to encourage the children to only use the English expressions as far as possible during the game. After each part of the game keep practising the English sentences in groups.

Tip: Coins, buttons or erasers can be used as tokens.

- Ask the children to look at ex. 9 on p. 38 in their Activity Book for about ten seconds. Then have the children close their books: *Close your books.* and name words that they can remember. Say: *Give me words.*
- Hold your book up. Point to one of the four areas (e.g. *body*) and say: *Give me words that go with body.* The children name body parts, e.g. *Nose, feet, head,…*
- The children open their books again. Now they put the words in ex. 9 into categories by allocating them to one of the four areas (*body, vegetables and fruit, furniture and clothes*) and copying them. Tell the children that the result should be four logical classifications.
- Finally, ask: *What goes with 'body'? Tell me the words.* Child: *Eyes, ears, nose, mouth, hand.* etc.

Solution:
body: eyes, ears, nose, mouth, hand
vegetable and fruit: potato, carrot, tomato, grapes, strawberry
furniture: chair, table, curtains, cupboard, sofa
clothes: shoes, jacket, pullover, cap, T-shirt

L E S S O N 5

Vocabulary, phrases and structures:

Max's favourite numbers are ...; My favourite number is...

Linguistic skills:

Saying what one's favourite number is.

Cognitive, motor and social skills:

Doing sums.
Solving a puzzle picture and finding hidden numbers in it.
Matching sentences to the corresponding numbers.

Cross-curricular integration:

Mathematics: Adding and numbers from one to one hundred.

Materials:

Activity Book, p. 39, ex. 10–11

---

⑩ Look and write.

Puzzle picture

- Ask the children to look at the picture in ex. 10 on p. 39 in their Activity Book. Tell them to find the three hidden numbers in the picture. Show them how to do this: Hold up your book and look at the picture from various perspectives *(Turn the book).*
- The children try to find the three hidden numbers in the picture and complete the sentence below: *Max's favourite numbers are (thirteen, fifty-one and eighty).*
- Finally, ask a child to read out the complete sentence. Write the written numbers on the board, so that the children can check.

⑪ Match the numbers to the pictures.

Step to creativity (ME-page)

My favourite number is ...

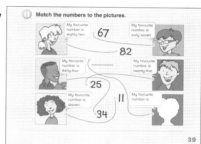

- Read out the sentences in the speech bubbles in ex. 11 on p. 39 in the Activity Book. The children read and point at the corresponding pictures (speech bubbles). Tell them to connect the pictures with the numbers in the middle of the page by drawing lines.
- To check the children's work, ask individual children: *What about this girl? (point to one speech bubble) What's her favourite number?* Children: *Eighty-two./Her favourite number is eighty-two.*
- One speech bubble and matching number has been left blank for children to write their own favourite numbers.

Let's count

C L I L:
Content and Language Integrated Learning

Objective:	Materials:
Formulating sums.	*Pupil's Book*, p. 43, ex. 6

Revision

- As revision ask one child to come out to the board. Say: *Forty ... plus twenty ... is ...* The child writes the sum on the board. Help through whispering cues. Get the other children to say the answer. Repeat this procedure with other tens several times.
- Write a few more simple sums (e.g.: 6 + 12 = ...) on the board and do them together with the children.
- Practise the expressions for this arithmetic operation thoroughly by getting the children to say and repeat it several times.

❻ Look and do the sums.

Arithmetic

- Get the children to look at ex. 6 on p. 43 in their Pupil's Book. Name the objects in the box on the upper half of the page: *Car – scissors –* etc. and elicit the prices from the children by saying e.g. 'How much is the car'?
- Then do the first sum together with the children. Hold your book up. Point at the respective pictures/prices while speaking: *Look, the teddy bear is ...* Look at the children. The children answer: *£12.* Say: *OK. 12 (pounds) plus ... The socks are ...* The children continue: *Three (pounds).* Repeat: *12 (pounds) plus 3 (pounds) is ...* Children: *15 (pounds).*
  Repeat the whole sum and say: *£12 plus £3 is £15. The teddy bear and the socks are £15.* The children do the remaining four sums in the book in pair work. Go round the class and help, if necessary.
- Finally, individual children read out the sums. Write them on the board at the same time and the children check their answers.

LESSON 1

Vocabulary, phrases and structures:
Checking of vocabulary acquisition in Units 5–6.

Linguistic skills:
Understanding and saying vocabluary from Units 5 and 6 on the topic areas 'clothes' and 'numbers' (from 10 to 100).

Cognitive, motor and social skills:
Matching words and sentences from the CD to the corresponding pictures.
Numbering these words and sentences according to the CD.
Checking the results with the aid of an answer key.

Materials:
CD 2/38–39; *Pupil's Book,* pp. 44–45, ex. 1–4; coloured pencils; answer key

Self-evaluation

Option: Divide *Show what you can do* into two lessons.

Note: For notes on the basic methodology of this section, see *Show what you can do* on p. 18 of the introduction in the Teacher's Book.

❶ **Listen and write the numbers.**

Listening exercise CD 2/38

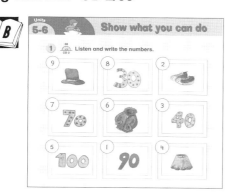

• Tell the children that they are going to find out which words in the Pupil's Book on p. 44, ex. 1, they can already understand well.

Tapescript:

Number one:	*Ninety.*
Number one:	*Ninety.*
Number two:	*Trainers.*
Number two:	*Trainers.*
Number three:	*Forty.*
Number three:	*Forty.*
Number four:	*Skirt.*
Number four:	*Skirt.*
Number five:	*One hundred.*
Number five:	*One hundred.*
Number six:	*Jacket.*
Number six:	*Jacket.*
Number seven:	*Seventy.*
Number seven:	*Seventy.*
Number eight:	*Thirty.*
Number eight:	*Thirty.*
Number nine:	*Hat.*
Number nine:	*Hat.*

• The children will check independently whether they can match the words and numbers to the corresponding pictures by numbering them from one to nine.
• Now play the listening exercise (CD 2/38).
• The children number the pictures in the book accordingly. The first picture has already been numbered.
• Go round the class and help the children, if necessary. Set out a completed sheet and let the children check their results independently.

❷ **Match the words to the pictures.**

Reading exercise

• Tell the children that they are going to find out which words in the Pupil's Book on p. 44, ex. 2 they can already read well.
• The children check independently whether they can match the written words to the corresponding pictures/numbers above, by copying the number written down in ex. 1 into the spaces in ex. 2.
• Set out a completed sheet and let the children check their results independently.

❸ Listen and write the numbers.

Listening exercise CD 2/39

- Tell the children to find out which sentences in the Pupil's Book on p. 45, ex. 3 they can already say.
- The children then check independently whether they can match the sentences they hear to the corresponding pictures.

Tapescript:

Number one:	*My cap is green.*
Number one:	*My cap is green.*
Number two:	*I've got £ 50 in my piggy bank.*
Number two:	*I've got £ 50 in my piggy bank.*
Number three:	*I can't do it!*
Number three:	*I can't do it!*
Number four:	*I hate it!*
Number four:	*I hate it!*

- Now play the listening exercise (CD 2/39).
- The children number the pictures in the book accordingly. The first picture has already been numbered.
- Go round the class and help the children, if necessary.
- Set out a completed sheet and let the children check their results independently.

❹ Match the sentences to the pictures.

Reading exercise

- Tell the children that they are going to find out which sentences in the Pupil's Book on p. 45, ex. 4 they can already read well.
- The children check independently whether they can match the written sentences in ex. 4 to the corresponding pictures in ex. 3.
- Set out a completed sheet and let the children check their results independently.

L E S S O N 1

Vocabulary, phrases and structures:

Vocabulary revision: arithmetic, numbers
mum; dad; brother; sister; grandpa; grandma; racoon
Receptive language: *In my family there's my mum etc...; Tom's/Daniel's... family; Kate's 4 years old; I've got a big family; What about Tom's family?*

Linguistic skills:

Learning the meaning, the pronunciation and the written form of the family words.
Understanding a rhyme from the CD.

Cognitive, motor and social skills:

Understanding family descriptions from the CD and matching them to the corresponding pictures in the book.

Understanding a rhyme from the CD and while listening, reading along in the book.
Learning by heart and reciting fluently one's own rhyme.
Composing a rhyme to fit a picture in the book.

Cross-curricular integration:

Topic: Speaking motivation 'Discussing members of a family'.

Materials:

Flashcards from *Payway 2:* 52–54; *Word Cards* from *Payway 2:* 89–91; CD 3/1–3; *Pupil's Book* pp. 46–47, ex. 1–3

Revision

- As revision, do a few simple sums together with the children. Write the calculations on the board while speaking.

Vocabulary revision and introduction

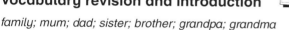

family; mum; dad; sister; brother; grandpa; grandma

- Revise the words already learnt for family members or introduce the new words in the following way: Draw a girl on the board. Have the children find a name for the girl, e.g.: Susan. This is Susan. Show the flashcard for dad and mum and say: This is Susan's dad. This is Susan's mum. Put the flashcards up on the board. Say the words dad and mum several times and have the children repeat them.
- Proceed in the same way with the remaining flashcards until the family is complete. Then point to the board and say: *This is Susan's family.* Repeat the word family several times and write it on the board. Then say: *In Susan's family there is a brother, a sister ...*
- Get the children to repeat all the family members again.
- Ask the children to bring photos of their closest family members with them. One child comes out in front of the class and presents his/her family members. Whisper: *My mum...* etc.

Vocabulary exercises with the support of the written forms

mum; dad; sister; brother; grandpa; grandma

- Hold up the word cards in quick succession. Do not allow the children enough time to read the words letter by letter. They should absorb the written form only as a single entity.
- When the children say the correct word, repeat it. Then get one of them to put the card up on the board next to the corresponding flashcard. Say: *Put it on the board, please.*
- Take down all the flashcards, but leave the word cards on the board. Read them out together with the children several times.

- Tell the children to close their eyes. Change the positions of the word cards. Say: *Open your eyes. What's wrong?* Ask individual children to put the cards back in their correct places.

Option: An alternative activity is for you to hold up the word cards one after another, saying the corresponding words. Then hand the cards out to individual children. Say the words in sequence. After each word, the child with the correct card comes out to the board and puts it up next to or below the flashcard.

❶ Listen and write the numbers. Say.

Listening exercise CD 3/1

- Now ask the children to open the Pupil's Book at p. 46 and look at the individual families.
- Tell the children that they are going to hear *Tom, Daniel, Emma* and *Anne* describing their families. They should listen carefully and number the families from one to four.

Tapescript:

One: Hi, my name's Tom. In my family there's my sister, my dad and me.

Two: Hi, I'm Emma. In my family there's my mum, my grandma, my sister Kate and me. Kate is 4 years old.

Three: Hi, I'm Daniel. I've got a big family. There's my mum, my dad, my brother Mike, my grandpa, my grandma and me.

Four: Hi, I'm Anne. In my family there's my mum, my dad and me.

- Play the listening exercise (CD 3/1). Stop the CD after each description so that the children can find and number the corresponding family.
- Write *Tom, Daniel, Emma* and *Anne* on the board and underline the initial letter of each. The children listen to the exercise again and write the corresponding initial letter next to the family photos.
- Check the children's answers by asking: *What about Tom's family?* Whisper clues to help them: *There's a …* Children: *… sister and a dad.* etc.
- The children compare their answers.

❷ **Listen and read.**
Listening and reading exercise CD 3/2

- Ask the children to open their Pupil's Book at p. 47 and look at ex. 2. Point at the picture of the racoon. Say the word *racoon* and get the children to repeat several times.

Tapescript:

My mum,
my dad,
three sisters,
two brothers and me.
This is my family.

- Then play the rhyme from CD 3/2. The children listen.
- Play the rhyme again and encourage the children to speak along. Then read out the rhyme line by line with the children several times.
- Get them to close their books and dictate the rhyme to you. Write a skeleton version of it on the board:

M m,
m d,
t s,
t b a m.
T i m f.

- Point to the skeleton version of the rhyme on the board letter by letter and ask the children to 'read' with you.
- Repeat this step two or three times. Tell them to learn the rhyme off by heart. This gives the children confidence and helps them remember important chunks of language that they will need for the creation of their own rhymes later.

❸ **Write. Listen and check.**
Writing exercise (Word Play) CD 3/3

- Tell the children that they are now to compose a parallel text for a family of mice as shown in the picture on p. 47 in the Pupil's Book.
- Get the children to complete the rhyme in ex. 3 so that it fits the picture. Go round the class and help, if necessary.

Tapescript:

My mum,
my two sisters and me.
This is my family.

- Then play the CD 3/3. The children listen and check.

Additional task for high-ability classes
Step to creativity (Word Play)

- Encourage the children to write their own rhyme about their family. Give them some prompts on the board and show them how they can extend or reduce this if they have a bigger or smaller family:

My …….
my …….. and me
This is my …

- Give the children sufficient time for this work. When they have finished the children learn their rhymes by heart. Go round the class and help if necessary.
- Finally, individual children may like to say their rhymes to the class. Remember to praise them for their work (*Let's give them a big hand*).

Note: Give the children the option of presenting their rhyme just to you on their own first, so that, if necessary, you can help with the pronunciation.

L E S S O N   2

Vocabulary, phrases and structures:

river; beaver; Cut off his tail!
Receptive language: *I've got an idea; Let's help him; Let's go to the river; Swim across the river; He is happy; We are happy.*

Linguistic skills:

Understanding a story (*The racoons and the beaver*) from the DVD and the CD and as narrated by the teacher.
Joining in with story-telling.
Mini-dialogues and (optional) acting out a role play.

Cognitive, motor and social skills:

Following the sequence of events in a story.
Sticking stick-in pictures from the appendix correctly in the picture story.
Matching pictures to the appropriate sentences.

Listening to a story on CD and putting pictures in the correct order.

Cross-curricular integration:

Topic: Speaking motivation *'The raccoons and the beaver'.*

Materials:

Flashcards from *Playway 2:* 52–55; *Word Cards* from *Playway 2:* 89–91
DVD (*The racoons and the beaver*); *Story Cards* from *Playway 2:* 30–41; CD 3/4–5; *Pupil's Book*, pp. 48–49, ex. 4; *Activity Book*, pp. 40–41, ex. 1–2; paper strips; photocopiable master from the appendix in the *Teacher's Book*, p. 159; answer key

Revision

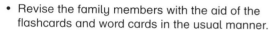

- Revise the family members with the aid of the flashcards and word cards in the usual manner.

Preparation of key words and phrases

river; racoon; beaver; cut off his tail

- Work on the new word *river* with the aid of the flashcard and word card in the usual manner.
- Stick on the board the story card where you can see the family of racoons and the beaver who has just been released. Revise and reinforce the words *racoon* and *beaver* with it. Point to the corresponding animals on the picture.
- Say: *Beaver* and make two long front teeth with your index fingers.
- Ask the children to do the actions with you and repeat the words.
- Explain the phrase *cut off his tail* in the following way: Take a beaver made from paper or draw a beaver on the board. Mime *cut off his tail* by pretending to cut off his tail with an imaginary knife.

Comment: Explain the habits of these two types of North American animals in L1. *Racoons* (also variant raccoons) [rəˈkuːnz] live in trees, sleep during the day and go hunting at night. They have long, bushy, black and white ringed tails. *Beavers* [biːvəz] live in Europe and North America. They have thick fur, a broad tail and fell whole trees with their sharp front teeth.

❹ Watch the story.

Cartoon Story: *The racoons and the beaver*

- Show the children the video sequence *The racoons and the beaver* twice (DVD).

DVD script: *The racoons and the beaver*

Storyteller:	The racoons are going for a picnic. Dad, Mum, Rosie and her brother, Ronnie.
Ronnie:	Let's go to the river.
Rosie:	Yes, great!
Mum and Dad:	OK.
Beaver:	Help!
Mum:	What's that?
Beaver:	Help! Help!
Ronnie:	It's a beaver. Over there!
Rosie:	Let's help him.
Storyteller:	Mum, Dad, Ronnie and his sister want to help. They swim across the river.
Beaver:	Help!
Rosie, Ronnie:	Pull! Pull!
Crow:	Cut off his tail. Cut off his tail.
Dad:	Go away.
Mum:	I've got an idea.
Beaver:	Help! Help!
Mum:	Just a minute.
Mum, Dad, Rosie, Ronnie:	One, two, three … jump.
Beaver:	It works.
Storyteller:	The beaver is very happy. Mum, Dad, Rosie and her brother Ronnie are happy too.
Rosie:	Now let's have our picnic.
All:	Yes. Great. Mmmh. That's good. Yummy.

Note: Not all the language in the DVD sequences or CD versions of the stories are presented in the cartoon story in the Pupil's Book. This is mainly because of the length of the stories but also this serves to encourage the children to listen for the necessary information in order to complete the gap fill in the Pupil's Book.

➍ Listen and stick.

Listening exercise: Sticker activity CD 3/4

- Play the listening version of the story twice (CD 3/4). The children listen and stick the pictures from the appendix in the corresponding blank spaces in the Pupil's Book (pp. 48–49).
- Check the children's work.

Option: To promote self-checking it is recommended that you put out a completed picture story in the classroom. The children go and check their own work themselves.

Telling the story

- Now tell the story with the aid of the story cards.
- Distribute the story cards to individual children. Tell the story again. Each child holding a picture comes out to the front at the correct point in the story. Finally all the children who were given the story cards are standing in the order that the story happens in front of the class. The pictures are held up so that they can be seen well by all.

Reconstructing the story

- Tell the story slowly and at the same time point to the child with the corresponding picture. Stop and ask the child to complete the sentence. If necessary, get the other children to help. Support with mimes and gestures.
  Say: *They are going for a …*
  Child: *… picnic.*
  Say: *Dad, Mum, Rosie and her brother, Ronnie. Let's go to the …*
  Child*: … river.*
  etc.

Role play

- The story can also be performed as a role play after appropriate intensive practice.

Additional task: Masks (racoon, beaver)

Materials:

- Copies, drawing paper, water colour paints, opaque white, paint brush, scissors, glue, elastic.

Expressions:

Take the copy of the mask.
Put some glue on it and stick it on the drawing paper.
Colour the mask.
Cut out the mask.
Cut out the eyes.
Push through the holes on each side of the mask.
Fix the elastic.
Put the mask on.

- Copy the masks (racoon, beaver) once from the photocopiable master in the appendix of the Teacher's Book, p. 159.
- Show the copy to the children. Ask the children each to choose one of the masks. Photocopy the appropriate number.
- Get the children to stick the copies on to drawing paper.
- The beaver mask is coloured in various shades of brown.
- The black and white drawing of the racoon's face is coloured with opaque white and black.
- Then the outlines and also the eyes of the mask are cut out.
- The holes on either side of the mask are pushed through. Then quite a strong piece of elastic is pulled through and knotted.
- Demonstrate the individual steps and give instructions in English.
- Perform the role play again wearing the masks.

Preparation of written phrases

That's good. Yummy; I've got an idea; Let's help him; Let's go to the river; Swim across the river; He's happy; We're happy.

- Write the sentences on strips of paper, large enough so that all the children in your class can comfortably read the sentences.

- Hold up one of the paper strips for about half a second only. The children call out the sentence. They should, however, not be able to read the words letter for letter. This helps to avoid interference between the written words and their pronunciation. Carry on as described above.

➊ Look, read and match.
Reading exercise

- Ask the children to look at the pictures in ex. 1 at p. 40 in their Activity Book.
- Read out the sentences below the pictures one after the other. The children read along.
- Read out the sentences in any order. The children point at the appropriate sentences.
- Tell the children to match the sentences to the corresponding pictures above by numbering them from one to six.
- To check say: 'He is happy.' What number is it? The children answer: Number three.

➋ Listen and write the numbers.
Listening exercise CD 3/5

- Ask the children to look at the pictures in ex. 2 at p. 41 in their Activity Book. Tell them that the pictures are printed in random order. They listen to the story on the CD and put the pictures in the correct order by numbering them accordingly.

Tapescript:

Announcer:	One.
Ronnie:	Mum, help me.
Mum:	OK.
	Ronnie, call your sister.
Announcer:	Two.
Ronnie:	Rosie, come here.
Announcer:	Three.
Rosie:	Pull, pull.
Announcer:	Four.
Mum:	Rosie, call dad.
Rosie:	OK.
Announcer:	Five.
Ronnie:	Pull dad, pull.
Announcer:	Six.
Rabbit:	Can I help?
Dad:	Yes, please.
Announcer:	Seven.
All:	Hooray!
Announcer:	Eight.
Mum:	Let's have a picnic!
All:	Yummy!

- Play CD 3/5 twice.
- Check the children's work: Draw a grid with eight boxes on the board. This grid represents p. 41 in the book. Have the children dictate the numbers for the corresponding box. Point to the first box on the board and say: What number is it? Children answer: Number eight.

Role play

- The story can also be performed as a role play after appropriate intensive practice.

LESSON 3

Vocabulary, phrases and structures:

Receptive language:*The clever racoons are helpful/strong; Oh, here they come; A bushy tail and two small ears; A funny face and a black nose; That's Ronnie, he's Rosie's brother.*

Linguistic skills:

Understanding a song (*The clever racoons*) from the CD.
Writing sentences using given words and phrases.

Cognitive, motor and social skills:

Pointing to the correct pictures while listening.
Maintaining rhythm and melody and doing actions to songs and rhymes.
Formulating categories.
Reading descriptions of families and matching them to the corresponding pictures.

Cross-curricular integration:

Music
Topic: Speaking motivation: 'Being helpful'.

Materials:

Story Cards from *Playway 2:* 30–41; masks from previous lesson
CD 3/6–7; *Pupil's Book*, p. 50, ex. 5; *Activity Book*, pp. 42–43, ex. 3–5

Revision

- Reconstruct the story *The racoons and the beaver* with the aid of the story cards.
- Have the children perform the story as a role play. Use the masks for this.

Vocabulary extension

helpful

- Explain *helpful* in L1.

❺ Listen and point. Sing the song.

Song: *The clever racoons* CD 3/6–7

- The children open their Pupil's Book at p. 50 and look at the pictures.

- Play the song (CD 3/6) and point at the correct pictures.
- Play the song again and do the corresponding actions.
- With the children, say the text together in the rhythm of the song, letting the children use the pictures in the book to jog their memory and point along again.
- The children stand up and put their masks on. Sing the song together and do the corresponding actions to it. Finally, sing to the karaoke version (CD 3/7).

❸ Find the odd one out.
Formulating categories

- Tell the children to look at the pictures in ex. 3 on p. 42 in their Activity Book for about five seconds only. They then close their books. Say: *Tell me the words you remember.* Record the words on the board. Ask: *What's missing?* Allow the children to have a brief look at ex. 3 and find out what's missing. They then name the missing words and you write them on the board again.
- Ask the children to open their books and look at ex. 3. Read out the first row: *Cucumber – onion – plum – potato – carrot.* Look at the children and ask: *What's wrong?* The children answer: *(The) plum.* Say: *Right. The plum is a fruit. And the others are …* Get the children to finish your sentence: *… vegetables.*
- The children try to find the odd one out in the remaining five rows and cross them out.
- When the children have finished with their work, they get together with a partner and check each other's results.

Option: To promote self-checking it is recommended that you put out an answer key. If an answer is unclear the children can go and check themselves.

❹ How many sentences can you make?
Sentence building

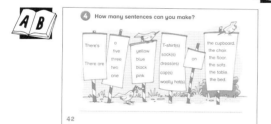

- Ask the children to look at ex. 4 on p. 42 in their Activity Book. Read out the words and phrases. The children read and point along in their books.
- Start a sentence, for example: *There's …* Stop and look at the children and get them to continue/finish the sentence. They say, for example: *…one yellow woolly hat … on … the bed.*
- The children try to find as many sentences as possible and write them on a sheet of paper.
- When they have finished their work, get them to count their sentences. Ask individual children, for example: *Martin, how many sentences have you got?* Martin answers accordingly, e.g.: *Ten.* Say: *Wow! That's a lot! Who has got more?* Get individual children to read their sentences.

❺ Look, read and write the names.
Reading exercise

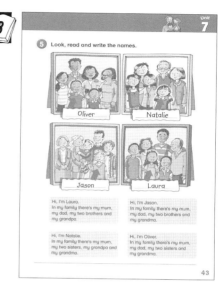

- The children look at ex. 5 on p. 43 in their Activity Book. Ask them to read the texts and write the names of the children below the corresponding pictures.
- Do the first text together with the children.
- Check the children's work: Hold up your book and point to the first picture. Ask: *What's his/her name?* The children answer accordingly.

L E S S O N   4

Vocabulary, phrases and structures:

Revision: family words
Receptive language: *Happy birthday, grandpa; Thank you Emily; Do you like pink roses?; They're from the garden; Oh, no, my roses; Yes; They smell wonderful; Here you are, grandma; Thank you, Ryan; Do you like the yellow bird?; Yes, thank you. It's wonderful; It's from your bedroom; Oh, no, my curtains!*

Linguistic skills:

Understanding a story in dialogue from the CD.
Understanding sentences from the CD.

Cognitive, motor and social skills:

Following a story and pointing to the corresponding pictures in the book.
Re-enacting the story as a role play.
Matching sentences from the CD to the pictures and then to the sentences in the book.
Drawing (or optional sticking in a photo) of one's own family and being able to describe them.

Cross-curricular integration:

Topic: Speaking motivation 'Describing your family and the people in it'.
Art

Materials:

CD 3/7; *Pupil's Book*, p. 50, ex. 5
CD 3/8–9; *Pupil's Book*, p. 51, ex. 6; *Activity Book*, pp. 44–45, ex. 6–9; coloured pencils

Revision

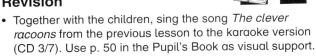

- Together with the children, sing the song *The clever racoons* from the previous lesson to the karaoke version (CD 3/7). Use p. 50 in the Pupil's Book as visual support.

Introduction of vocabulary

They smell wonderful; garden

- Clarify the meaning of the sentence *They smell wonderful,* through gestures and mimes.
- Translate – if necessary – the word *garden* into L1.

❻ Listen and point.
Listening exercise CD 3/8

- The children look at the picture story on p. 51, ex. 6 of their Pupil's Book.

Tapescript:

Emily:	*Happy birthday, Grandpa.*
Grandpa:	*Thank you, Emily.*
Emily:	*Do you like pink roses?*
Grandpa:	*Yes. Mmmh. They smell wonderful.*
Emily:	*They're from the garden.*
Grandpa:	*Oh, no, my roses.*

- Play the listening exercise several times (CD 3/8). The children look at the pictures in the book.
- Check whether the children have understood the text. Say the individual sentences in random order. The children point to the corresponding pictures/speech bubbles in the book.

❻ Listen and point.
Listening exercise CD 3/9

- The children open their Activity Book and look at the pictures in ex. 6, on p. 44.

Unit **7**

Tapescript:

Boy:	*Here you are, Grandma.*
Grandma:	*Thank you, Ryan.*
Boy:	*Do you like the yellow bird?*
Grandma:	*Yes, thank you. It's wonderful.*
Boy:	*It's from your bedroom.*
Grandma:	*Oh, no, my curtains!*

- Play the CD 3/9 twice. The children look at the pictures in their books.

❼ Match the sentences to the pictures.
Reading exercise

- Ask the children to look at ex. 7 on p. 44 in their Activity Book. Read out the sentences one after the other. The children read along.
- Tell them to put the sentences in the correct order by matching them to the pictures above.
- Do sentence number one together with the children. Hold your book up so that all can see well. Say: *What's number one?* Children: *Here you are, Grandma.* Pretend to write one in the circle in front of the corresponding sentence.
- Then the children order the remaining sentences. When they have finished ask them to read out the sentences in the correct order.

Additional task for high-ability groups
Role play: Act out

- With high-ability groups work on the role play *The pink roses.*
- Change your voice to say *Happy birthday, grandpa!* and change places to reply as *Grandpa* with *Thank you, Emily.* Point to the first two pictures in the book at the same time.
- In this way develop the whole dialogue and act it out several times in front of the class.
- Then encourage one child to play the part of *Emily.* Whisper cues to help. Then ask another child to play the part of *Grandpa.* In this way act out the dialogue in front of the class with several children.
- After that the children practise the dialogue in pairs and act it out as a role play in front of the whole class. Remember to give them a clap (*Let's give them a big hand!*).

❽ Look and say.
Speaking exercise

- Ask the children to look at the picture in ex. 8 on p. 45 in their Activity Book where *Rosie* is presenting her family.
- Get the children to read the text in the speech bubble with you: *In my family there's mum, dad, my brother Ronnie and me.* Practise the sentence thoroughly by getting the children to say and repeat it several times.

❾ Draw and say.
Step to creativity (ME-page)

In my family there's ...

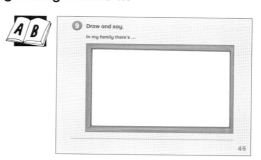

- Get the children to draw a picture of themselves in the space provided in ex. 9 on p. 45 in their Activity Book. Point to the empty frame. Tell them they should draw their family or stick in a photo of their closest family.
- Ask individual children to describe their family: *In my family there's ...* Help through whispering cues, if necessary.

LESSON 1

Vocabulary, phrases and structures:

Vocabulary revision: numbers from 1 to 12; *cat; dog; mouse; duck; butterfly; bee; hen earthworm; horse; pig; cow; sheep; egg/s*
Receptive language: *Put on your shoes; Take some corn; Go outside; Call the hens; Feed the hens; Go to the hen house; Look for eggs; Pick up an egg; Crack; There's a chick; Pick up your trainers; Put on your trainers; Call the cat; Look for the cat; Feed the cat.*

Linguistic skills:

Learning the meaning, the pronunciation and the written form of the new words.
Understanding instructions from an action story *(Feed the hens).*
Understanding instructions from the CD and matching with the corresponding pictures.

Cognitive, motor and social skills:

Practising the new words in pair work.
Understanding words from the CD and numbering the pictures in the book to correspond.
Understanding and carrying out jumbled instructions.

Cross-curricular integration:

Topic: Speaking motivation 'Talking about animals that live on a farm' and *'Feed the hens'.*

Materials:

Flashcards from *Playway 1:* 29–30, 32–33, 53–54, 85; *Flashcards* from *Playway 2:* 56–62; *Word Cards* from *Playway 2:* 29, 93–105; CD 3/10–12; *Pupil's Book* pp. 52–53, ex. 1–2; *Activity Book,* p. 46, ex. 1–2; paper strips

Vocabulary revision

numbers from one to twelve; cat; dog; mouse; duck; butterfly; bee; hen

- Revise numbers one to twelve in the usual manner.
- Revise the animal names already learnt with the aid of the flashcards.

Introduction of vocabulary

pig; cow; earthworm; sheep; horse

- Reinforce the new words with the aid of the flashcards in the usual manner.

Exercises for anchoring the vocabulary in the children's recognition memory

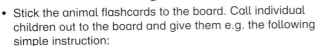

- Stick the animal flashcards to the board. Call individual children out to the board and give them e.g. the following simple instruction:
  Christina, touch the cow.
  Markus, swap the pig and the horse.
  Anna, take the earthworm and put it on Marie's desk.
  Sandro, take the cat and give it to Thomas.
  etc.

Exercises for anchoring the vocabulary in the children's productive memory

- Say all the words together with the children.
- Then play *What's missing?* with the flashcards on the board.
- Then remove all the flashcards from the board. Take one card and keep it hidden. Ask: *What is it? Guess.* Have individual children guess using the following expressions:
  Child: *Is it a cow?*
  Teacher: *No, sorry.*
  Child: *Is it a horse?*
  Teacher: *Yes, Tom, you are right. Come out. It's your turn now.*

- The child who has guessed correctly can now continue in your place etc.

Option: Mime an animal (sound or movement) and the children guess what it is. The child that has guessed right is the next to mime another one etc.

Vocabulary exercises with the support of the written forms

dog; mouse; duck; cat; bee; butterfly; hen; earthworm; horse; pig; cow; sheep

- Hold up the word cards in quick succession. Do not allow the children enough time to read the words letter by letter. They should absorb the written form only as a single entity.
- When the children say the correct word, repeat it. Then get one of them to put the card up on the board next to the corresponding flashcard. Say: *Put it on the board, please.*
- Take down all the flashcards, but leave the word cards on the board. Read them out together with the children several times.
- Tell the children to close their eyes. Turn the word cards face down on the board and tell the children to open their eyes. Point to the word cards in any order and say, each time: *What is it? What do you think?*

Option: An alternative procedure is for you to hold up the word cards one after another, saying the corresponding words. Then hand the cards out to individual children. Say the words in sequence. After each word, the child with the corresponding card comes out to the board and puts it up next to or below the flashcard.

❶ Listen and write the numbers.
Listening exercise CD 3/10

Tapescript:

One:	Bee.
Two:	Earthworm.
Three:	Horse.
Four:	Cat.
Five:	Butterfly.
Six:	Mouse.
Seven:	Pig.
Eight:	Cow.
Nine:	Sheep.
Ten:	Duck.
Eleven:	Hen.
Twelve:	Dog.

- The children work in pairs with one Pupil's Book at p. 52, ex. 1. Child A names individual animals, child B points to the corresponding illustration/word in the book. Then they swap roles.
- Play the listening exercise twice (CD 3/10). The children listen and number the pictures in the Pupil's Book on p. 52.
- Check the children's answers by saying the numbers. The children say the names of the corresponding animals.

Vocabulary extension

eggs; corn; chick

- Introduce the new words with the aid of the flashcards, drawings, gestures and mimes in the usual manner.

Action Story: *Feed the hens*

- For reinforcement of the Action Story carry out the following steps in the usual manner (see also Introduction of the Teacher's Book, p. 16).
  - Listening and imitating
  - Carrying out instructions
  - Carrying out the instructions in a jumbled order.

❷ Listen and point.
Write the numbers.

Action Story: *Feed the hens* CD 3/11

- The children open their Pupil's Book at p. 53, ex. 2. The nine pictures are printed in random order. Give the children sufficient time to look at the pictures.

Tapescript:

Put on your shoes.
Take some corn.
Go outside.
Call the hens.
Feed the hens.
Go to the hen house.
Look for eggs.
Pick up an egg.
Crack. There's a chick.

- Play the listening exercise (CD 3/11). At first the children just listen and point at the pictures in the book.
- Play the listening exercise again. Now the children number the pictures in the book.
- Go round the class and check the children's work.

Pronunciation tip: Pay attention in the pronunciation of chick [tʃɪk] to the voiceless [tʃ]. This sound is clearly different from the [dʒ] in jump.

❶ Listen and write the numbers.
Listening exercise CD 3/12

- The children open their Activity Book at p. 46, ex. 1. The six pictures are printed in random order. Now give the children sufficient time to look at the pictures.

Tapescript:

One:	*Pick up your trainers.*
Two:	*Put on your trainers.*
Three:	*Go outside.*
Four:	*Look for the cat.*
Five:	*Call the cat.*
Six:	*Feed the cat.*

- Play the listening exercise (CD 3/12). At first the children just listen and point at the respective pictures in the book.
- Play the listening exercise again. Now the children number the pictures in the book.
- Check the children's work: Ask: *Put on your trainers. What number is it?* Children: (*Number*) *two.*

Preparation of written phrases

Feed the cat; Look for the cat; Put on your trainers; Call the cat; Pick up your trainers; Go outside.

- Write the sentences on strips of paper, large enough so that all the children in your class can comfortably read the sentences.
- Hold up one of the paper strips for about half a second only. The children call out the sentence. They should, however, not be able to read the words letter for letter. This helps to avoid interference between the written words and their pronunciation. Carry on as described with the other sentences.

Option: You can also write the sentences on the board. In this case point to the sentences in quick succession and get the children to say the corresponding sentences. Close the board and say: *Give me the sentences you remember.* The children say the sentences they can remember. Allow them a brief look on the board and they check which sentence/s is/are missing.

❷ Look at the pictures in ❶ and write.
Writing exercise

- Read out the sentences in ex. 2 on p. 46 in the Activity Book. The children read along and point at the respective sentences.
- Then they write the sentences below the corresponding pictures in ex. 1 on the lines provided in the book.
- Go round the class and help, if necessary.
- Check the children's work by holding up one paper strip after the other only for about half a second (for example paper strip showing the sentence: *Feed the cat.*) Ask: *What number is it?* Children: (*Number*) *six.*

C L I L:
Content and Language Integrated Learning
Work Instructions: Folding a cat

Objective:
Practising fine motor skills.
Talking about domestic cats and wildcats and their habits.

Materials:
for each child a copy of the assembly instructions in the appendix from the *Teacher's Book*, p. 160; scissors; coloured pencils

Folding a cat

Art

- For each child in the class prepare a copy of the assembly instructions in the appendix of the Teacher's Book, p. 160. Distribute the copies and get the children to cut out the squares.

Photocopiable master:

- The children fold the squares diagonally into a double triangle.
- They place the double triangle with the fold down.
- Then they fold the top corner over backwards.
- The side corners are folded up and back.
- Then the children colour the cat's face with coloured pencils.
- Demonstrate the individual steps and accompany your activities with the corresponding English instructions. Keep to the right pace so that each child can follow the folding activity.
- Keep repeating your instructions and praise the children when they get it right.

Expressions:

Cut the square out.
Fold it like this. Yes, very good.
Put it down like this. Look at me. Yes, good.
Now fold the top corners down. Down, like this. Well done.
Fold one bottom corner up. Up, like this. Be careful. OK. That's right.
Now the other one. Fold it up, like this.
Colour your cat's face. Wonderful!

All about cats: fact sheet

- Ask children to write a fact sheet explaining all about cats.
- Elicit from the children:
  - what cats eat
  - where cats sleep
  - what cats do.
- Children write a list of what they know about domestic cats.
- Do they know any facts about wild cats?

L E S S O N   2

Vocabulary, phrases and structures:

Vocabulary revision: *bee; hen; eggs; cow; earthworm; milk; honey; vegetables; trees; flowers. There's…; There are…; butterflies; Who are you?; Eddie is happy; Bees make honey; Eddie is sad; Hens lay eggs; Everybody loves you.*

Linguistic skills:

Understanding a story (*Eddie, the earthworm*) from the DVD and the CD and from the teacher's narration.
Joining in with the story-telling.
Carrying out role plays.

Cognitive, motor and social skills:

Following the narrative structure of a story on DVD and CD.
Role playing.
Building sentences with given phrases.
Doing a word search.

Cross-curricular integration:

Topic: Speaking motivation 'The role of earthworms in gardens'.

Materials:

Flashcards from *Playway 1:* 53, 74, 85; *Flashcards* from *Playway 2:* 56, 59, 61–62; *Word Cards* from *Playway 2:* 97–105; *Story Cards* from *Playway 2:* 42–53; DVD (*Eddie, the earthworm*); CD 3/13; *Pupil's Book,* pp. 54–55, ex. 3; stick-in pictures from the appendix of the *Pupil's Book; Activity Book,* pp. 47–48, ex. 3–5; (optional) answer key for self-checking

Revision

- For revision play the game *Max says…* with the children using the instructions of the Action Story: *Feed the hens* from the previous lesson.

Revision for high-ability groups

- Get the children to sit on their chairs in a circle. Give each child the name of an animal. Go round the outside of the circle and say: *I like animals. I like rabbits.* All the rabbits join you and go round the circle and say: *I like animals. I like rabbits and I like …* etc.
- Continue in this way for a while. Then say: *… But I don't like monsters.* All those who are marching round the circle now try to sit on seats. As you too want to sit down there is one seat too few. The child who is left starts the next round: *I like animals. I like cows.* etc.

Revision and preparation of key words

bee; eggs; hen; cow; earthworm; milk; honey; vegetables; trees; flowers

- Revise the words *earthworm, cow, hen, eggs, milk, honey* and *bee* with the aid of the flashcards.
- For reinforcing the words *vegetables, trees* and *flowers* take the story card on which *Eddie, trees, flowers* and *vegetables* can be seen. Point to the individual illustrations and name them.

❸ Watch the story.

Cartoon Story: *Eddie, the earthworm*

- Show the children the video sequence *Eddie, the earthworm* twice (DVD).

DVD script: *Eddie, the earthworm*

Storyteller:	*It's a lovely morning on the farm. This is Eddie, the earthworm.*
Eddie:	*Hi, everybody.*
Cow:	*Moo. Who are you?*
Eddie:	*Hi. I'm Eddie, the earthworm.*
Cow:	*I give milk. What about you?*
Eddie:	*Erm, erm … I live underground.*
Cow:	*Underground? Stupid.*
Storyteller:	*Eddie is sad.*
Hen:	*Who are you?*
Eddie:	*Hi. I'm Eddie, the earthworm.*
Hen:	*I lay eggs. What about you?*
Eddie:	*Erm, erm … I live underground.*
Hen:	*Underground? Stupid.*
Storyteller:	*Eddie is very sad.*
Bee:	*Who are you?*
Eddie:	*Hi. I'm Eddie, the earthworm.*
Bee:	*I make honey. What about you?*
Eddie:	*Erm, erm … I live underground.*
Bee:	*Underground? Stupid.*
Storyteller:	*Eddie is very, very sad.*
Girl:	*Hello, Eddie. You look sad. What's the problem?*
Eddie:	*I can't give milk. I can't lay eggs and I can't make honey.*
Girl:	*Eddie, you're the king of the garden.*
Eddie:	*Really?*
Girl:	*Yes. The flowers love you, the vegetables love you, and the trees love you.*
Chorus:	*Eddie, Eddie is the king of the garden. Eddie, Eddie, everybody loves you.*
Storyteller:	*Eddie is happy again.*
Eddie:	*Oh, thank you. Thank you very much.*

Note: Not all the language in the DVD sequences or CD versions of the stories are presented in the cartoon story in the Pupil's Book. This is mainly because of the length of the stories but also this serves to encourage the children to listen for the necessary information in order to complete the gap fill in the Pupil's Book.

❸ Listen and stick.

Listening exercise: Sticker activity CD 3/13

- Play the listening version of the story twice (CD 3/13). The children stick the stick-in pictures from the appendix in the corresponding blank spaces in the Pupil's Book (pp. 54 and 55) while they are listening.
- Check the children's work.

Option: To promote self-checking it is recommended that you put out a completed picture story. The children go and check their own work themselves.

Telling the story

- Tell or reconstruct the story with the aid of the story cards in the usual manner.

Role play

- Tell the story again. Have two children play and say the parts of *Eddie, the cow, the hen and the bee*. Practise the parts thoroughly by getting the children say and repeat them several times.
- Then give the part of the girl to two children.
- Re-enact the story as a role play. You play the part of the storyteller and help the children, if necessary, by whispering cues.

Comment: In the rehearsal phase two children can take one part to help each other along. After that let the children speak their parts alternately and not at the same time to keep the performance natural.

❸ Find the ten names of the animals. ↓ →

Word search

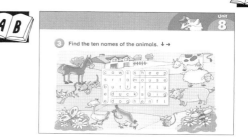

- Ask the children to open their Activity Book at p. 47 and look at ex. 3. There are ten names of animals hidden in the word search. Tell the children to find the words and circle them.
- Allow the children to do this exercise together with a partner. When the children have finished, ask: *Who's got seven words?* The children who have found seven words raise their arms. Say: *Good.* Ask: *Who's got eight words or more? – Great! Well done!*
- Get the children that have found all ten animals to read them out.

Option: To promote self-checking it is recommended that you put out an answer key in the classroom. The children go and check their own work themselves.

❹ Read. Tick the correct pieces to make a sentence (✓).

Sentence building

- Start to draw a butterfly on the board. Stop your drawing and get the children to guess what it is. Continue with the drawing until the children have guessed the animal. Then get the children to close their eyes or turn around. Draw a few more butterflies on the board and close it. The children open their eyes or turn around again. Ask: *How many butterflies are there now? What do you think? Guess.* When the children have guessed right, open the board and show your drawings. Say: *Right, there are five butterflies.* Write the word *butterflies* on the board.
- Then get the children to look on ex. 4 on p. 47 in their Activity Book. Hold your book up and point at the respective puzzle pieces while speaking. Say: *Four dogs.* Look at the children questioningly. Point to the puzzle pieces that show *There's* and *There are.* Get the children to say: *There are.* Say: *Right.* and repeat the whole sentence: *There are four dogs.* Pretend to tick the appropriate puzzle piece in the book.
- Tell the children to tick: *There's* or *There are* on the remaining puzzle pieces.
- To check, get individual children to read out the sentences.

Preparation of written phrases

Who are you?; Eddie is happy; Bees make honey; Eddie is sad; Hens lay eggs; Everybody loves you.

- Write the sentences on strips of paper, large enough so that all the children in your class can comfortably read the sentences.
- Hold up one of the paper strips for about half a second only. The children call out the sentence. They should, however, not be able to read the words letter for letter. This helps to avoid interference between the written words and their pronunciation. Carry on as described with the other sentences.

Option: Write the sentences on the board and work on them in the usual manner.

❺ Look, read and match.
Reading exercise

- Ask the children to look at the pictures in ex. 5 on p. 48 in their Activity Book.
- Then read out the sentences below the pictures one after the other. The children read along in their books.
- Read out the sentences in any order. The children point at the appropriate sentences. Tell the children to match the sentences to the corresponding pictures above by numbering them from one to six.
- To check say: *'Eddie is sad.' What number is it?* The children answer: *(Number) five.*

L E S S O N   3

Vocabulary, phrases and structures:

Revision: *Hens lay eggs; Cows give milk; And bees make honey; Lots of eggs/milk/honey; But Eddie is the king of the garden; Everybody loves you; In picture A there are three ducks; In picture B there's just one.*

Linguistic skills:

Learning the meaning and pronunciation of the new words.
Singing a song *(The earthworm song)*.
Understanding questions and matching them to the corresponding answers.

Cognitive, motor and social skills:

Pointing to the correct pictures while listening.

Maintaining rhythm and melody while speaking in unison and singing.
Role playing different characters.
Completing sentences using information from pictures.

Cross-curricular integration:

Music
Topic: Speaking motivation 'Talking about animals that live on a farm'.

Materials:

DVD *(Eddie, the earthworm); Story Cards* from *Playway 2:* 42–53
CD 3/14–15; *Pupil's Book*, p. 56, ex. 4; *Activity Book*, pp. 49–50, ex. 6–8

Revision

- For revision, show the story *Eddie, the earthworm* again on DVD and reconstruct the story together with the children. Use the story cards for this.

❹ Listen and point. Sing the song.

Song: *The earthworm song* CD 3/14–15

- The children look at the picture on p. 56, ex. 4 in the Pupil's Book for about five seconds. They close their books and give you words. Say: *Tell me some words.*

The earthworm song

Lyrics: Gerngross/Puchta
Music: Lorenz Maierhofer
© Helbling, Rum/Innsbruck

- Play the song (CD 3/14). At first the children just listen and follow in the book.
- Then say the lyrics line by line and do the appropriate actions to it or point to the pictures in the book to facilitate understanding of the text. The children imitate your actions or point at the respective pictures in the book.
- Play the song several times. The children point along in the Pupil's Book.
- Say the text with the children in the rhythm of the song, while the children point at the pictures in the book again.
- Stand in a circle with the children. Hum the tune of the song. Gradually the children join in with you and hum along. When they are all humming start to sing the words.
- Act out the story of *Eddie, the earthworm* again.
- After that sing the earthworm song with all the children using the karaoke version (CD 3/15).

On the farm

❻ Look and write.

Reading exercise

- Ask the children to look at picture A in ex. 6 on p. 49 in their Activity Book for about ten seconds. Get them to close their books and ask: *How many ducks/sheep/ brown hens/... are there?* Write their guesses on the board.
  Proceed in the same way as above with picture B.
- Read out the first sentence below the pictures. Get the children to count the ducks in picture A and give you the right answer. *(In picture A there are three ducks.)*
- Then the children complete the remaining sentences. Read out the last sentence and if necessary translate the words *just* and *missing* into L1.
- To check the children's work, ask individual children to read out the sentences.

❼ Read and match.

Mini-dialogues

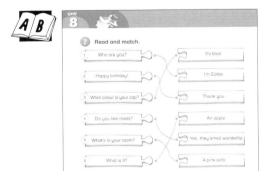

- Before you ask the children to open their Activity Books on p. 50 and look at the sentences in ex. 7, you may prefer to write questions and answers on separate pieces of paper.
  Fix them to the board in random order. Point at a question and the children call out the answer. Put the correct answer next to the question.
- Then read out the questions and answers aloud and close the board or remove them from the board.

- Now, read out the sentences in ex. 7 on p. 50 in the Activity Book one after the other. The children point at the sentences in their book and read along. Later, jumble the order of the sentences.
- Tell the children to match the questions to the corresponding answers. Do the first example together with the children. Hold your book up so that all can see well. Point to the first question and ask: *Who are you?* Then pretend to look for the correct answer. Read out the possible answers in a low voice. Look at the children and get the children to give you the correct answer: *I'm Eddie.*
- The children match the remaing questions to the answers individually.
- Check the children's work: Read out the first part of the dialogues and get the children to say the appropriate answers/second part of the dialogues.

❽ Look, read and complete.

Writing exercise

- Tell the children to look at ex. 8 on p. 50 of the Activity Book. Hold up your book so that all the children can see it well. Read out the first question and answer and clap when you get to the gap, e.g.: *What do <clap> make? – They make milk.* Point to the gap and the picture next to it and ask: *What goes here?* Make sure the children produce the correct response: *cows.* Show how one letter fits on each line. The children fill in the gaps in the rest of the sentences individually.
- Check the children's work: Hold up your book so that all the children can see it and get individual children to read out the sentences. Write the missing word on the board and get the rest of the class to say whether or not they think it's correct.

L E S S O N   4

Vocabulary, phrases and structures:

Vocabulary revision: *How many…*

Cognitive, motor and social skills:

Drawing one's own farm and describing it.

Cross-curricular integration:

Music
Topic: Speaking motivation 'Talking about animals that live on a farm'.

Materials:

CD 3/15
Activity Book, p. 51, ex. 8–9

Revision

- Sing *The earthworm song* with the children using the karaoke version CD 3/15.

❾ Look and read.
Reading exercise

- Get the children to look at the picture in ex. 8 on p. 51 in their Activity Book for about five seconds only. Get them to close their books. Ask: *How many horses are there?* The children answer accordingly: *Six*. Say: *Right. There are six horses.* Continue with the remaining animals. Write the number and plural forms of the animals on the board.
- Then get the children to open their books again. Read the text below the picture. The children repeat several times. This text is to serve as a model text for their own text in the next step.

❿ Draw, write and say.

Step to creativity (ME-page)

On my farm there are …

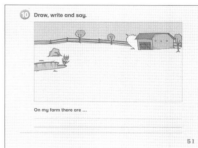

- Tell the children to draw on their own farm the animals that live in the space provided in ex. 9 on p. 51 in their Activity Book.
- Then the children write a short text about their farm based on the model in ex. 8 above. They write their sentence/short text underneath the drawing in ex. 9 on p. 51 in their Activity Book.
- Go round the class and help, if necessary.
- The children practise their sentence/short text when they have finished their drawing. Also help with the pronunciation, if necessary.
- Then put two desks together. The children put their Activity Books with p. 51 face up on them and stand around the desks, so that all can see each others' drawings. Finally, get individual children to read out their sentence/text.

C L I L:
Content and Language Integrated Learning

Objectives:

Understanding facts concerning the earthworm.
Matching questions to answers.

Materials:

Pupil's Book, p. 57, ex. 5

❺ **Match the sentences to the pictures.**
   Write the numbers.

Reading exercise

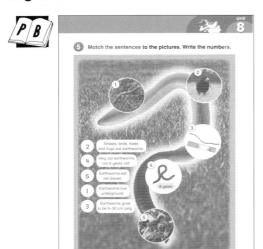

- Explain the words the children do not know through mime and gestures or – if necessary through translation in L1.
- Read out the sentences in any order and get the children to point to the corresponding pictures in their books.
- Then the children match the sentences to the pictures by numbering them accordingly. Number one is already done.
- To check the children's work read out the sentences one after another. The children read along in their books: *Earthworms live underground. What number is it?* Children: *Number one.*

- Ask the children to point along in ex. 5 on p. 57 in their Pupil's Book. Hold your book up and point to the pictures while speaking:
  Picture 1: Earthworms live underground.
  Picture 2: Snakes, birds, foxes and frogs eat earthworms.
  Picture 3: Earthworms grow to be 9–30cm long.
  Picture 4: Very old earthworms are eight years old.
  Picture 5: Earthworms eat old leaves.

L E S S O N   1

Vocabulary, phrases and structures:
Checking of vocabulary acquisition in Units 7–8.

Linguistic skills:
Understanding and saying important words from Units 7–8 on the topic areas 'family' and 'on the farm'.

Cognitive, motor and social skills:
Matching words and sentences from the CD to corresponding pictures.
Numbering words and sentences according to the CD.
Checking results with the aid of an answer key.
Self-evaluation

Materials:
CD 3/16–17; *Pupil's Book*, pp. 58–59, ex. 1–4; coloured pencils; answer key

Self-evaluation

Option: Divide *Show what you can do* into two lessons.

Note: For notes on the basic methodology of this section, see *Show what you can do* on p. 18 of the introduction in the Teacher's Book.

❶ Listen and write the numbers.
Listening exercise CD 3/16

- Tell the children that they are going to find out which words in the Pupil's Book on p. 58, ex. 1 they can already understand well.
- The children are going to see whether they can match the words they hear to the corresponding pictures by numbering them from one to twelve.

Tapescript:

Number one:	*Picnic.*
Number one:	*Picnic.*
Number two:	*Hen.*
Number two:	*Hen.*
Number three:	*River.*
Number three:	*River.*
Number four:	*Earthworm.*
Number four:	*Earthworm.*
Number five:	*Cow.*
Number five:	*Cow.*
Number six:	*Sheep.*
Number six:	*Sheep.*

Number seven:	*Bee.*
Number seven:	*Bee.*
Number eight:	*Duck.*
Number eight:	*Duck.*
Number nine:	*Rose.*
Number nine:	*Rose.*
Number ten:	*Pig.*
Number ten:	*Pig.*
Number eleven:	*Eggs.*
Number eleven:	*Eggs.*
Number twelve:	*Horse.*
Number twelve:	*Horse.*

- Now play the listening exercise (CD 3/16).
- The children number the pictures in the book correspondingly. The first picture has already been numbered.
- Go round the class and help the children, if necessary.
- Set out a completed sheet and let the children check their results independently.

❷ Match the words to the pictures.
Reading exercise

- Tell the children that they are going to find out which words in the Pupil's Book on p. 58, ex. 2 they can already read well.
- The children now check independently whether they can match the written words in ex 2. to the corresponding pictures in ex. 1.
- Set out a completed sheet and let the children check their results independently.

---

❸ Listen and write the numbers.

Listening exercise CD 3/17

- Tell the children to find out by themselves which sentences in the Pupil's Book on p. 59, ex. 3 they can already say.
- The children check independently whether they can match the sentences they hear to the corresponding pictures.

Tapescript:

Number one:	*I've got an idea.*
Number one:	*I've got an idea.*
Number two:	*My sister is very sad.*
Number two:	*My sister is very sad.*
Number three:	*They smell wonderful.*
Number three:	*They smell wonderful.*
Number four:	*Happy birthday, Anna!*
Number four:	*Happy birthday, Anna!*

- Now play the listening exercise (CD 3/17).
- The children number the pictures in the book accordingly. The first picture has already been numbered.
- Go round the class and help, if necessary.
- Set out a completed sheet and let the children check their results independently.

❹ Match the sentences to the pictures.

Reading exercise

- Tell the children that they are now to find out themselves which sentences in the Pupil's Book on p. 59, ex. 4 they can already read well.
- The children now check independently whether they can match the written sentences to the corresponding pictures in ex. 3.
- Set out a completed sheet and let the children check their results independently.

L E S S O N   1

Vocabulary, phrases and structures:

car; train; plane; boat; bike; walk; left; right
Receptive language: *Point to the boat/person/...
turning left/right.*

Linguistic skills:

Learning the meaning, the pronunciation and the
written form of the new words.
Understanding new words from the CD.

Cognitive, motor and social skills:

Understanding the new words from the CD and
pointing along in the book.
Left and right.

Cross-curricular integration:

Topic: Speaking motivation 'Recognising different
modes of transport'.

Materials:

Flashcards from *Playway 2:* 63–70; *Word Cards*
from *Playway 2:* 106–113; CD 3/18; *Pupil's Book,*
p. 60, ex. 1; *Activity Book,* p. 52, ex. 1

Revision and preparation of key words

car; train; plane; boat; bike; walk; left; right

- Revise the words *car, train, plane* and *boat* with the aid
  of corresponding gestures/sounds and by drawing the
  transport on the board. Elicit each one from the class
  and label the pictures. Repeat the process for *walk* and
  bike.
- Reinforce the words left and right as follows: Turn
  around. Stretch out your left arm and say, *Left.* Do the
  same with *right.* Repeat this several times. Draw an
  arrow showing to the left and one showing to the right on
  the board.

Vocabulary game to anchor the words in the children's recognition memory

- Say one new word after the other and get the children to
  make the corresponding gestures.
- Get the children to stand up. Give instructions like: Say:
  *Point to the left/right. Turn to the left./Turn to the right.
  Walk. Walk to the left. Walk to the right.*
- The children make the corresponding movements.

Vocabulary exercises with the support of the written forms

boat; car; train; plane; bike; walk

- Hold up the word cards in quick succession. Do not
  allow the children enough time to read the words letter
  by letter. They should absorb the written form only as a
  single entity.
- When the children say the correct word, repeat it. Then
  get one of them to put the card up on the board next to
  the corresponding flashcard. Say: *Put it on the board,
  please.*
- Take down all the flashcards, but leave the word cards
  on the board. Read them out together with the children
  several times.
- Then play: *What's missing?* with the cards.

❶ Listen and point.
Listening exercise CD 3/18

- Ask the children to open their Pupil's Book at p. 60 and
  look at the pictures in ex. 1.
- Hold up your book. Say: *Look. Left. Right.* Point to the
  red arrows on the left side on the bottom of the page.
- Then say: *Look. A car turning left.* Point at the yellow
  car.
- Say: *Now you. Point to the boat turning right.* Now the
  children try to find the boat turning right and point to it in
  their books. Give some more similar instructions with the
  words *train, person, bike* and *plane.*

Tapescript:

Point to the boat turning left.
Point to the boat turning right.
Point to the car turning left.
Point to the car turning right.
Point to the bike turning right.
Point to the bike turning left.
Point to the person turning left.
Point to the person turning right.
Point to the train turning right.
Point to the train turning left.
Point to the plane turning right.
Point to the plane turning left.

- Tell them to listen to the CD and to point at the respective pictures in their books. Play CD 3/18 twice.

❶ Look and write.

Writing exercise

- Ask the children to open their Activity Book and look at ex. 1 on p. 52. Hold your book up so that all can see. Say: *Look. A car turning right.* Point to the first picture and to the sentence below the first picture.
- Then point to the third picture. Say: *A bike ...* Look at the children and get them to finish the sentence. Children: *... turning left.* Help through whispering cues, if needed.

Repeat the sentence: *A bike turning left.* Get the children to repeat several times.
- Then the children individually write the appropriate sentences to the pictures in their books. Go round the class and help, if necessary.
- Check the children's work: Ask, for example: *Barbara, what about picture four?* Barbara reads out her sentence: *A car turning left.* etc. Write the sentences on the board so that the children can check their results.

L E S S O N   2

Vocabulary, phrases and structures:

By bus/car/ ...; How do you get to ...?
Receptive language: *What about Simon? How does he get to school?; Go by plane; Come to my party on Saturday at eight; Listen how to get there; And don't be late; you can't go by underground/ bike/car/bus/plane; You can't walk; I live far away; I live on a star; Take my rocket, Aaaah!*

Linguistic skills:

Understanding short dialogues from the CD.
Speaking a chant rhythmically (*Come to my party*).

Cognitive, motor and social skills:

Carrying out pair work.
Matching the answers given in interviews on the CD with the right pictures in the book.

Speaking rhythmically in a group.
Carrying out the appropriate actions while speaking rhythmically.

Cross-curricular integration:

Topic: Speaking motivation 'Describing how you get to school'.
Music

Materials:

Flashcards from *Playway 2*: 63–70; *Word Cards* from *Playway 2*: 106–113
CD 3/19–21; *Pupil's Book*, p. 61, ex. 2–3; CD 3/22; *Activity Book*, p. 53, ex. 2; glove puppet; percussion instruments

Revision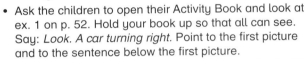

- Revise all the means of transport already learnt with the aid of the flashcards and the word cards.
- Then present a means of transport in a mime and get the children to guess what it is. The child who has guessed correctly may act out a means of transport next etc.

Preparation of key phrases

How do you get to school?; By bus/car ...;
Go by bus/car ...

- Take the glove puppet and ask as Max: *How do you get to school?* Give an appropriate answer, e.g. *By bike.* Max can ask you first as an example, then make the glove puppet ask individual children. Help with the answer, if necessary. The answer should always be ***By bike. By bus.*** etc. or ***I walk.***

Comment: You can say *to go by tram*. However in Britain there are only a few towns with *trams*.

Vocabulary extension

(go by) car; (go by) train; (go by) plane; (go by) bike; (go by) boat; walk; (go by) bus; (go by) underground

- Introduce the phrases for *(go by) bike*, *(go by) train* and *(go by) bus* with the aid of the flashcards and word cards.
- Say, e.g.: *Go by bike.* The children pretend to go by bike by doing the movements. etc.

Game

- Stick the flashcards of the types of transport on the board.
- Make two or three groups. Draw a chalk line on the floor. Each group lines up behind each other. The first child in each line waits ready to start at your command behind the line. You say one type of transport, e.g. *Go by bus.* The first one to touch the corresponding flashcard gets a point for their group. The first ones go to the end of their line. The second ones are thus moved forward and carry out the next instruction etc.

Pair work: Speaking exercise

- The children open p. 61 in their Pupil's Book and look at ex. 2. Name the means of transport illustrated in random order increasing the pace as you go. The children point at the respective pictures in the book.
- The children practise in pairs with one book. Child A names a means of transport and child B points to the corresponding picture.

❷ Listen and draw lines. Say.

Listening exercise CD 3/19

- Tell the children that they are now going to hear how four children called *Maria, Simon, Pamela* and *Ben*, get to school every day. Looking at p. 61, ex. 2. in their Pupil's Book, they should match the children with the right means of transport by drawing lines.

Tapescript:

Speaker:	*Maria, how do you get to school?*
Maria:	*I walk.*
Speaker:	*And what about you, Simon? How do you get to school?*
Simon:	*By car. My father takes me.*
Speaker:	*And you, Pamela?*
Pamela:	*By underground.*

Speaker:	*Mmh. And you, Ben, how do you get to school?*
Ben:	*By bus.*

- Play the listening exercise from the CD 3/19 several times.
- Check the answers to the listening exercise: Ask: *What about Simon? How does he get to school?* The children answer: *By car.*

Vocabulary extension

rocket

- Start drawing a rocket on the board and keep stopping to ask: *What is it?* Keep on until the children have guessed the word. Say: *A rocket.* and write the word on the board.

❸ Listen and point. Say the chant.

Chant: *Come to my party* CD 3/20–21

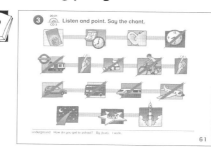

- Have the children open their Pupil's Book at p. 61 and look at the pictures in ex. 3. Then say a few words in random order and the children point to the corresponding pictures: *star, rocket, car, plane …*
- Explain to the children in L1 that in the following chant someone is being invited to a party. There is a description of how to get there.

Tapescript:

Speaker 1:	*Come to my party on Saturday at eight. Listen how to get there. And don't be late.*
Speaker 2:	*You can't go by underground. No, no, no. You can't walk or go by bike. No, no, no.*
Speaker 1:	*You can't go by car. You can't go by bus. You can't go by train. You can't go by plane.*
Speaker 2:	*I live far away. I live on a star. Take my rocket. Aaaaaaah!*

- Then play the chant from the CD 3/20 several times. Hold your book up to that they can all see and at first point at the respective pictures in the book. Play the chant again. Now the children look and point at the respective pictures in their books.

- Say the first verse slowly and do the appropriate gestures to it.
- Practise with the children the second and third verses by saying and having them repeat, support the understanding of the text by appropriate mimes and actions.
- Recite the last four lines and make the meaning clear with gestures. For example hang up a small star/planet in one corner of the classroom and point to it when you say: *I live on a star.* At the last sentence point to the picture of a rocket on the board.
- Then practise the last four lines (fourth verse) with the children by saying and repeating several times.
- Play the chant again a few times. The children join in the second and fourth verses (Speaker 2).
- Play the first part of the karaoke version (CD 3/21). The children say the missing parts of the text in unison.
- Practise the first verse intensively. Finally, play the karaoke section of the CD 3/21 and the children say the whole text.
- Give individual children various percussion instruments to support the rhythm or as instrumental representation of the sounds made by the vehicles.

❷ Listen and write the names.

Listening exercise CD 3/22

- Ask the children to look at the box with the names at the top of ex. 2 on p. 53 in their Activity Book for five seconds. Get the children to close their books and give you the names. Write the names on the board.
- Tell the children that they are now going to hear how these six children called *Ella, Tom, Polly, Patrick, Mia* and *Ken* get to school every day. They should match the children to the right means of transport by writing their name underneath the corresponding picture.

Tapescript:

Speaker:	*Polly, how do you get to school?*
Amy:	*By bus, I take the bus.*
Speaker:	*Patrick, how do you get to school?*
Mia:	*I walk. It's not far.*
Speaker:	*Mia, what about you?*
	How do you get to school?
Lily:	*By car. My dad takes me.*
Speaker:	*Ken, how do you get to school?*
Ken:	*By bike.*
Speaker:	*By bike?*
Ken:	*Yes, I go with my mum. We go by bike.*
Speaker:	*Ella, how do you get to school?*
Ella:	*By train. I live far from school.*
Speaker:	*OK, now Tom. How do you get to school?*
Tom:	*By underground.*
Speaker:	*Thank you children.*

- Play the listening exercise from the CD 3/22 several times.
- Check the answers to the listening exercise: Ask: *What about Polly? How does she get to school?* The children answer: *By bus.*

L E S S O N   3

Vocabulary, phrases and structures:

Revision: *rain; wind; apples; go by bike; go by bus; go by train; peaches; juicy; bus stop; station; walk (faster)*

Linguistic skills:

Understanding a story (*Timmy*) from the DVD and the CD.
Performing a role play.
Understanding sentences from the CD.
Formulating categories.
Writing how children get to school.

Cognitive, motor and social skills:

Following the narrative structure of a story.
Role playing different characters.

Understanding sentences from the CD and matching them to pictures in the book.
Matching written sentences to pictures.
Being able to write how children get to school with the aid of information from pictures.

Cross-curricular integration:

Topic: Speaking motivation *'Timmy'*.

Materials:

Flashcards from *Playway 1:* 25, 46, 48; *Flashcards* from *Playway 2:* 64, 66, 69; *Word Cards:* 107, 109, 112; *DVD (Timmy); CD* 3/23–24; *Pupil's Book,* pp. 62–63, ex. 4; *Activity Book,* pp. 54–55, ex. 3–6; stick-in pictures from the appendix of the *Pupil's Book;* paper strips; (optional) answer key for self-checking

Revision and preparation of key words and phrases

rain; wind; apples; go by bike; go by bus; go by train; peaches; juicy; bus stop; station; walk (faster)

- Revise the words *bike, rain, wind* and *apples* with the aid of the flashcards from *Playway to English 1.*
- Revise the phrases *go by train, go by bus, go by bike* and *walk* with the aid of corresponding gestures, the flashcards and the word cards.
- Explain *juicy* in L1 and get the children to say a few times: *juicy peaches, juicy apples.*
- Clarify the meaning of the phrase *walk faster* through appropriate movements. Say, for example: *Sylvia, walk to the bus stop, please. Walk faster. Andi, walk to the station. Walk faster.*
- Explain *bus stop* and *station* in L1, if necessary.

Pronunciation tip: Pay attention to the pronunciation of *juicy* ['dʒuːsi]: The [dʒ] is pronounced clearly voiced as in *jump.*

❹ Watch the story.
Cartoon Story: *Timmy*

- Show the children the video sequence *Timmy* twice (DVD).

Note: Not all the language in the DVD sequences or CD versions of the stories are presented in the cartoon story in the Pupil's Book. This is mainly because of the length of the stories but also this serves to encourage the children to listen for the necessary information in order to complete the gap fill in the Pupil's Book.

DVD script: *Timmy*

Storyteller:	Lovely peaches. Juicy peaches. Oh … and here's Timmy.
Timmy:	One peach, two peaches, three peaches, four. Five peaches, six peaches, seven peaches, more! One peach, two peaches, three peaches, four. Five peaches, six peaches, seven peaches, more! Phew! What a heavy basket.
Storyteller:	Timmy goes by bike to the bus stop.
Two boys:	What lovely peaches. Can we have one?
Timmy:	OK. Here you are.
Storyteller:	Timmy goes by bus to the station.
Two girls:	What lovely peaches. Can we have one?
Timmy:	OK. Here you are.
Storyteller:	Then Timmy goes by train.
Woman and two children:	What lovely peaches. Can we have one?
Timmy:	OK. Here you are.
Storyteller:	It starts raining. Timmy walks faster. What a strong wind.
Friend:	Oh, hi, Timmy. What's in your basket?
Timmy:	Sorry, no peaches.
Friend:	Oh, apples. I love apples. One apple, two apples, three apples, four. Five apples, six apples, seven apples, more! One apple, two apples, three apples, four. Five apples, six apples, seven apples, more!

❹ Listen and stick.

Listening exercise:

Sticker activity CD 3/23

- Play the listening version of the story twice (CD 3/23). The children stick the stick-in pictures from the appendix in the corresponding blank spaces in the Pupil's Book pp. 62 and 63 ex. 4, while they are listening.
- Check the children's work or put out an answer key for self-checking in the classroom.

Rhyme

- Say the rhyme: *One apple, two apples, three apples, four … and five apples, six apples, seven apples, more* with the children.
- For this stand in a circle with the children. Say the rhyme as a counting rhyme and point at children as you count, so that each child has a number. At *four* the child involved must sit down. The children gradually take over the counting themselves.

Telling the story

- Now prepare the next part of the work on the story as follows: Draw a tree with peaches on the board. Stick the flashcards with *bus* and *train* on a side wall of the classroom, paper strips with the signs for *bus stop* and *station* on the opposite one. The flashcard for *rain* is fixed on the rear wall of the classroom. A little distance away from it, put the cards with *apple* and *wind*.
- Now tell the story and as you do so go to the corresponding cards that represent the individual locations. Start by taking the shopping basket and going to the peach tree. Pretend to take peaches from the tree and put them in the basket. Say: *Phew! What a heavy basket.* Put the basket on an imaginary bike and cycle to the bus stop. Say: *Timmy goes by bike to the bus stop.*
- Continue with the story in this way.

Role play

- Tell the story again. Now have two or three of the children act out the scenes one after the other. The counting rhyme is spoken by all the children together.

Preparation of written phrases

What a heavy basket; What a strong wind!; Nicole goes by bus; Can I have an apple?; What's in your basket?; It starts raining.

- Write the sentences on strips of paper, large enough so that all the children in your class can comfortably read them.
- Hold up one of the paper strips for about a second only. The children call out the sentence. They should, however, not be able to read the words letter for letter. This helps to avoid interference between the written words and their pronunciation. Carry on as described with the other sentences.

Option: Write the sentences on the board and work on them in the usual manner.

❸ Listen and write the numbers.

Listening exercise CD 3/24

- Ask the children to look at the pictures in ex. 3 on p. 54 in their Activity Book.
- Tell them that they should listen to the CD and number the pictures accordingly from one to six.

Tapescript:

One:	*It starts raining.*
Two:	*What a strong wind!*
Three:	*What's in your basket?*
Four:	*Can I have an apple?*
Five:	*Nicole goes by bus.*
Six:	*What a heavy basket.*

- Play CD 3/24 twice. The children listen and fill in the numbers.
- Play the CD again and the children check.

❹ Match the sentences to the pictures.
Reading exercise

- Read out the sentencs in ex. 4 on p. 54 in the Activity Book one after the other, then in jumbled order. The children point at the respective sentences in their books.
- Tell the children to match the sentences to the corresponding pictures in ex. 3 above by numbering them from one to six.
- To check say: *'Nicole goes by bus.' What number is it?* The children answer: *Number five.*

❺ Find the odd one out.
Formulating categories

- Tell the children to look at the words in ex. 5 on p. 55 in their Activity Book for about five seconds only. They then close their books. Say: *Give me the words you remember.* The children say words they can remember. Write them on the board. Ask: *What's missing?* Allow the children to have a brief look at ex. 5 again and find out what's missing. They then name the missing words and you write them on the board.

- Ask the children to open their books again at p. 55 and look at ex. 5. Read out the first row: *Peach – onion – plum – orange – banana.* Look at the children and ask: *What's wrong?* The children answer: *(The) onion.* Say: *Right. The onion is a vegetable. All the others are …* Get the children to finish your sentence: *… fruits.*
- The children try to find the odd one out in the remaining three rows and cross them out.
- When the children have finished with their work, they go together with a partner and check each other's results.

Option: To promote self-checking it is recommended that you put out an answer key. If an unclarified point occurs the children can go and check themselves.

❻ Look and write.
Writing exercise

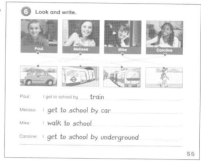

- The children look at ex. 6 on p. 55 in their Activity Book. Read out the names and get the children to say how the children in the book get to school. For example: *Paul. How does he get to school?* Children: *By train.*
- Then read the sentence below the picture. *I get to school by _____ .* The children complete the sentence and say: *… train.* Repeat the sentence, say: *Right. I get to school by train.* The children write the word *train* on the line provided in the book.
- Practise the phrase (*I get to school by …*) thoroughly by getting the children to say and repeat it several times.
- Then the children write how *Melissa, Mike* and *Caroline* get to school.
- To check ask individual children to read out their sentences.
- Write the sentences on the board for the children to check their spelling.

L E S S O N   4

Vocabulary, phrases and structures:

Revision: *What colour is your...?; Go by bike/bus etc; I love juicy apples; I eat them every day; They keep me fit; So listen to what I say; Oh, please eat...;*
Receptive language: *Put some pears in your basket; Pick up the basket; Put it on your bike; Ride to the station; Get on the train; Oh no! Where's your basket?*

Linguistic skills:

Singing a song (*Juicy apples*).
Asking about the colour of various means of transport.
Understanding a short story from the CD.

Cognitive, motor and social skills:

Learning the words of a song with the aid of actions and pictures.
Exchanging information about the colour of various means of transport and colouring the drawings in the book to correspond.
Maintaining rhythm and melody while speaking in unison and singing.
Understanding a short story from the CD, pointing to the corresponding pictures in the book and completing a text by choosing words.

Cross-curricular integration:

Music
Topic: Speaking motivation 'Recognising different modes of transport'.

Materials:

CD 3/25–28; *Pupil's Book*, p. 64, ex. 5–6; *Activity Book*, p. 56, ex. 7–8; coloured pencils

Revision

- Tell the story *Timmy* from the previous lesson again.

Optional: Have individual children re-enact the scenes. Everyone says the rhyme together (see previous lesson).

❺ Listen and point.
   Sing the song.

Song: *Juicy apples* CD 3/25–26

Juicy apples

Lyrics: Gerngross/Puchta
Music: Lorenz Maierhofer
© Helbling, Rum/Innsbruck

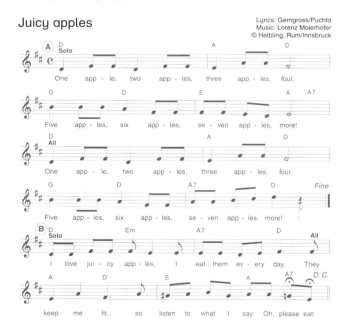

- The children open their Pupil's Book at p. 64 and look at the pictures in ex. 5.

- Play the song (CD 3/25). At first the children just listen and follow in the book.
- Reinforce the lyrics in the usual manner with the aid of the pictures in the book and appropriate gestures.
- After practising thoroughly, sing the song with the children using the karaoke version (CD 3/26).

Revision of key phrases

What colour is your ...?

- Revise the phrase *What colour is your...?* Ask individual children, e.g.: *Daniel, what colour is your favourite T-shirt?* Daniel: *(It's) blue.*
- Practise the question (*What colour is your...?*) by saying and repeating several times.

❻ Colour and say.
Pair work: Communication game

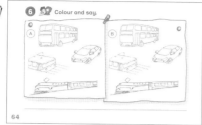

- The children open their Pupil's Book at p. 64 and look at ex. 6.
- Tell them that they should set up a schoolbag or a book between their books so that their partners cannot see how the drawings are coloured.
  Child A colours the types of transport in picture A as she/he chooses. Child B does the same with picture B. Tell the children to use one colour only for each means of transport. Child A asks child B what colours the means of transport in child B's picture are, e.g.: *What colour is your train?*
  Child B answers e.g.: *Red.*
- Child A colours the train in picture B in his book to correspond. Child A continues with the remaining means of transport in the same way. When child A has coloured all the illustrations, it is child B's turn.
- When both children have finished colouring the means of transport they compare their pictures.

❼ Listen and point.
Listening exercise CD 3/27

- Ask the children to look at ex. 7 on p. 56 in their Activity Book. Tell them to listen to the CD and to point at the respective pictures in the book.

Tapescript:

Put some pears in your basket.
Pick up the basket.
Put it on your bike.
Turn left into the station.
Get on the train.
Oh, no! Where's your basket?

- Play CD 3/27 twice.

❽ Listen again and write.
Listening and writing exercise CD 3/28

- The children look at the words in the box in ex. 8 on p. 56 in their Activity Book. Read out the words in order, then jumbled. The children read along.
- Now read the text line by line. Say: *Put some…in your basket.* Pause and look at the children. The children say: *… pears.* Proceed in this way with the rest of the text.
- Play the CD 3/28 several times, if necessary. The children write the missing sentences under the pictures in ex. 7.
- Check the children's work: Get individual children to read out their sentences. Say: *Picture five: What is it?*

Unit 9 — Travelling

LESSON 5

Vocabulary, phrases and structures:

First by bike, then by train…; Travelling from six to one; Travelling, travelling is such fun!

Linguistic skills:

Understanding a poem from the CD and reading along in the book while listening.
Learning a rhyme by heart and reciting one's own poem fluently.

Cognitive, motor and social skills:

Drawing the means of transport one likes and composing one's own poem.
Reciting one's own poem rhythmically.

Drawing one's own way to school and writing about it.

Cross-curricular integration:

Topic: Speaking motivation 'Recognising different modes of transport'.

Materials:

CD 3/26; *Pupil's Book*, p. 64, ex. 5; *Flashcards* from *Playway 2:* 63–70; *Word Cards* from *Playway 2:* 106–113
CD 3/29–30; *Pupil's Book*, p. 65, ex. 7–8; *Activity Book*, p. 57, ex. 9

Revision

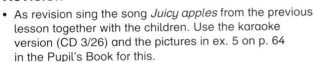

- As revision sing the song *Juicy apples* from the previous lesson together with the children. Use the karaoke version (CD 3/26) and the pictures in ex. 5 on p. 64 in the Pupil's Book for this.
- Stand in a circle together with children. Get a child to choose a word card and have a brief look at it. The child mimes the means of transport (movement or sound) and the others try to guess. When guessed correctly, put the card in the middle of the circle. The child who has guessed the word draws the next card etc.
- Play a memory game with the flashcards and the word cards.

❼ Listen and say the rhyme.

Listening and reading exercise CD 3/29

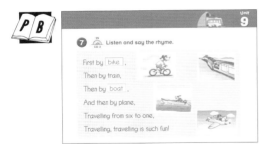

- Ask the children to open their Pupil's Book at p. 65 and look at ex. 7. Read out the rhyme line by line and point at the respective lines.

Tapescript:

First by bike,
Then by train,
Then by boat,
And then by plane,
Travelling from six to one,
Travelling, travelling is such fun!

- Then play the rhyme from CD 3/29 twice. The children listen.
- Play the rhyme again and encourage the children to speak along.
- Read the rhyme line by line with the children several times.
- Get them to close their books and dictate the rhyme to you. Write a skeleton version of the rhyme on the board:

    F b b,
    T b t,
    T b b,
    A t b p, …

- Point to the skeleton version of the rhyme on the board letter by letter and ask the children to 'read' with you.
- Repeat this step two or three times. Then get the children to learn the rhyme off by heart. Show the children the best way to do this. Hold up your book. Recite the rhyme several times in a low voice and point at the respective lines in the book. This gives the children confidence and helps them remember important chunks of language that they will need for the creation of their own poems later.

❽ Draw. Create your own poem.

Step to creativity (Word Play) CD 3/30

- Tell the children to compose their own poem. The children first draw two means of transport of their own choice in the blank space provided in the Pupil's Book, ex. 8, p. 65. Then they complete the poem on the left according to their drawing.
- Give the children sufficient time for this work. When they have finished, the children learn the text of their poems by heart. Go round the class and help, if necessary.
- Finally, individual children present their poems to the class. Remember to praise the children for their work (*Let's give them a big hand*).
- Individual children may like to say their poems to the karaoke version of track 3/30 on the CD.

Note: Give the children the option of presenting their poems just to you on their own first, so that, if necessary, you can help with the pronunciation.

❾ Look and read. Then draw and say.
Step to creativity (ME-page)
My transport

- Ask the children to open their Activity Book at p. 57. Hold up your book so that all can see well. Point as you explain.
- The children look at the pictures first and read the texts in the speech bubbles in ex. 9.
- Then they draw their own face or stick a photo of themselves in the last picture and draw the means of transport they use to get to school.
- Next, they write an appropriate text in the speech bubble provided in the book to describe how they get to school.
- Go round the class and help, if needed.
- Check the children's work: Get individual children to read out how they get to school.

LESSON 1

Vocabulary, phrases and structures:

Revision: body parts; travelling; farm; family *beach; swimming; sailing; fishing; I'm bored.*
Receptive language: *Dad, we're bored; Let's go to the beach/home; It's a lovely day; Build a sandcastle; What about your sandcastle?; It's finished. I'm bored; It's there!; Wow! Dad, that's great; No, not that!; It's this one here; I'm still bored; Go swimming/sailing/fishing, Dad; That's the sport for me!; He's fine; I hate swimming/the beach; Get them off!; No. I can't. No boat; Where's Dad?; He's fishing, look!; Look, I think he's got a fish; Quick, come on; It's a big fish. It's a big one; But it's not a fish. What do we do now?; Some things are different in picture A from picture B. What are they?*

Linguistic skills:

Understanding a story *(A day on the beach)* from the DVD.

Understanding mini-dialogues (scenes from the story) from the CD.

Cognitive, motor and social skills:

Understanding mini-dialogues from the CD and numbering the pictures in the book to correspond. Comparing two pictures, finding out differences and writing them down.

Cross-curricular integration:

Topic: Speaking motivation *'A day on the beach'*.

Materials:

soft ball
Flashcard from *Playway 2:* 71; *Word Cards* from *Playway 2:* 114; *DVD (A day on the beach);* CD 3/31; *Pupil's Book,* p. 66, ex. 1; *Activity Book,* p. 58, ex. 1; (optional) answer key for self-checking

Revision

- Stand in a circle with the children. Throw a soft ball to one child and say e.g. *arm.* The child who catches the ball names another word on the topic of *body* and throws the ball to another child etc. Also revise the topic areas *travelling, on the farm* and *family* in this way.

Introduction of vocabulary and preparation of phrases

beach; swimming; sailing; fishing; I'm bored.

- Introduce the new word *beach* with the aid of the flashcard and word card.
- Clarify the meaning of the remaining words and the phrase *I'm bored* through corresponding actions, gestures or by translating into L1.

❶ Watch the story.

Mr Matt Story: *A day on the beach*

- Show the children the video sequence *A day on the beach* twice (DVD).

DVD script: *A day on the beach*

Danny:	Dad, we're bored.
Daisy:	Let's go to the beach.
Mr Matt:	But … All right.
Danny and Daisy:	Yeah!
Mr Matt:	I'm bored. Let's go home.
Danny:	No, Dad. It's a lovely day.
Daisy:	Build a sandcastle.
Mr Matt:	All right.
Danny:	What about your sandcastle?
	Mr Matt It's finished. I'm bored.
Daisy:	It's finished?
Mr Matt:	Yeah, look. It's there!
Danny:	Wow! Dad, that's great.

Mr Matt:	No, not that!
	It's this one here.
Mr Matt:	I'm still bored. Let's go home.
Danny:	Go swimming, Dad.
Mr Matt:	Good idea.
	Swimming, swimming!
	That's the sport for me!
	Swimming, swimming!
Danny and Daisy:	Good.
Danny:	He's fine.
Daisy:	Dad?
Mr Matt:	I hate swimming.
Danny:	What's the matter?
Mr Matt:	Get them off!
	I'm bored. Let's go home.
Daisy:	No, Dad. It's a lovely day.
Danny:	Go sailing, Dad!
Mr Matt:	Good idea.
	No. I can't. No boat!
Danny and Daisy:	Take that.
Girl:	Stop! Stop!
Mr Matt:	Let's go home. I hate the beach.
Danny:	Come, on, Dad. It's a lovely day.
	Go fishing.
Mr Matt:	OK. Ha Ha!!
Daisy:	Where's Dad?
Danny:	He's fishing, look!
Daisy:	Look, I think he's got a fish.
Danny:	Quick, come on.
Mr Matt:	Oooh! It's a big fish. It's a big one.
Daisy:	Dad!
Mr Matt:	Yes?
Daisy:	It's big.
Mr Matt:	Yes.
Daisy:	But it's not a fish. Look!
Mr Matt:	What?
Girl's dad:	You again!
Mr Matt:	What do we do now?
Danny and Daisy:	Let's go home.

❶ Listen and write the numbers.
Listening exercise CD 3/31

- The children open their Pupil's Book on p. 66 and look at the pictures.
- Tell the children that they are going to hear individual sentences or short dialogues on the CD.

Tapescript:

Announcer:	Picture one.
Mr Matt:	Get them off!
Announcer:	Once again.
	Picture one.
Mr Matt:	Get them off!
Announcer:	Picture two.
Mr Matt:	I'm bored. Let's go home.
Announcer:	Once again.
	Picture two.
Mr Matt:	I'm bored. Let's go home.
Announcer:	Picture three.
Danny:	Go sailing, Dad!
Mr Matt:	Good idea.
Announcer:	Once again.
	Picture three.
Danny:	Go sailing, Dad!
Mr Matt:	Good idea.
Announcer:	Picture four.
Mr Matt:	No, not that! It's this one here.
Announcer:	Once again.
	Picture four.
Mr Matt:	No, not that! It's this one here.

- Play the listening exercise twice (CD 3/31). The children listen and number the pictures in the book.
- Then hold your book up so that it can be seen by all. Point to the fourth picture and ask: *What number is it?* Children: *Three.*

Tip: You can also check the children's answers by saying e.g.: *Go sailing, Dad! – Good idea.* Children: *(It's number) three.*

❶ Look and write.
Writing exercise

- Ask the children to open their Activity Book on p. 58 and look at the pictures in ex. 1 for five seconds only. Get the children to close their books and tell you what's in the pictures. Write the words the children name on the board.
- The children open their books again and look at the two pictures very carefully. Say: *Look at the two pictures. Some things are different in picture A from picture B. What are they?*
- The children should find out the differences.
- Read out the sentence below the pictures. The children read along in their books. Say: *In picture A there are three children. In picture B there are…* Look at the children and get them to complete the sentence: *… four.* Say: *Correct./Right. In picture B there are four children.*
- Now, the children try to find out the differences individually and complete the sentences.
- Check the children's work: Tell the children to get together with a partner, swap books and check each others' work.

Option: To promote self-checking it is recommended that you put out an answer key in the classroom. The children can go and check.

L E S S O N   2

Vocabulary, phrases and structures:

lake
Receptive language: *Jump in. Take off your jeans;*
Go to the swimming pool; Swim; You're hot; cool
off.

Linguistic skills:

Understanding instructions in an action story (*The lake*).
Understanding instructions from the CD and
matching with the corresponding pictures.

Cognitive, motor and social skills:

Combining instructions with actions.
Understanding and carrying out instructions
jumbled up.
Understanding sentences from the CD and
matching them with pictures and written sentences
in the book.

Cross-curricular integration:

Topic: Speaking motivation *'The lake'*.

Materials:

DVD *(A day on the beach)*
Flashcard from *Playway 2:* 72, *Word Card* from
Playway 2: 115; CD 3/32–33; *Pupil's Book,* p. 67,
ex. 2; *Activity Book,* p. 59, ex. 2–3; paper strips

Revision

- Revise the story *A day on the beach* with the aid of the
  DVD.

Vocabulary extension

lake

- Introduce the new word with the aid of the flashcard and
  word card in the usual manner.

Action Story: *The lake*

- For reinforcement of the action story carry out the
  following steps in the usual manner (see Introduction of the
  Teacher's Book, p. 16):
  – Listen and imitate
  – Carry out instructions
  – Carry out the instructions jumbled up

❷ Listen and point. Write the numbers.
Action Story: *The lake* CD 3/32

- The children open their Pupil's Book at p. 67. The nine
  pictures in ex. 2 are printed in random order. Now give
  the children sufficient time to look at the pictures.

Tapescript:

You're riding your bike.
You're hot.
Stop and get off your bike.
You can see a lake.
Go down to the water.
Cool off.
Dive into the water.
Aargh! There's something in your mouth.
It's a frog.

- Play the listening exercise (CD 3/32). At first the children
  just listen and follow in the book.
- Play the listening exercise again. Now the children
  number the pictures in the book.
- Go round the class and check the children's work.

Option 1: Draw a grid with nine boxes on the board. This grid
represents p. 67 in the book. Have the children dictate
the numbers for the corresponding box. (*What number
is it?*)

Option 2: Say e.g.: *Number three. Do it.* The children carry out
the action corresponding to it, in this case they imitate
getting off a bike etc.

Preparation of written phrases

Jump in; Take off your jeans and T-shirt;
Go to the swimming pool; Swim; You're hot; Cool off.

- Write the sentences on strips of paper, large enough so
  that all the children in your class can comfortably read
  the sentences.

- Hold up one of the paper strips for about half a second only. The children call out the sentence. They should, however, not be able to read the words letter for letter. This helps to avoid interference between the written words and their pronunciation. Carry on as described with the other sentences.

Option: Write the sentences on the board and work on them in the usual manner.

❷ Listen and point.
Listening exercise CD 3/33

- Ask the children to look at the pictures in ex. 2 at p. 59 in their Activity Book.
- Tell them to listen to the CD and point at the corresponding pictures.
- Play the CD 3/33 twice. The children listen and point.

Tapescript:

You're hot.
Go to the swimming pool.
Take off your jeans and T-shirt.
Cool off.
Jump in.
Swim.

---

❸ Match the sentences to the pictures.
Reading exercise

- Read the sentences in ex. 3 at p. 59 in the Activity Book one after the other and then in any order. The children point at the respective sentences in their books.
- Tell them to match the sentences in ex. 3 with the corresponding pictures in ex. 2 above by numbering them accordingly.
- Check the children's work: Say: *Swim. What number is it?* The children answer: *(Number) six.*

L E S S O N 3

Vocabulary, phrases and structures:

tiger; jungle; Let's be quiet; It's asleep; Let's jump in; Too late; Careful; Look at its big teeth.

Linguistic skills:

Understanding a story (*The jungle safari*) from the DVD and from narration by the teacher.
Joining in with the storytelling.
Acting out a role play.

Cognitive, motor and social skills:

Following the sequence of events in a story.
Sticking stick-in pictures from the appendix correctly in the picture story.

Matching sentences to the corresponding pictures by numbering them.

Cross-curricular integration:

Topic: Speaking motivation *The jungle safari.*

Materials:

Flashcards from *Playway 2:* 73–74; *Word Cards* from *Playway 2:* 116–117; *DVD (The jungle safari) Story Cards* from *Playway 2:* 54–63; CD 3/34; *Pupil's Book,* pp. 68–69, ex. 3; stick-in pictures from the appendix of the *Pupil's Book;* paper strips; *Activity Book,* p. 60, ex. 4

Revision

- Play *Max says …* with the instructions of the action story *The lake* from the previous lesson.

Introduction of vocabulary and preparation of important phrases

tiger; jungle; Let's be quiet; It's asleep.

- Reinforce the new words *tiger* and *jungle* with the aid of the flashcards and word cards.
- Explain the meaning of the sentences *Let's be quiet.* and *It's asleep.* by making the corresponding gestures for them.

❸ **Watch the story.**

Cartoon Story: *The jungle safari*

- Show the children the DVD sequence: *The jungle safari* twice (DVD).

DVD script: *The jungle safari*

Benny:	Sssshhhh!
Linda:	Let's be quiet.
Max:	It's asleep.
Linda:	Wow! What a big snake!
Benny:	Careful!
Max:	Don't worry. It's asleep.
Linda:	An elephant!
Benny:	Look at its big ears!
Max:	It's asleep too. Hee hee hee hee!
Max:	Atishoo! Atishoo! Atishoo!
Linda:	They're coming!
Benny:	Oh, no!
Max:	Let's run!
Linda:	Look, there's a boat!
Benny:	Let's jump in!
Max:	Help me, Benny.
Linda:	Row, row, Benny!
Benny:	OK!
Max:	Too late! Hee hee hee hee!
Benny, Linda:	Bye, bye, bye, bye, see you again!
and Max:	Bye, bye, bye, bye, see you again!

Note: Not all the language in the DVD sequences or CD versions of the stories are presented in the cartoon story in the Pupil's Book. This is mainly because of the length of the stories but also this serves to encourage the children to listen for the necessary information in order to complete the gap fill in the Pupil's Book.

- Put the story cards in random order up on the board. Ask two children to put the story cards in the right order.
- Get the children to name individual words and phrases from the story that they can recall. Now show the video sequence *The jungle safari* (DVD) again and compare together with the children whether the order of the story cards on the board is correct. Then take the cards down from the board.

❸ **Watch the story. Listen and stick.**

Listening exercise:
Sticker activity CD 3/34

- Play the listening version of the story twice (CD 3/34). The children listen and stick the stick-in pictures from the appendix in the corresponding blank spaces in the Pupil's book pp. 68 and 69.
- Check the children's work.

Note: To promote self-checking you can place a completed picture story out in the classroom. The children go and check their own work.

Preparation of written phrases

Let's jump in; Too late; It's asleep; Careful! Let's be quiet; Look at its big teeth.

- Write the sentences on strips of paper, large enough so that all the children in your class can comfortably read the sentences.
- Hold up one of the paper strips for about a second only. The children call out the sentence. They should, however, not be able to read the words letter for letter. This helps to avoid interference between the written words and their pronunciation. Carry on as described with the other sentences.

Option 1: To pre-teach the written form of the sentences, you can also read out the texts from the speech bubbles in the Pupil's Book in any order. The children point along in their books.

Option 2: Write the sentences on the board. Point in quick succession to the sentences and the children call them out.

Telling the story

- Now tell the story with the aid of the story cards.
- Ask the children for individual words and phrases to complete it.
  Say e.g.: *Sssshhhh! Let's be quiet. It's …*
  Look at the children.
  Children: … *asleep.* etc.

Story reconstruction game

- Tell the children that you are tired and you may get some of the facts wrong while telling the story. The children should listen particularly carefully and correct the mistakes.
  Say e.g.: *The tiger is sad.*
  The children correct the mistake: *No. … asleep.*
  Repeat the sentence with the right wording: *The tiger is asleep.*
- Continue in this way.

Role play

- In high-ability groups the story can be performed as a role play after intensive practice.

❹ Look and write.
Writing exercise

- Ask the children to open their Activity Book at p. 60 and look at the sentences in the box at the top of the page.
- Read out the sentences and tell the children to write them underneath the corresponding pictures in ex. 4.
- Check the children's work: Hold your book up so that all can see. Point to the pictures and get individual children to read out the corresponding sentences.

Option: To promote self-checking it is recommended that you put out an answer key in the classroom. The children go and check their own work themselves.

Unit 10 — Holidays

L E S S O N   4

Vocabulary, phrases and structures:

Let's go to the (show); Let's go swimming; Let's build a sandcastle; Let's watch TV;This is the holiday boogie, yeah!; Come on boys/girls; Let's have fun in the sun; See you again.
Receptive language: *There's an elephant; Let's run; Look there's a boat; Let's get in; Where's the elephant? Here he is.*

Linguistic skills:

Singing a song (*Holiday boogie*).
Understanding sentences from the CD and matching them to the written form of the sentences.

Cognitive, motor and social skills:

Following pictures in the book while listening.

Maintaining rhythm and melody and doing corresponding actions while speaking in unison and singing.
Understanding sentences from the CD and numbering pictures accordingly.
Understanding sentences from the CD and colouring them accordingly.
Matching texts to the corresponding pictures.

Cross-curricular integration:

Music
Topic: Speaking motivation 'Planning free time activities'.

Materials:

CD 3/34; *Pupil's Book*, pp. 68–69, ex. 3
CD 3/35–38; *Activity Book*, p. 61–62, ex. 5–7;
Pupil's Book, p. 70, ex. 4; plastic plate; paper strips

Revision

- Revise the story *The jungle safari* from the previous lesson. For this use the listening version (CD 3/34) and pp. 68 and 69 in the Pupil's Book. Finally, have children perform the story as a role play.

❺ Listen and write the numbers.
Listening exercise CD 3/35

- Ask the children to open their Activity Book at p. 61 ex. 5. The pictures are printed in random order. Give the children sufficient time to look at the pictures.

Tapescript:

One:	*There's an elephant.*
Two:	*Let's run.*
Three:	*Look, there's a boat.*
Four:	*Let's get in.*
Five:	*Where's the elephant?*
Six:	*There he is!*

- Tell them to listen to the CD and number the pictures in the order they happen from one to six.
- Play CD 3/35 twice. The children listen and fill in the numbers.
- Play the CD again and the children check.
- To check say: *Where's the elephant? What number is it?* The children answer: *(Number) five.*

❹ Listen and point. Sing the song.
Song: *Holiday boogie* CD 3/36–37

Holiday boogie

Lyrics: Gerngross/Puchta
Music: Lorenz Maierhofer
© Helbling, Rum/Innsbruck

- The children open their Pupil's Book at p. 70.
- Play the song (CD 3/36). The children listen and look at the illustrations in the book.
- Now recite the lyrics once and make the meaning clear in the following way:

  This is the holiday boogie, yeah! – clap in time and move with it in the rhythm of the song.
  Yeah! – *stretch your arms up.* Ask the children to imitate your actions:
  Come on, boys. – Stamp your right foot three times and make a gesture of invitation towards the boys. Ask the girls to imitate these actions:
  Come on, girls. – Stamp your left foot three times and make a gesture of invitation towards the girls. Ask the boys to imitate your actions.
  Let's sing the holiday boogie, yeah! – clap again in time and move with it to the rhythm of the song.
  Let's have fun in the sun. – Run on the spot. All the children imitate your actions.
  Bye-bye, bye-bye, see you again. – Clap again.
  At *See you again.* Wave goodbye. All the children copy your actions.

- Recite the lyrics again a few times and again do the corresponding actions to them. Ask the children to join in the speaking and doing the actions. Recite the text several times rhythmically together with the children and sing the song to the CD.
- Finally, the children go round the class singing the song and doing the corresponding actions. Use the karaoke version (CD 3/37).

Option: Only the girls sing the line *Come on, boys.* The line *Come on, girls.* is only sung by the boys.

A game: Spin the plate

- Ask the children to arrange their chairs in a circle. Give each child a number from one to ten and then in tens to one hundred. The children have to remember their number. If necessary give individual numbers out twice.
- One child goes into the middle of the circle and spins a plastic plate like a top *Spin the plate.* As soon as the plate is spinning the child says one of the previously named numbers, e.g. *twenty.*
- The child with this number must run to the middle and try to catch the plate before it stops spinning. If the child succeeds, he/she may now spin the plate and name a number. If he/she does not succeed, the child whose turn it is continues to play.

Option: This game can also be played with the words from other language areas, for example names of animals, means of transport, etc.

Preparation of written phrases

Let's build a sandcastle; Let's go fishing; Let's go home; I'm bored; Let's go sailing; Let's go to the show.

- Write the sentences on strips of paper, large enough so that all the children in your class can comfortably read the sentences.
- Hold up one of the paper strips for about a second only. The children call out the sentence. They should, however, not be able to read the words letter for letter. This helps to avoid interference between the written words and their pronunciation. Carry on as described with the other sentences.

Option: Write the sentences on the board and work on them in the usual manner.

❻ Listen and colour.
Listening exercise CD 3/38

- Ask the children to take out the following coloured

pencils: *green, blue, yellow, red, orange and pink.*
- Ask the children to look at the sentences in ex. 6 on p. 62 in their Activity Book.
- Tell them to listen to the CD and to colour the frames around each sentence according to what they hear.

- Play CD 3/38 twice. The children listen and first mark the frames in the corresponding colours. Later they complete colouring the frames.
- Play the CD again and the children check.
- To check say: *Let's go swimming. What colour is it?* The children answer: *It's orange.*

Tapescript:

Green:	*Let's go home.*
Green:	*Let's go home.*
Blue:	*Let's go to the show.*
Blue:	*Let's go to the show.*
Pink:	*Let's go fishing.*
Pink:	*Let's go fishing.*
Orange:	*Let's build a sandcastle.*
Orange:	*Let's build a sandcastle.*
Red:	*I'm bored.*
Red:	*I'm bored.*
Yellow:	*Let's go sailing.*
Yellow:	*Let's go sailing.*

❼ Read, match and colour.
Reading exercise

- Tell the children to colour the empty speech bubbles in ex. 7, on p. 62 in their Activity Book according to ex. 6 above.
- Then ask, for example: *What colour is 'Let's go to the show'?* The children answer: *Blue.*

L E S S O N   5

Vocabulary, phrases and structures:

My favourite holiday: at home with Benny and Linda; on a beach/farm; at home.

Linguistic skills:

Reading about Max's favourite holiday.
Writing about one's own holiday.

Cognitive, motor and social skills:

Drawing, writing and speaking about one's own holiday.

Materials:

CD 3/37
Activity Book, p. 63, ex. 8–9

Revision

- Sing the *Holiday boogie* from the previous lesson together with the children. Use the karaoke version (CD 3/37).

❽ Look and read.
Reading exercise

- The children open their Activity Book at p. 63 ex. 8 and look at the pictures.
- Read out the phrases above the pictures in jumbled order. The children point at the respective phrases in their books. Then hold your book up so that all can see well. Point to the pictures and get individual children to read out the corresponding phrases.
- Practise the expressions thoroughly by getting the children to say and repeat them several times.

❾ Draw, write and say.
Step to creativity (ME-page)
My favourite holiday

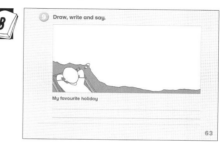

- The children look at ex. 9 in their Activity Book on p. 63.
- Tell them that they are now to draw themselves on their favourite holiday and write about it.
- Give the children sufficient time for this task. Go round the class and help if needed.
- Put together two desks and the children put their Activity Books onto the desks, so that they can see each others' work.
- Get individual children to talk about their favourite holiday. Help through whispering cues, if necessary.

C L I L:
Content and Language Integrated Learning

Objectives:

Understanding facts about the sea world.
Becoming aware of environmental protection.

Materials:

Pupil's Book, p. 71, ex. 5

❺ **Read and write the numbers.**
Speaking exercise

- Ask the children to open their Pupil's Book on p. 71 and look at the pictures in ex. 5.
- Hold up your book. Underneath the pictures there are sentences printed in jumbled order. Read them out twice. The children read along in their books.
- Clarify the meaning of new words through the help of the pictures in the book, through simple drawings on the blackboard or if necessary translate into L1.
- Clarify the meaning of the sentence *Don't throw old bottles and bags into the sea.* through appropriate gestures and mime.
- Get the children to read the sentences again and to number the pictures. Allow them to do this together with a partner.
- Check the children's work by holding up your book, pointing to the first picture above and asking:
  What number is it? Children answer: *(Number) one.*

LESSON 1

Vocabulary, phrases and structures:
Checking of vocabulary acquisition in Units 9–10.

Linguistic skills:
Understanding and saying important words from Units 9 and 10 on the topic areas 'travelling' and 'holidays'.

Cognitive, motor and social skills:
Matching words and sentences from the CD to the corresponding pictures.
Numbering these words and sentences according to the CD.
Checking the results with the aid of an answer key.
Self-evaluation

Materials:
CD 3/39–40; *Pupil's Book,* pp. 72–73, ex. 1–4; coloured pencils; answer key

Self-evaluation

Option: Divide *Show what you can do* into two lessons.

Note: For notes on the basic methodology of this section, see *Show what you can do* on p. 18 of the introduction in the Teacher's Book.

❶ **Listen and write the numbers.**

Listening exercise CD 3/39

• Tell the children that they are going to find out by themselves which words in the Pupil's Book on p. 72, ex. 1 they can already say.
• The children check independently whether they can match the words they hear to the corresponding pictures by numbering them from one to nine.

Tapescript:

Number one: Boat.
Number one: Boat.

Number two: Go by underground.
Number two: Go by underground.

Number three: Walk.
Number three: Walk.

Number four: Go by bike.
Number four: Go by bike.

Number five: Go by plane.
Number five: Go by plane.

Number six: Go by train.
Number six: Go by train.

Number seven: Lake.
Number seven: Lake.

Number eight: Go by bus.
Number eight: Go by bus.

Number nine: Elephant.
Number nine: Elephant.

• Now play the listening exercise (CD 3/39).
• The children number the pictures in the book accordingly. The first picture has already been numbered.
• Go round the class and help the children, if necessary.
• Set out a completed sheet and let the children check their results independently.

❷ **Match the words to the pictures.**

Reading exercise

• Tell the children that they are going to find out by

themselves which words in the Pupil's Book on p. 72, ex. 2 they can already read well.
• The children now check independently whether they can match the written words to the corresponding pictures in ex. 1.
• Set out a completed sheet and let the children check their results independently.

❸ Listen and write the numbers.
Listening exercise CD 3/40

- Tell the children to find out themselves which sentences in the Pupil's Book on p. 73, ex. 3 they can already say.
- The children now check independently whether they can match the sentences they hear to the corresponding pictures.

Tapescript:

Number one:	Bye-bye, see you again.
Number one:	Bye-bye, see you again.
Number two:	What a big snake.
Number two:	What a big snake.
Number three:	Tom is asleep.
Number three:	Tom is asleep.
Number four:	Let's be quiet.
Number four:	Let's be quiet.

- Now play the listening exercise (CD 3/40).
- The children number the pictures in the book accordingly. The first picture has already been numbered.
- Go round the class and help the children, if necessary.
- Set out a completed sheet and let the children check their results independently.

❹ Match the sentences to the pictures.
Reading exercise

- Tell the children that they are going to find out by themselves which sentences in the Pupil's Book on p. 73, ex. 4 they can already read.
- The children now check independently whether they can match the written sentences to the corresponding pictures in ex. 3.
- Set out a completed sheet and let the children check their results independently.